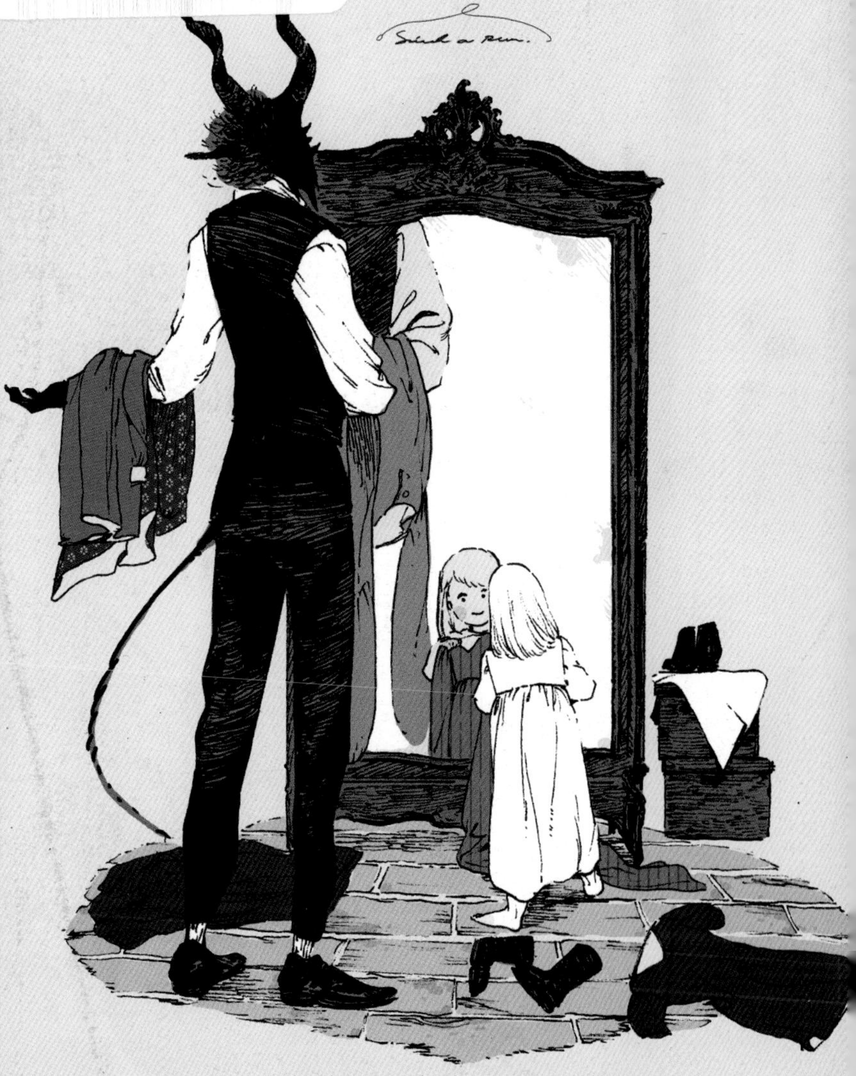

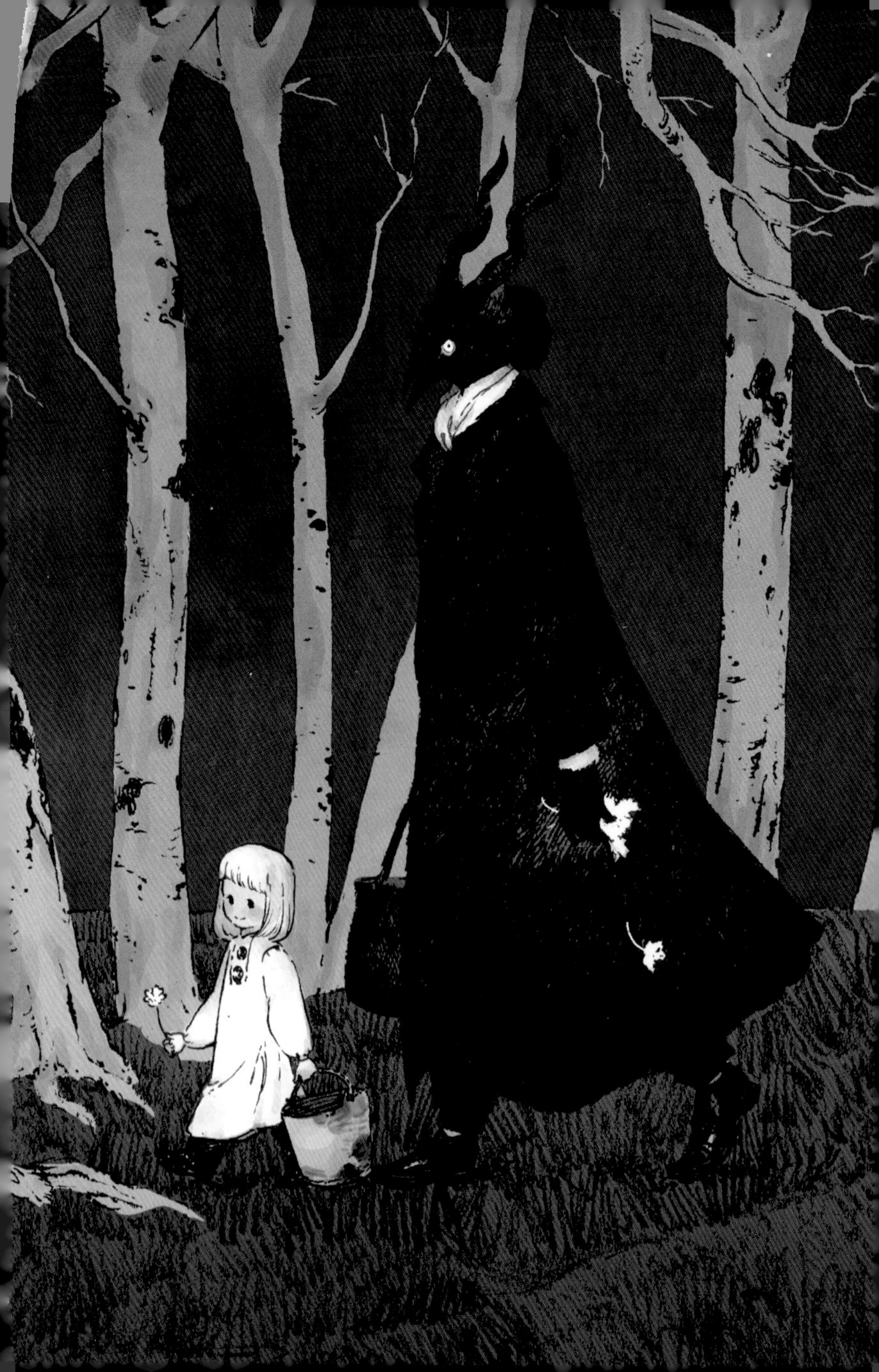

Chapter 1

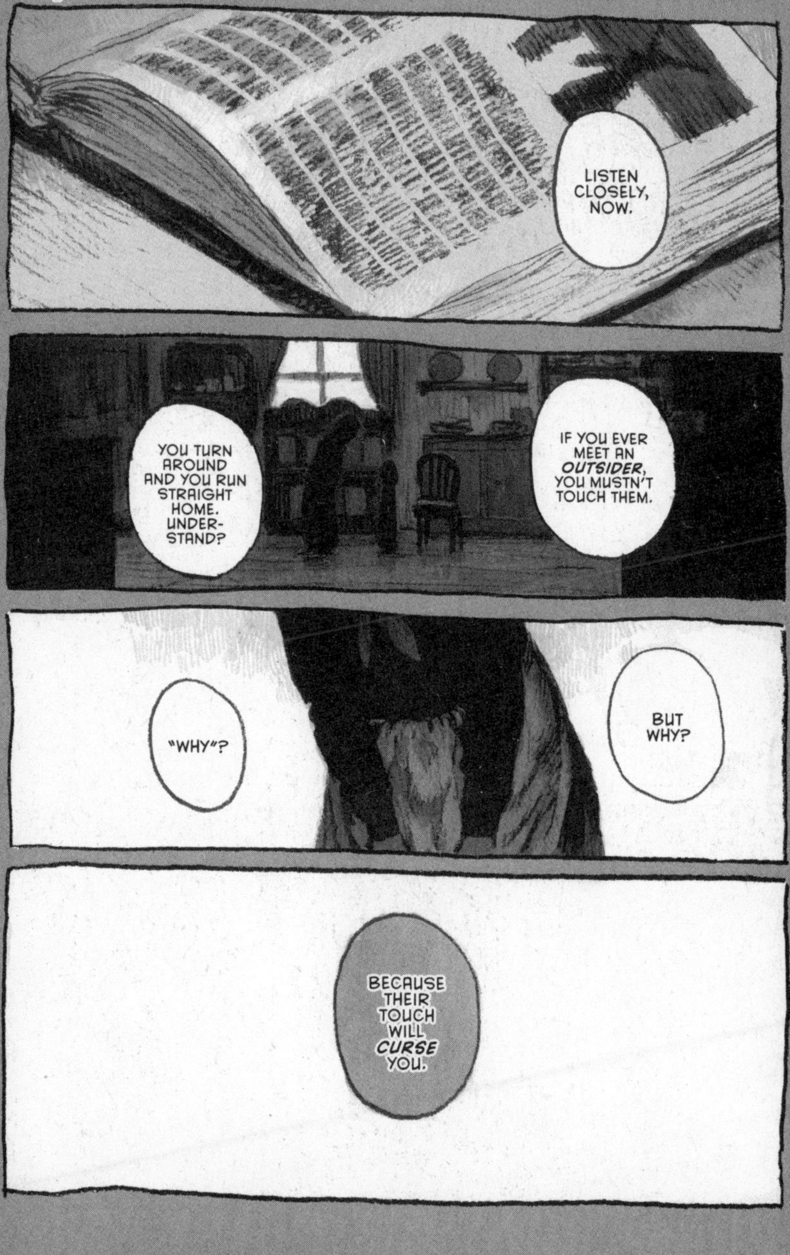
LISTEN CLOSELY, NOW.
IF YOU EVER MEET AN *OUTSIDER*, YOU MUSTN'T TOUCH THEM.
YOU TURN AROUND AND YOU RUN STRAIGHT HOME. UNDER-STAND?
BUT WHY?
"WHY"?
BECAUSE THEIR TOUCH WILL *CURSE* YOU.

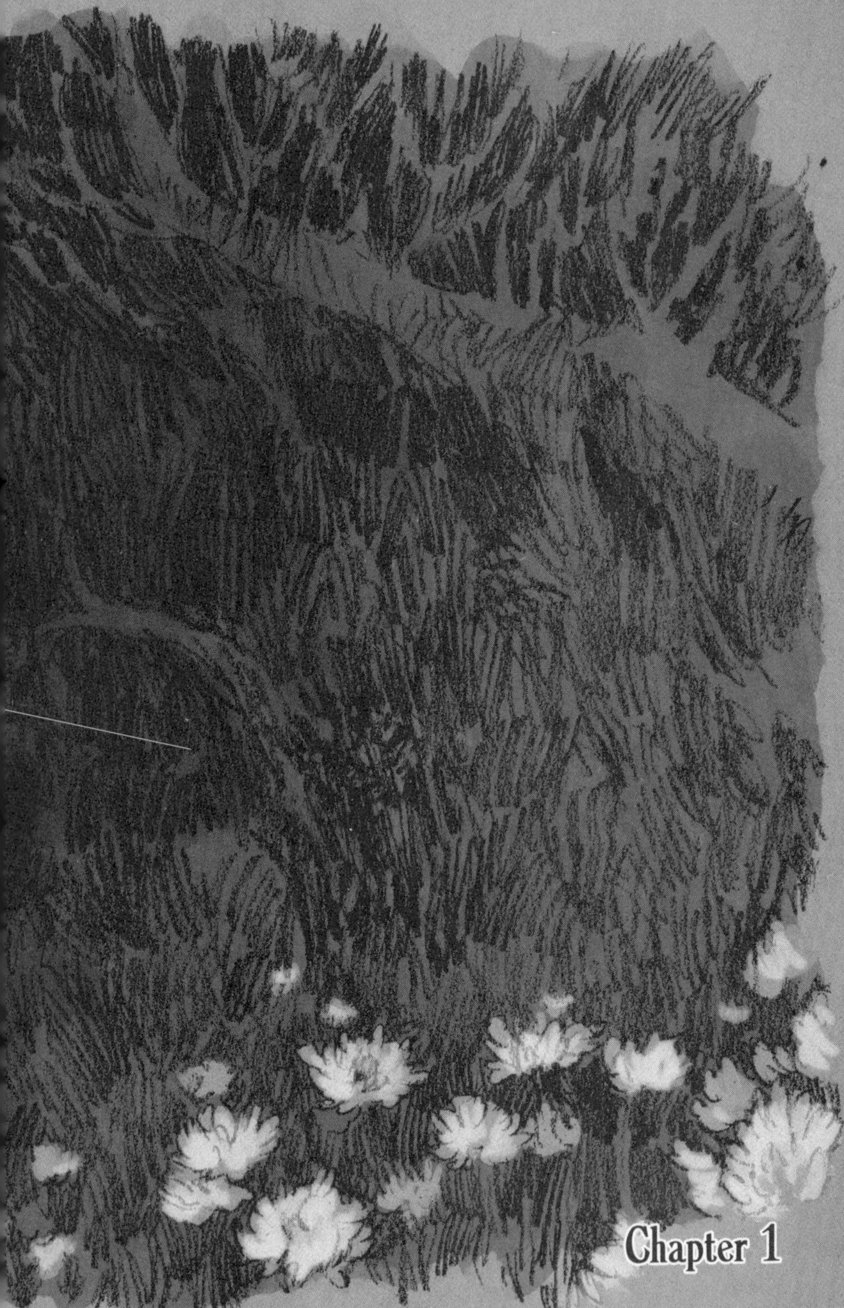

Chapter 1

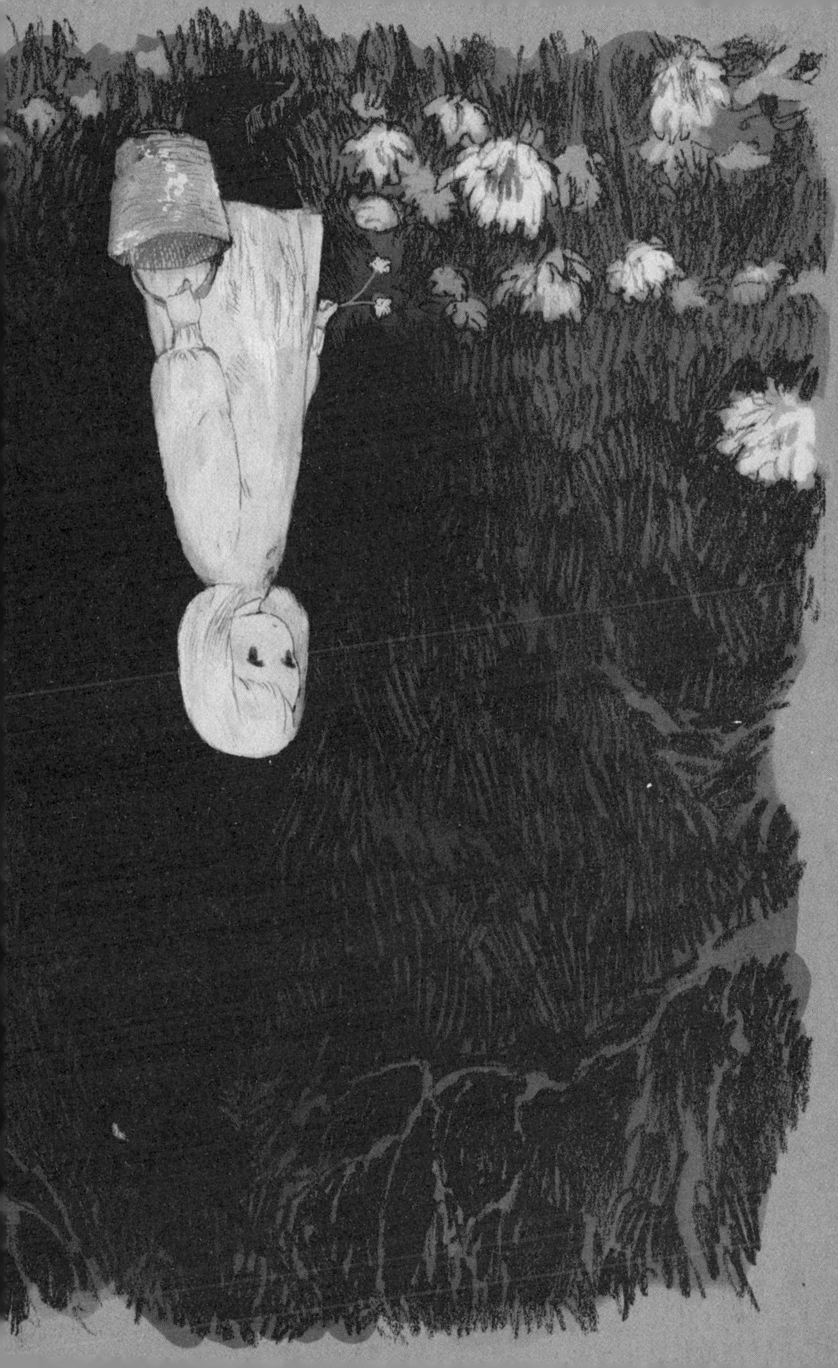

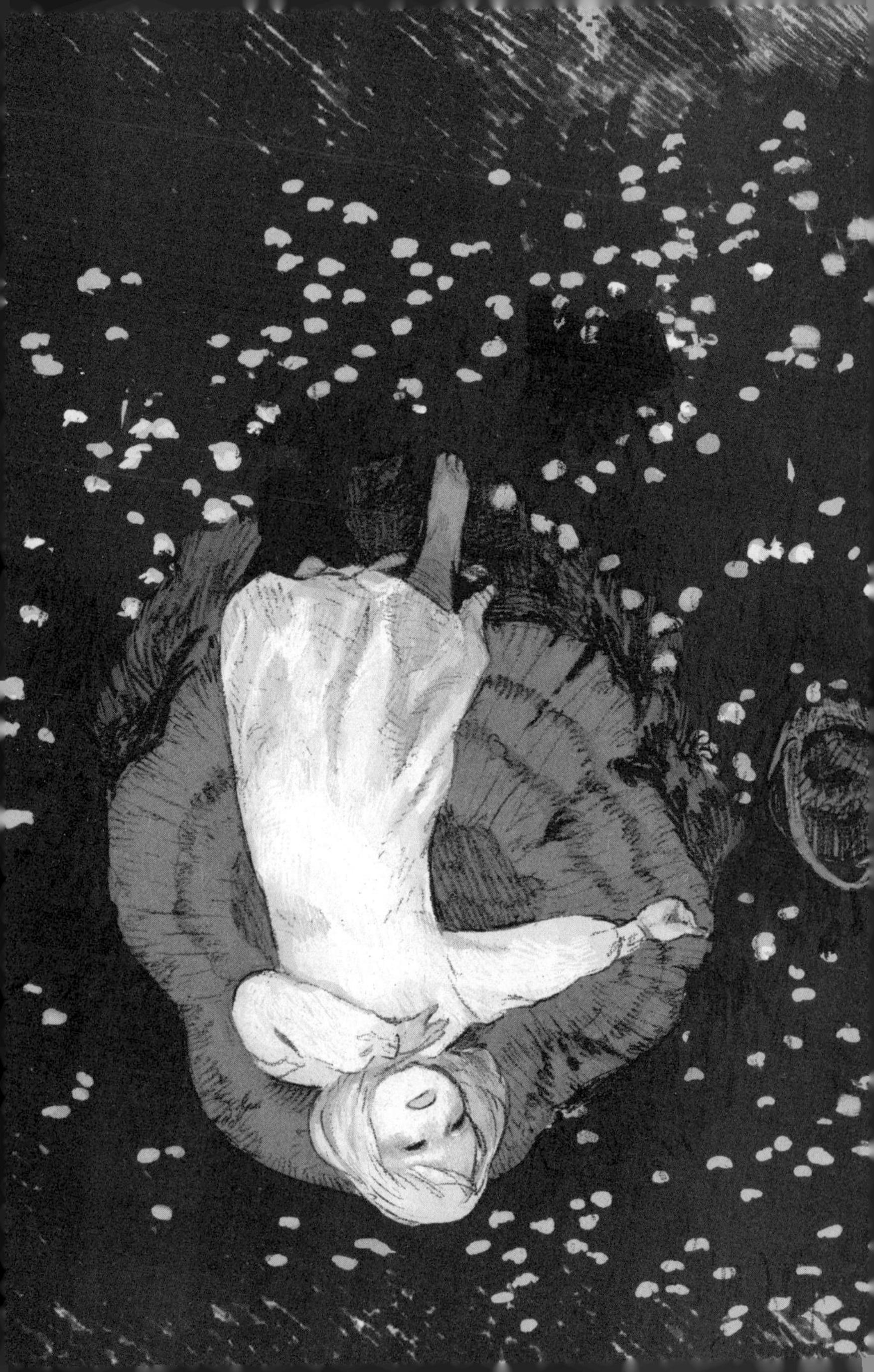

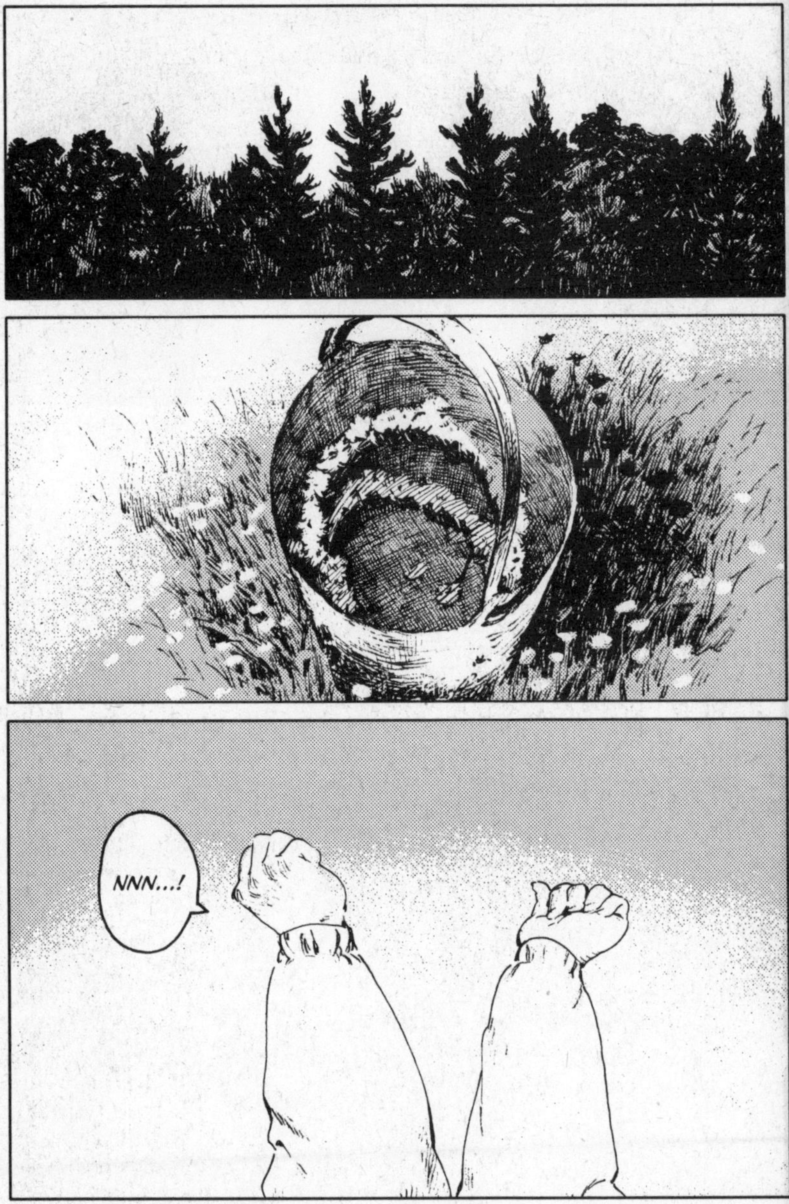
NNN...!

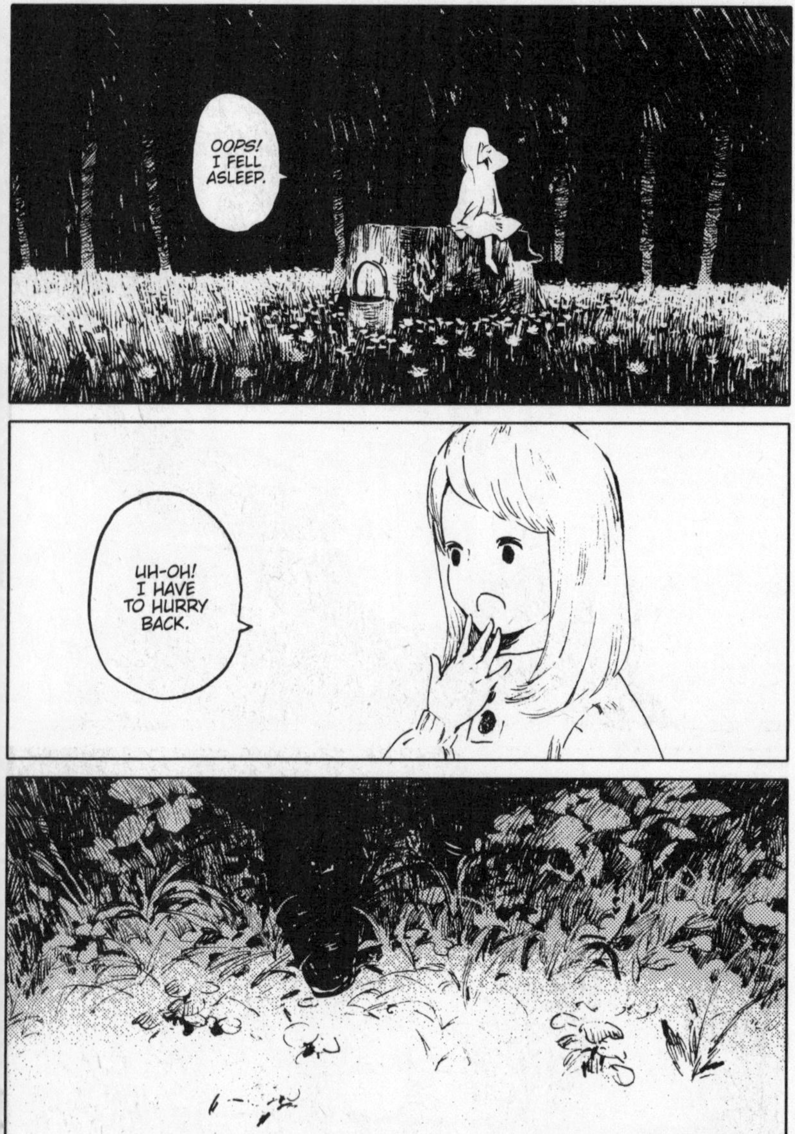
OOPS! I FELL ASLEEP.
UH-OH! I HAVE TO HURRY BACK.

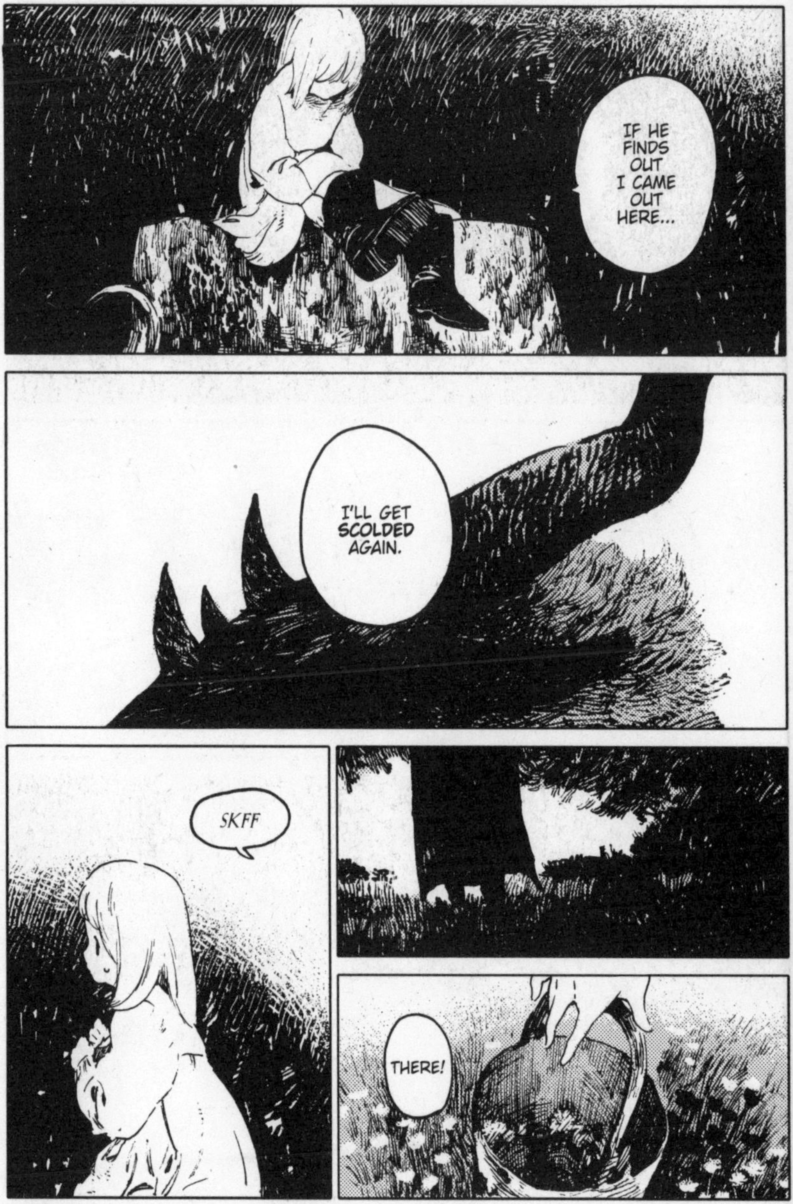
IF HE FINDS OUT I CAME OUT HERE...
I'LL GET SCOLDED AGAIN.
THERE!
SKFF

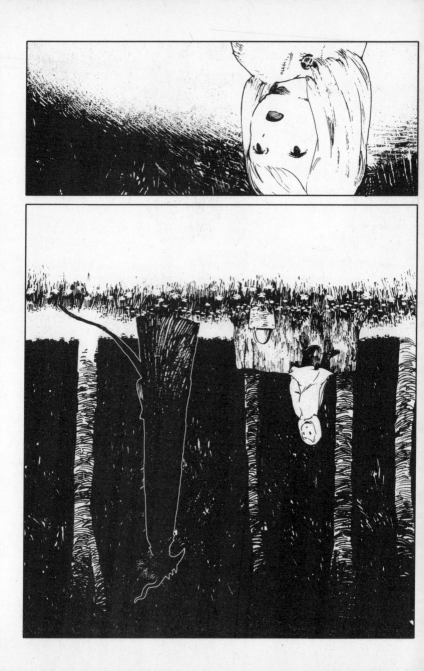

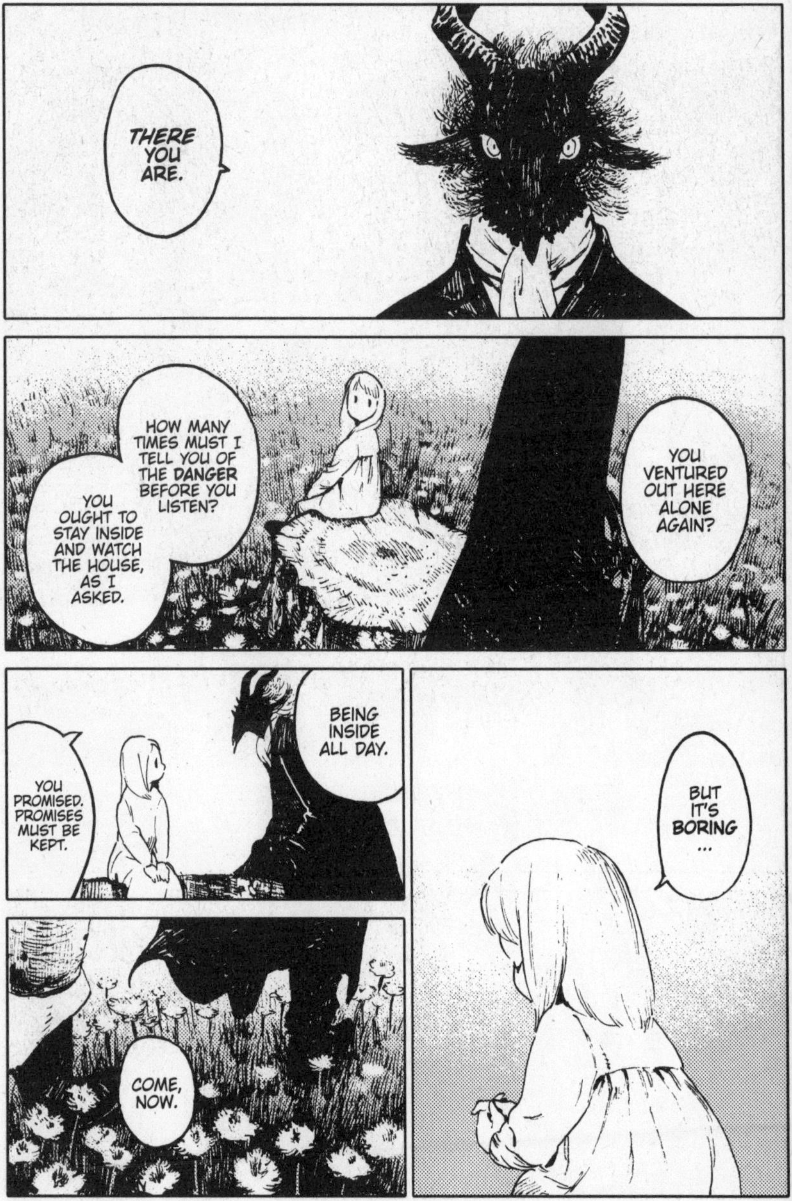
THERE YOU ARE.
YOU VENTURED OUT HERE ALONE AGAIN?
HOW MANY TIMES MUST I TELL YOU OF THE DANGER BEFORE YOU LISTEN?
YOU OUGHT TO STAY INSIDE AND WATCH THE HOUSE, AS I ASKED.
BUT IT'S BORING...
BEING INSIDE ALL DAY.
YOU PROMISED. PROMISES MUST BE KEPT.
COME, NOW.

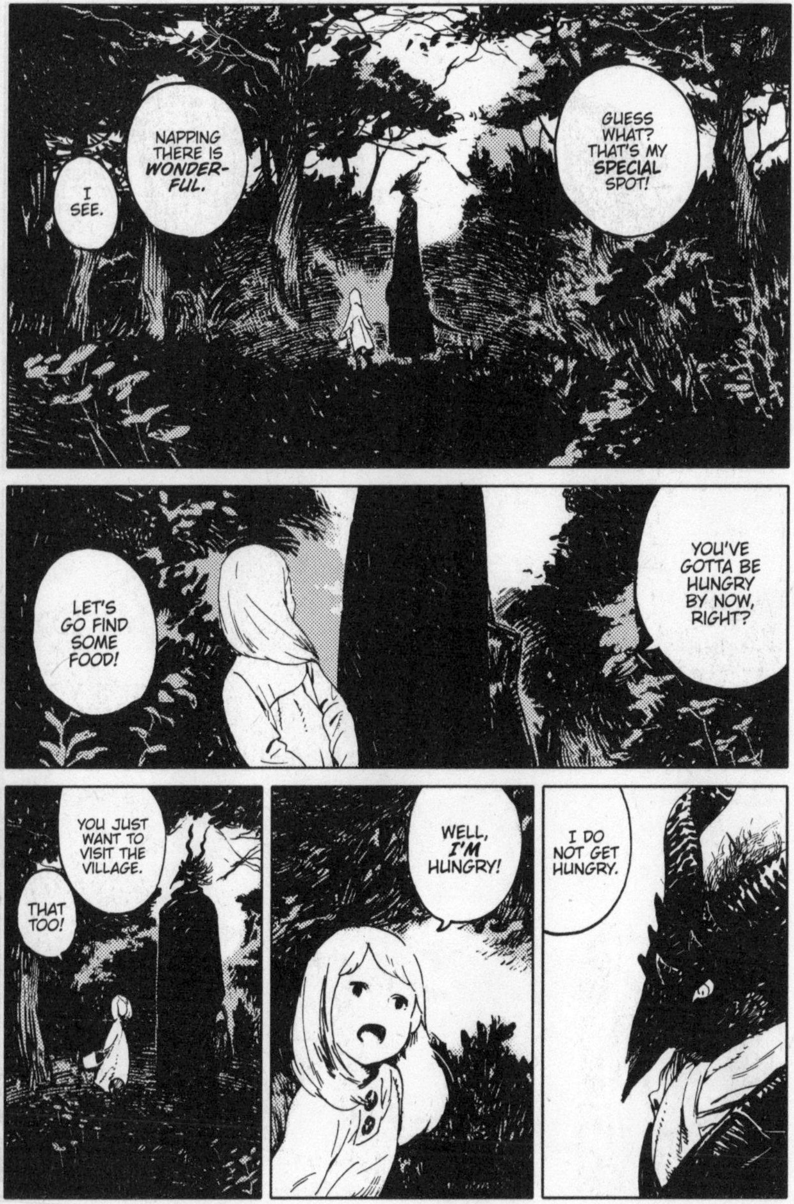
GUESS WHAT? THAT'S MY **SPECIAL** SPOT!
NAPPING THERE IS ***WONDERFUL.***
I SEE.
YOU'VE GOTTA BE HUNGRY BY NOW, RIGHT?
LET'S GO FIND SOME FOOD!
I DO NOT GET HUNGRY.
WELL, ***I'M*** HUNGRY!
YOU JUST WANT TO VISIT THE VILLAGE.
THAT TOO!

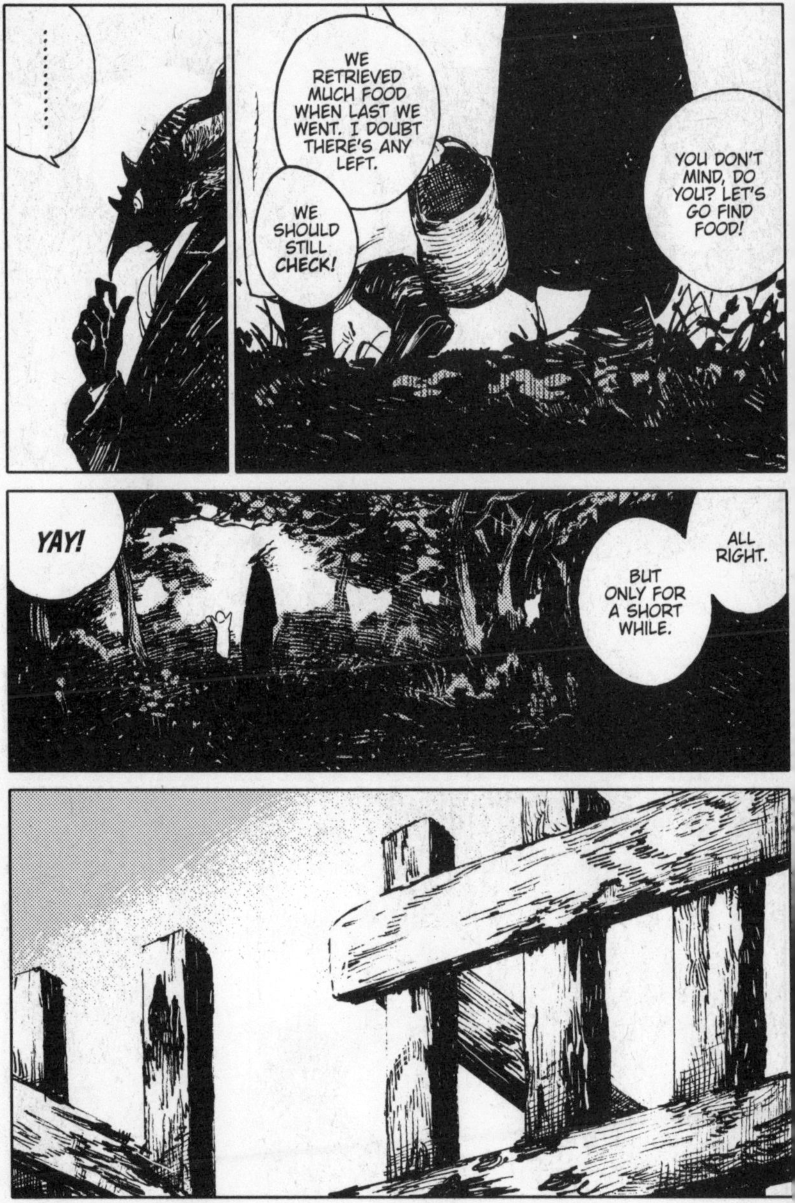
YOU DON'T MIND, DO YOU? LET'S GO FIND FOOD!
WE RETRIEVED MUCH FOOD WHEN LAST WE WENT. I DOUBT THERE'S ANY LEFT.
WE SHOULD STILL CHECK!
......
ALL RIGHT.
BUT ONLY FOR A SHORT WHILE.
YAY!

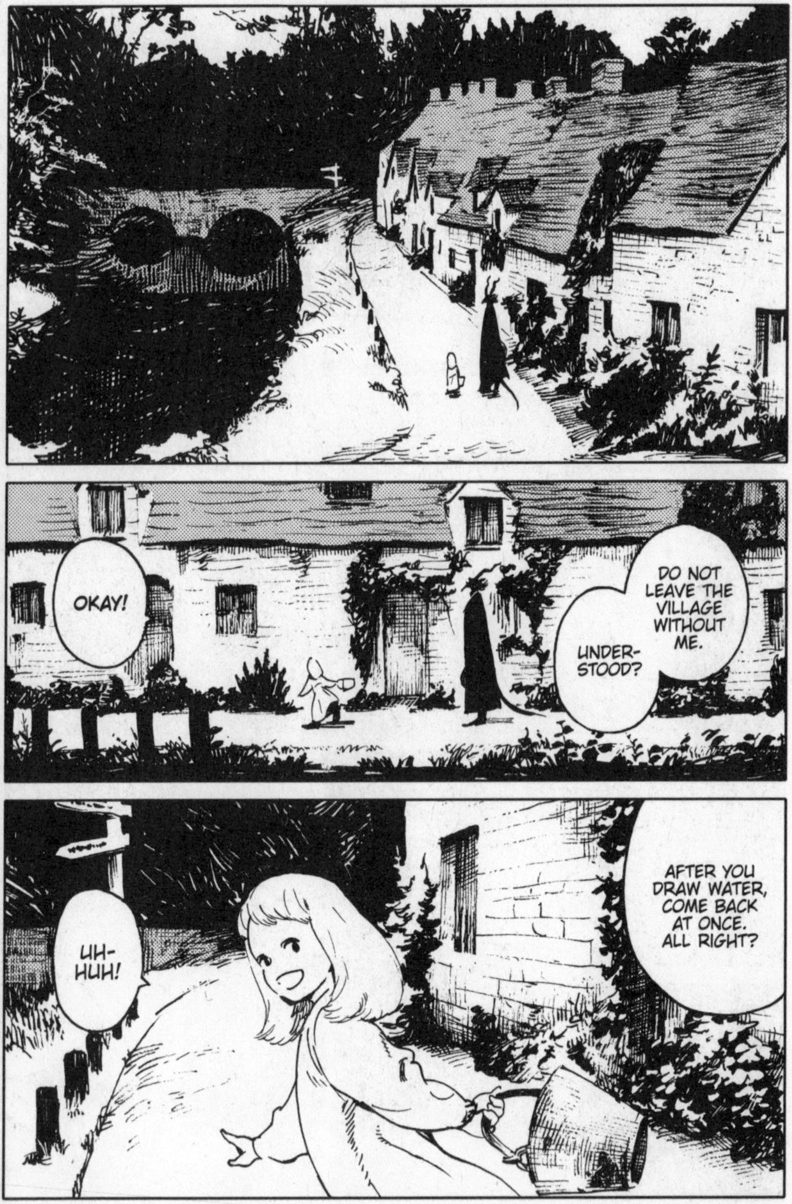
DO NOT LEAVE THE VILLAGE WITHOUT ME.
UNDER-STOOD?
OKAY!
AFTER YOU DRAW WATER, COME BACK AT ONCE. ALL RIGHT?
UH-HUH!

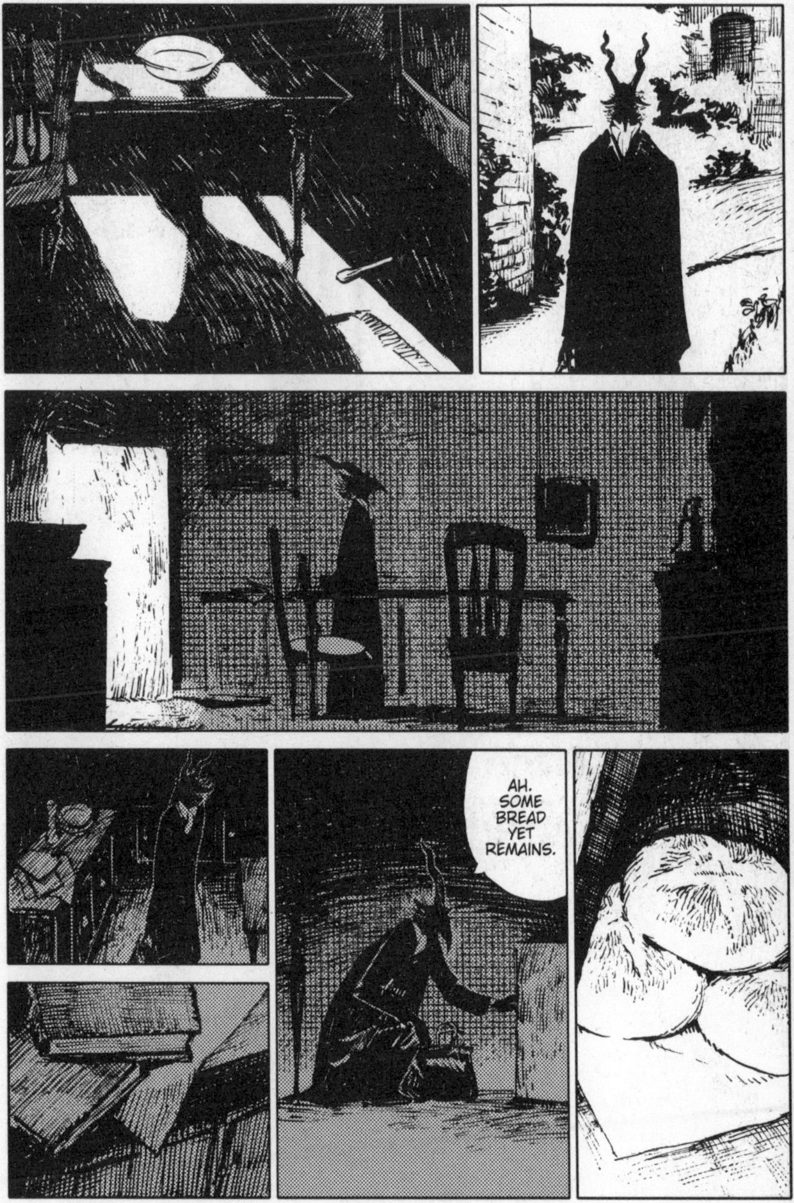
AH. SOME BREAD YET REMAINS.

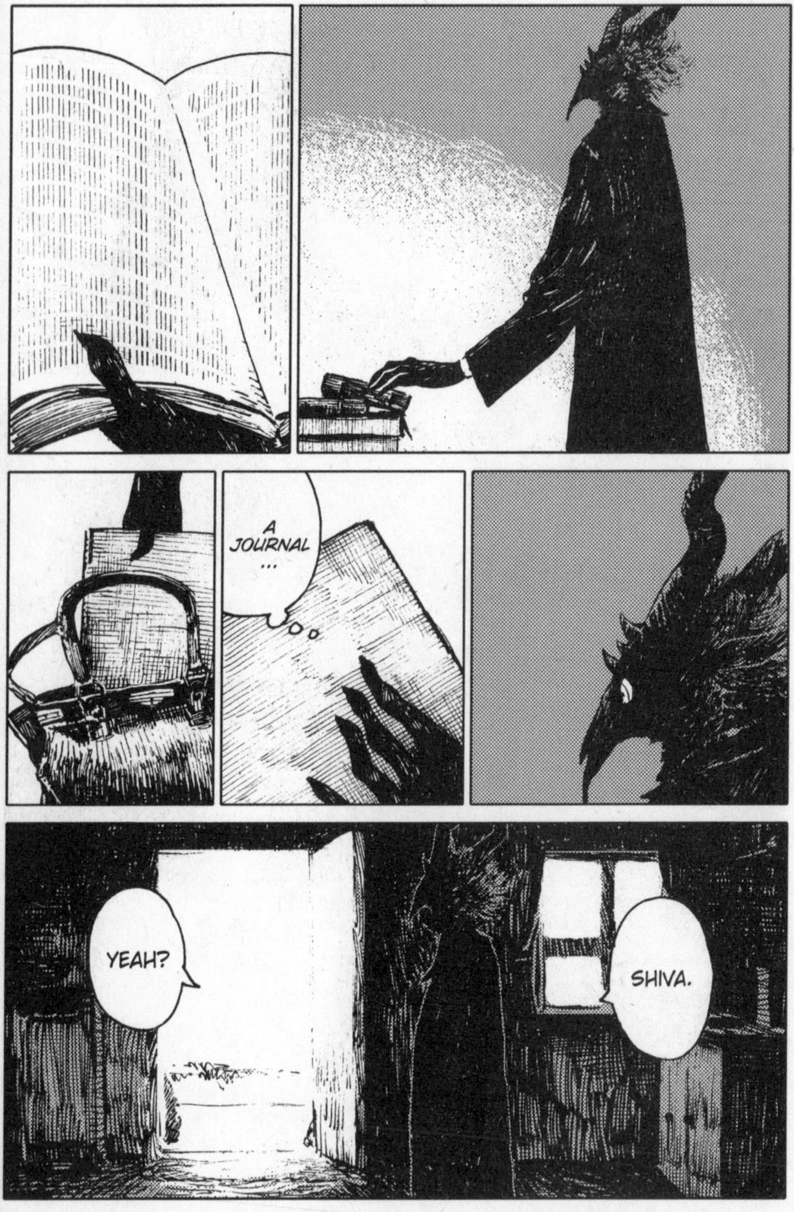
A JOURNAL ...
SHIVA.
YEAH?

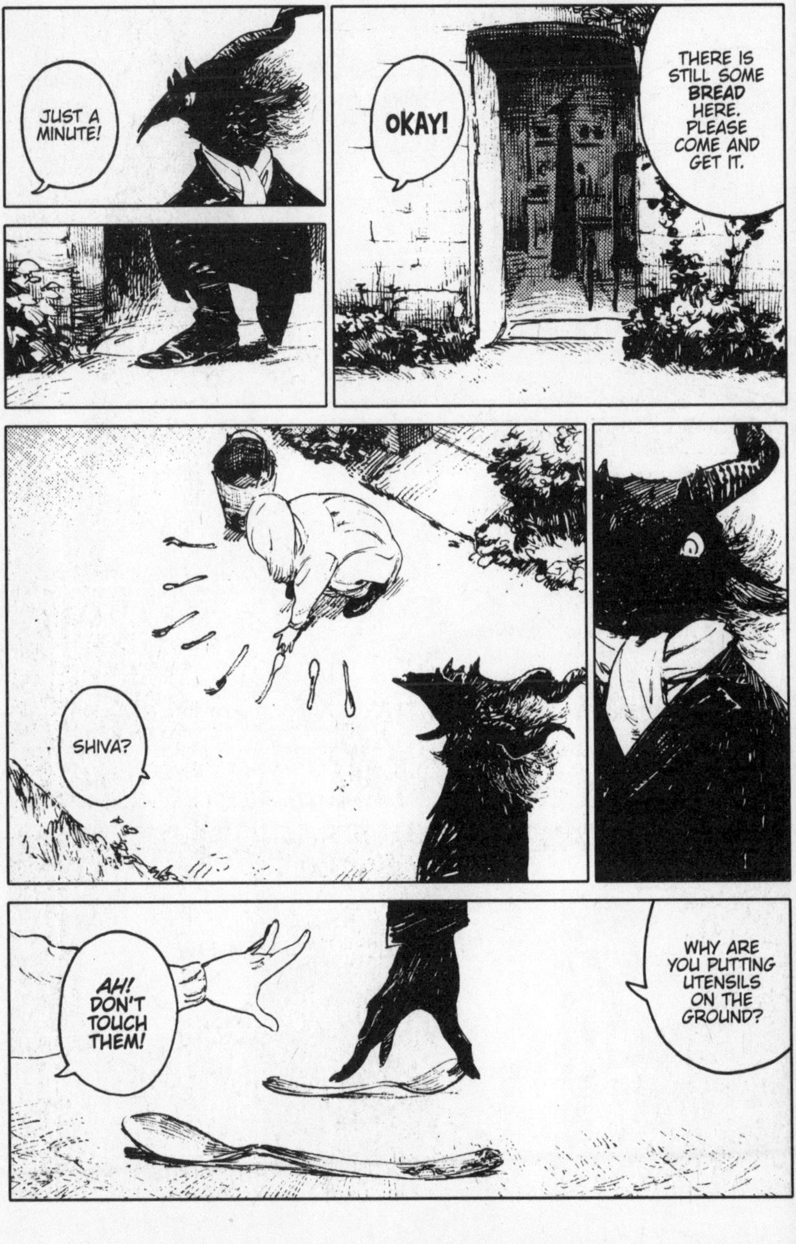
THERE IS STILL SOME BREAD HERE. PLEASE COME AND GET IT.
OKAY!
JUST A MINUTE!
SHIVA?
WHY ARE YOU PUTTING UTENSILS ON THE GROUND?
AH! DON'T TOUCH THEM!

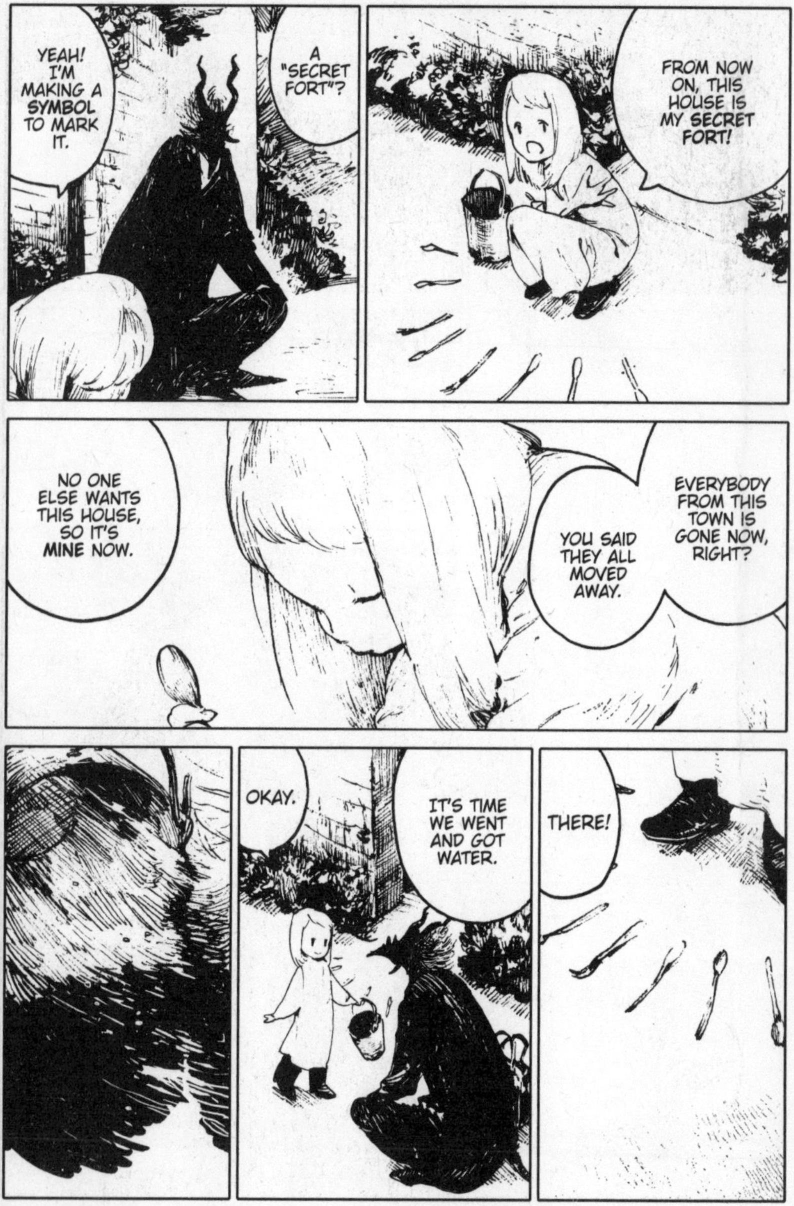
FROM NOW ON, THIS HOUSE IS MY SECRET FORT!
A "SECRET FORT"?
YEAH! I'M MAKING A SYMBOL TO MARK IT.
EVERYBODY FROM THIS TOWN IS GONE NOW, RIGHT?
YOU SAID THEY ALL MOVED AWAY.
NO ONE ELSE WANTS THIS HOUSE, SO IT'S MINE NOW.
THERE!
IT'S TIME WE WENT AND GOT WATER.
OKAY.

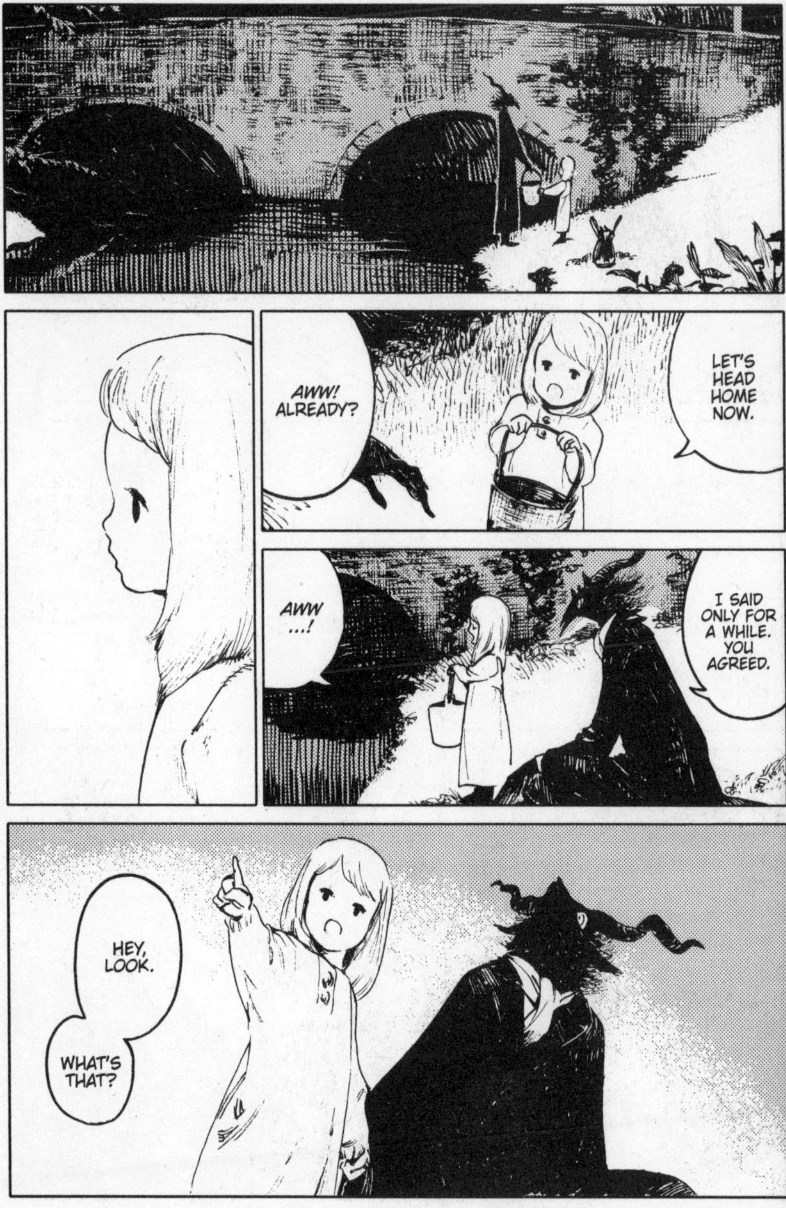
LET'S HEAD HOME NOW.
AWW! ALREADY?
I SAID ONLY FOR A WHILE. YOU AGREED.
AWW ...!
HEY, LOOK.
WHAT'S THAT?

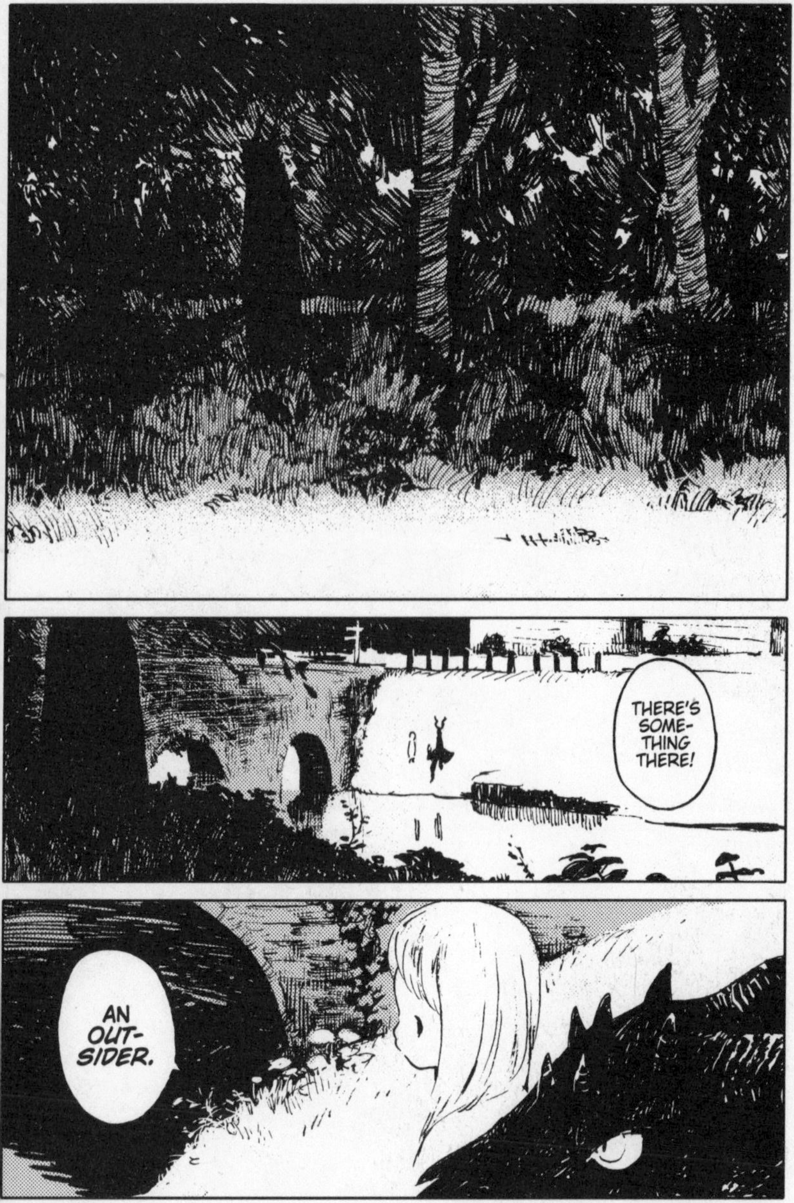
THERE'S SOME-THING THERE!
AN OUT-SIDER.

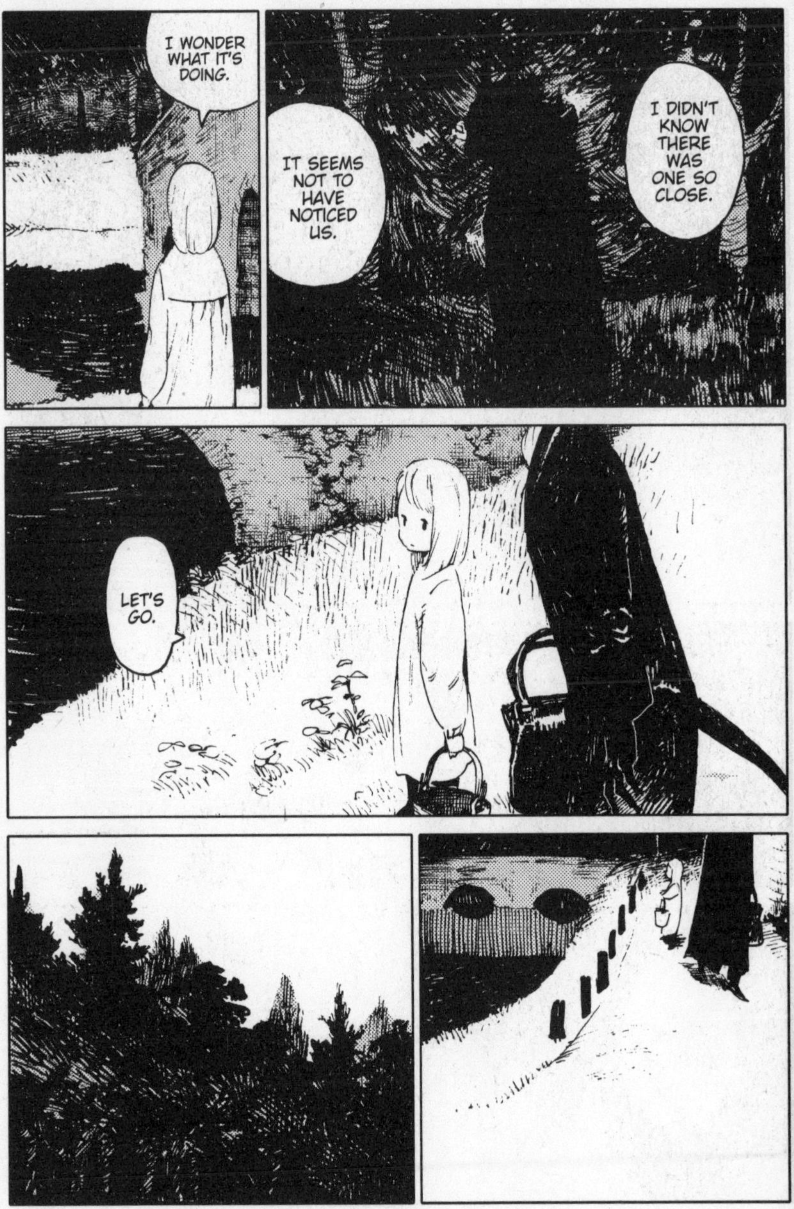
I DIDN'T KNOW THERE WAS ONE SO CLOSE.
IT SEEMS NOT TO HAVE NOTICED US.
I WONDER WHAT IT'S DOING.
LET'S GO.

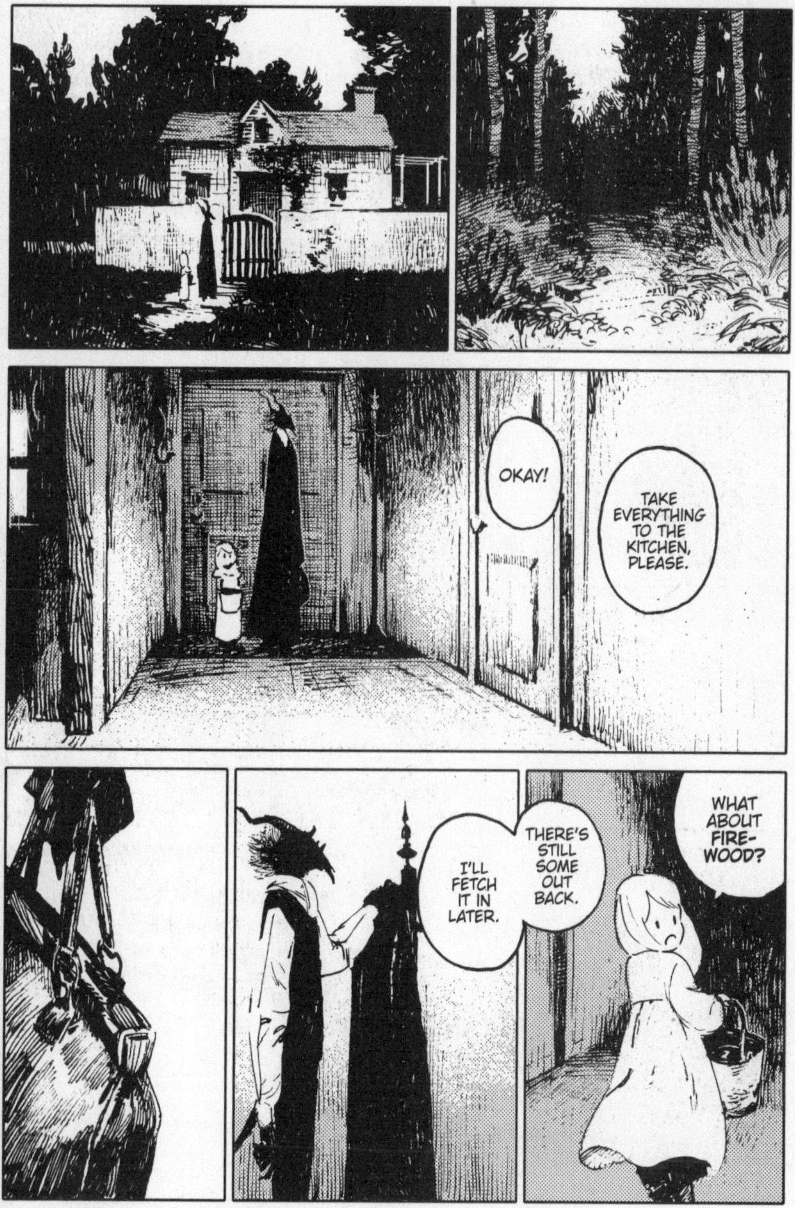
TAKE EVERYTHING TO THE KITCHEN, PLEASE.
OKAY!
WHAT ABOUT FIRE-WOOD?
THERE'S STILL SOME OUT BACK.
I'LL FETCH IT IN LATER.

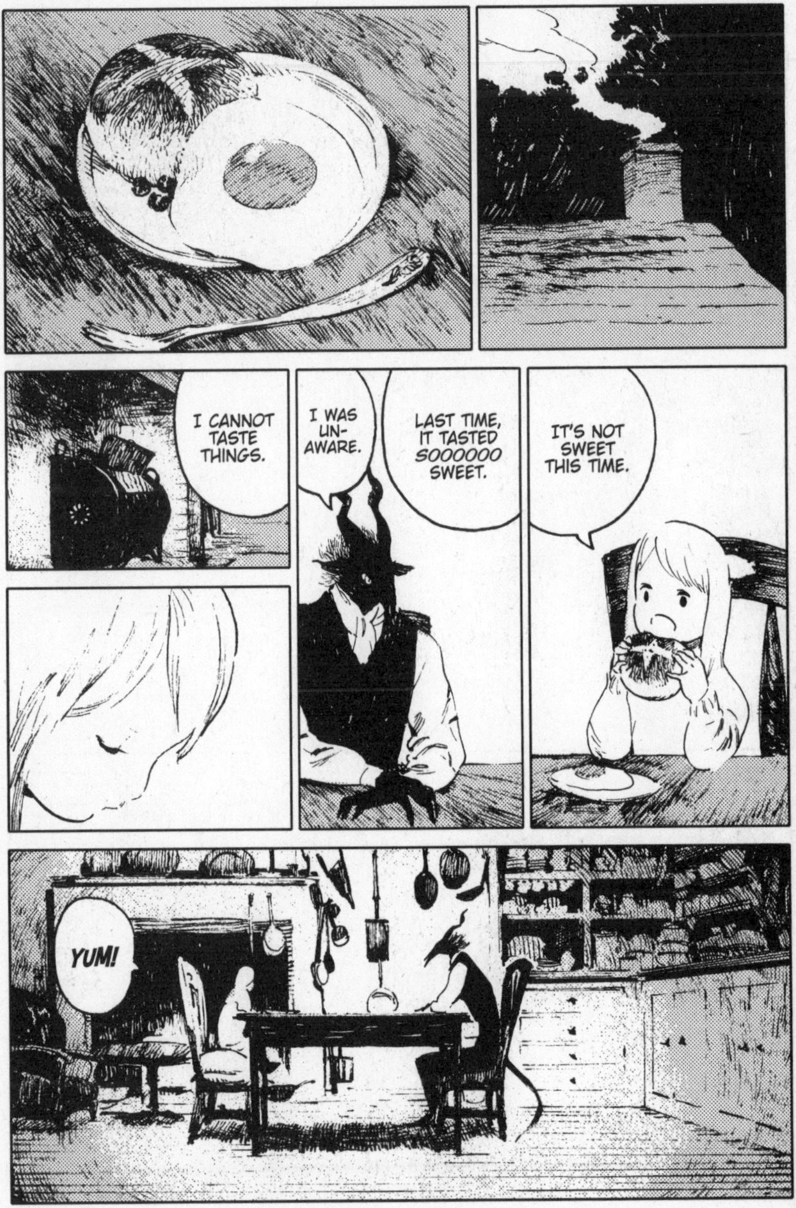
IT'S NOT SWEET THIS TIME.
LAST TIME, IT TASTED SOOOOOO SWEET.
I WAS UN-AWARE.
I CANNOT TASTE THINGS.
YUM!

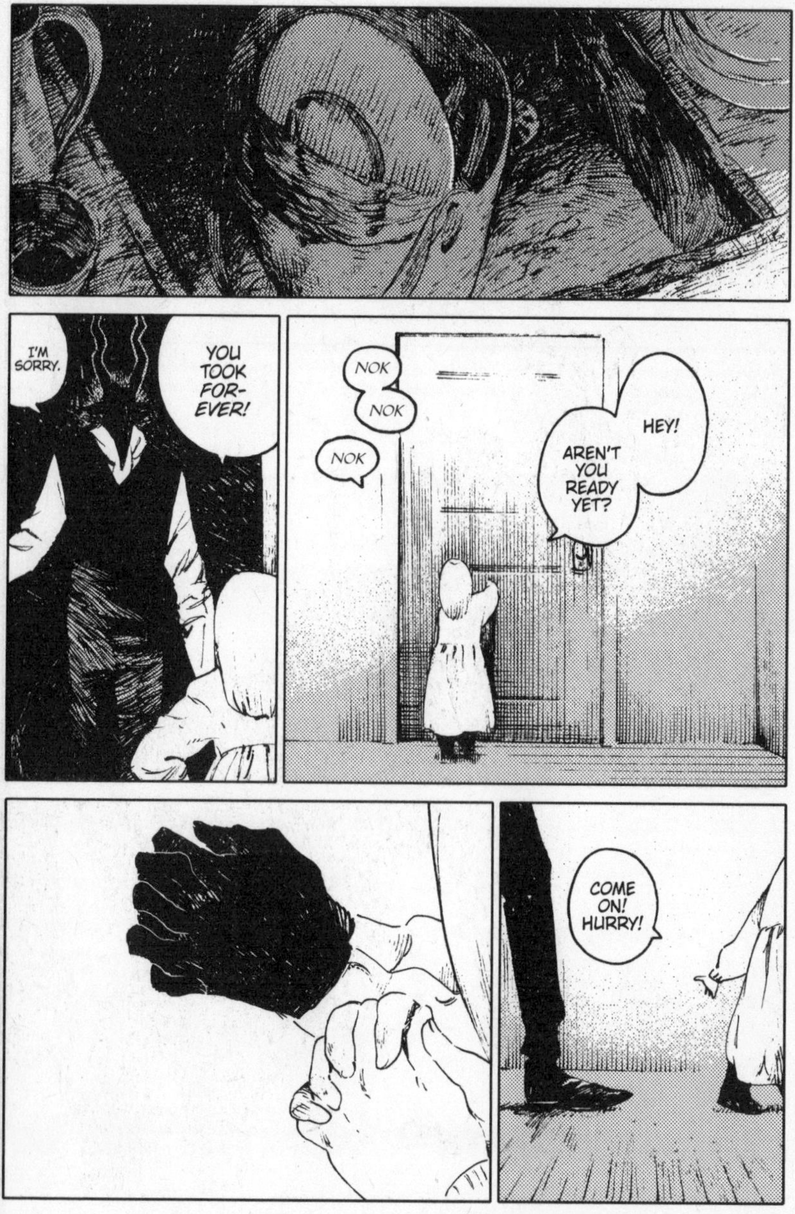
HEY!
AREN'T YOU READY YET?
NOK
NOK
NOK
YOU TOOK FOR-EVER!
I'M SORRY.
COME ON! HURRY!

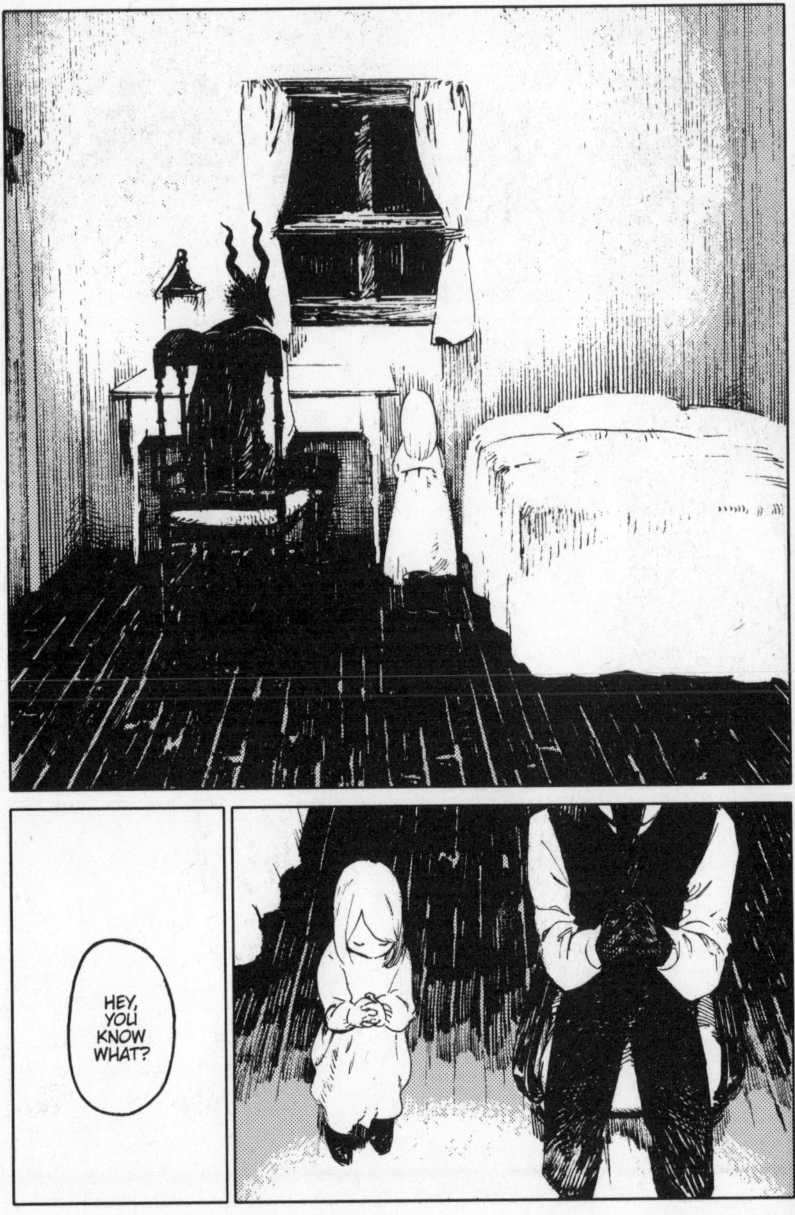
HEY, YOU KNOW WHAT?

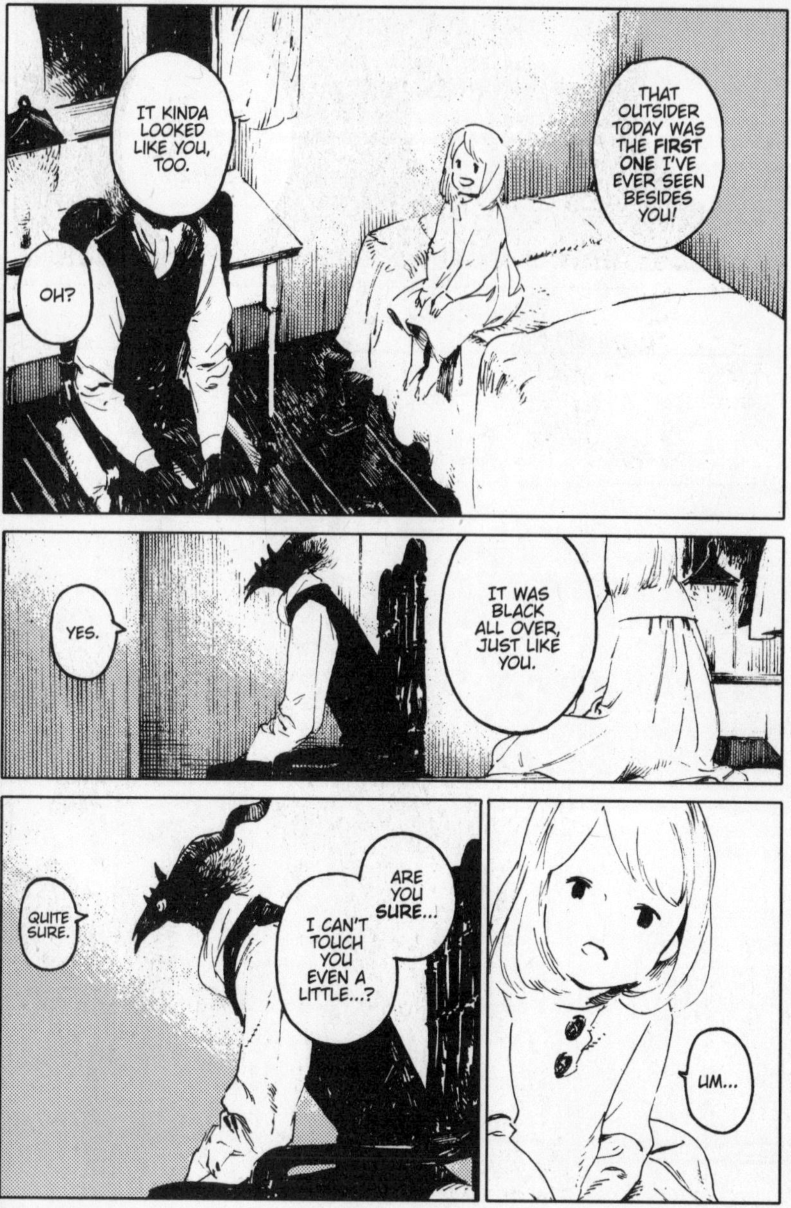
THAT OUTSIDER TODAY WAS THE FIRST ONE I'VE EVER SEEN BESIDES YOU!
IT KINDA LOOKED LIKE YOU, TOO.
OH?
IT WAS BLACK ALL OVER, JUST LIKE YOU.
YES.
UM...
ARE YOU SURE...
I CAN'T TOUCH YOU EVEN A LITTLE...?
QUITE SURE.

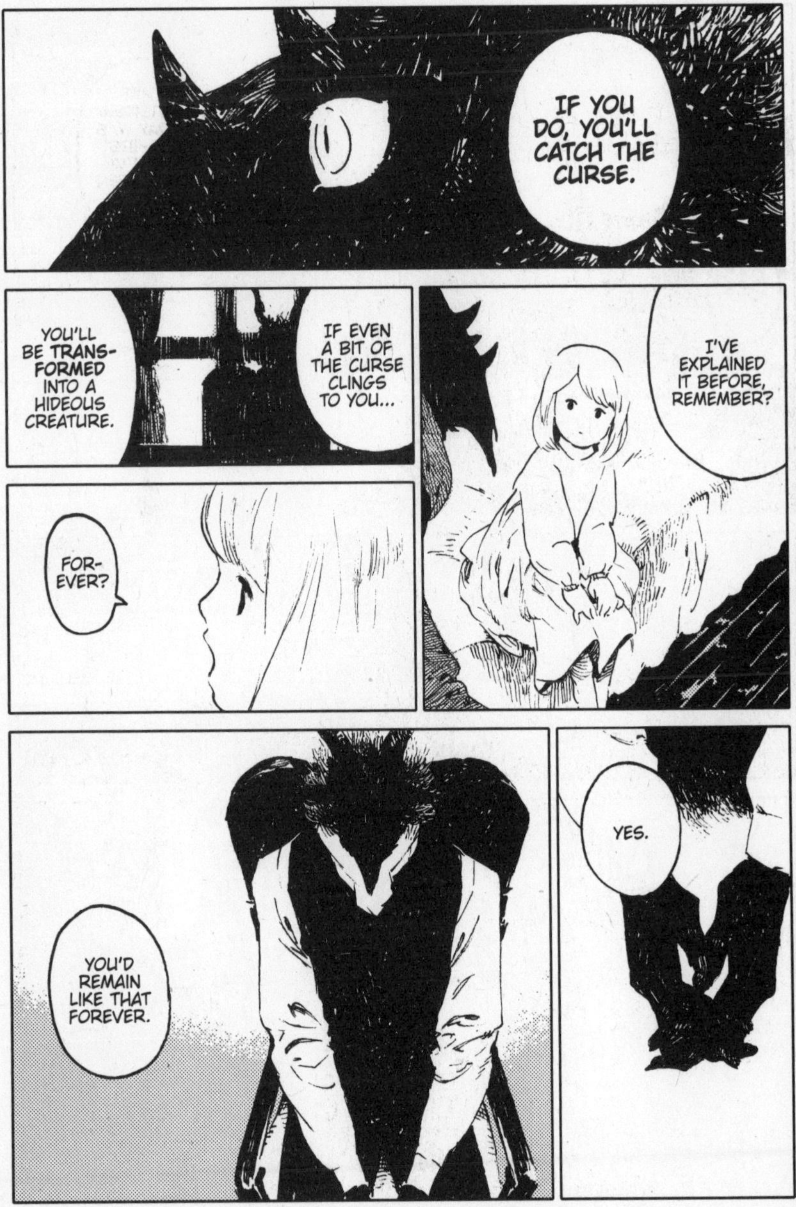
IF YOU DO, YOU'LL CATCH THE CURSE.
I'VE EXPLAINED IT BEFORE, REMEMBER?
IF EVEN A BIT OF THE CURSE CLINGS TO YOU...
YOU'LL BE TRANSFORMED INTO A HIDEOUS CREATURE.
FOREVER?
YES.
YOU'D REMAIN LIKE THAT FOREVER.

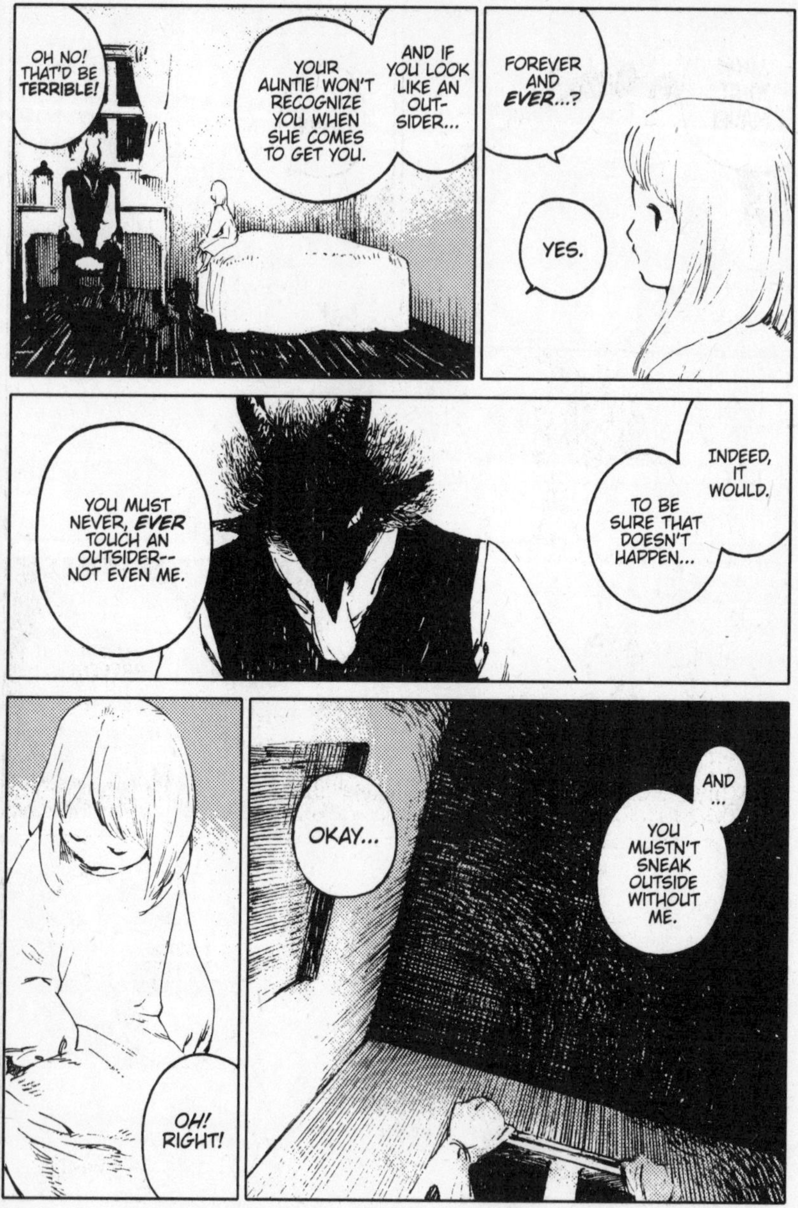
FOREVER AND *EVER*...?
YES.
AND IF YOU LOOK LIKE AN OUT-SIDER...
YOUR AUNTIE WON'T RECOGNIZE YOU WHEN SHE COMES TO GET YOU.
OH NO! THAT'D BE TERRIBLE!
INDEED, IT WOULD.
TO BE SURE THAT DOESN'T HAPPEN...
YOU MUST NEVER, *EVER* TOUCH AN OUTSIDER-- NOT EVEN ME.
AND ...
YOU MUSTN'T SNEAK OUTSIDE WITHOUT ME.
OKAY...
OH! RIGHT!

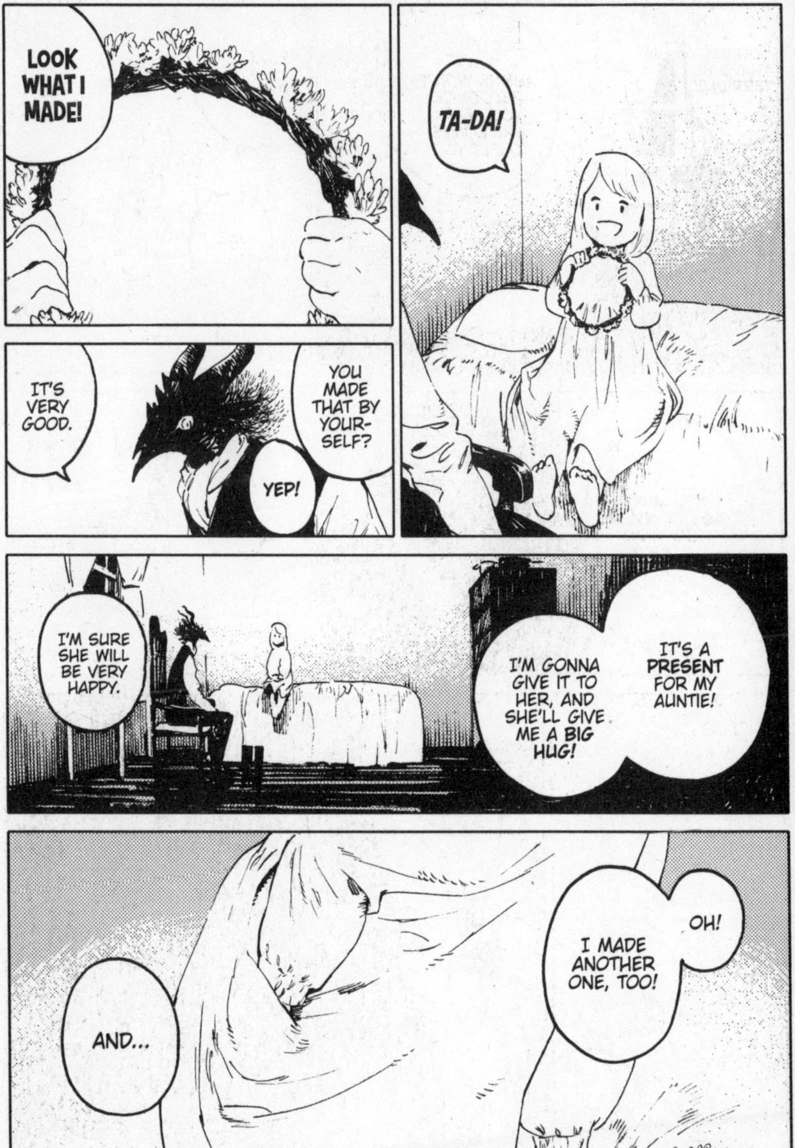
TA-DA!
LOOK WHAT I MADE!
YOU MADE THAT BY YOUR-SELF?
YEP!
IT'S VERY GOOD.
IT'S A PRESENT FOR MY AUNTIE!
I'M GONNA GIVE IT TO HER, AND SHE'LL GIVE ME A BIG HUG!
I'M SURE SHE WILL BE VERY HAPPY.
OH!
I MADE ANOTHER ONE, TOO!
AND...

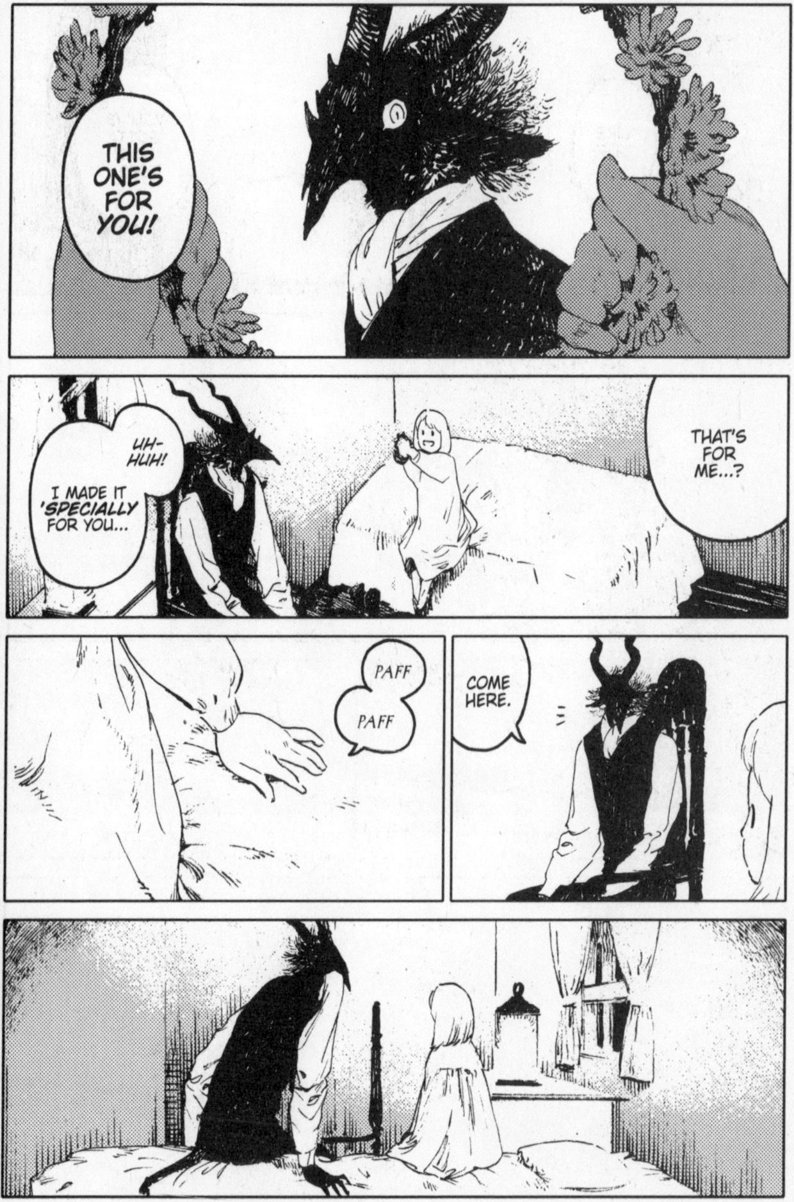
THIS ONE'S FOR YOU!
THAT'S FOR ME...?
UH-HUH!
I MADE IT 'SPECIALLY FOR YOU...
COME HERE.
PAFF
PAFF

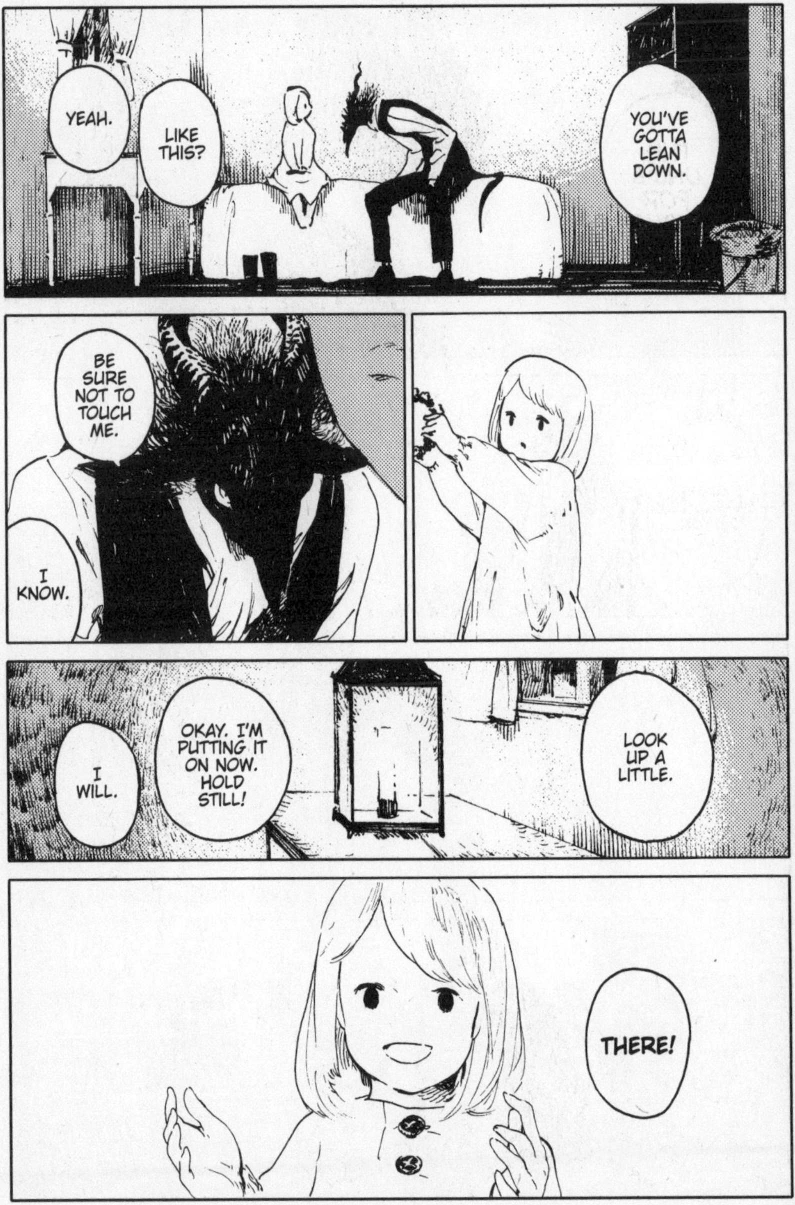
YOU'VE GOTTA LEAN DOWN.
LIKE THIS?
YEAH.
BE SURE NOT TO TOUCH ME.
I KNOW.
LOOK UP A LITTLE.
OKAY. I'M PUTTING IT ON NOW. HOLD STILL!
I WILL.
THERE!

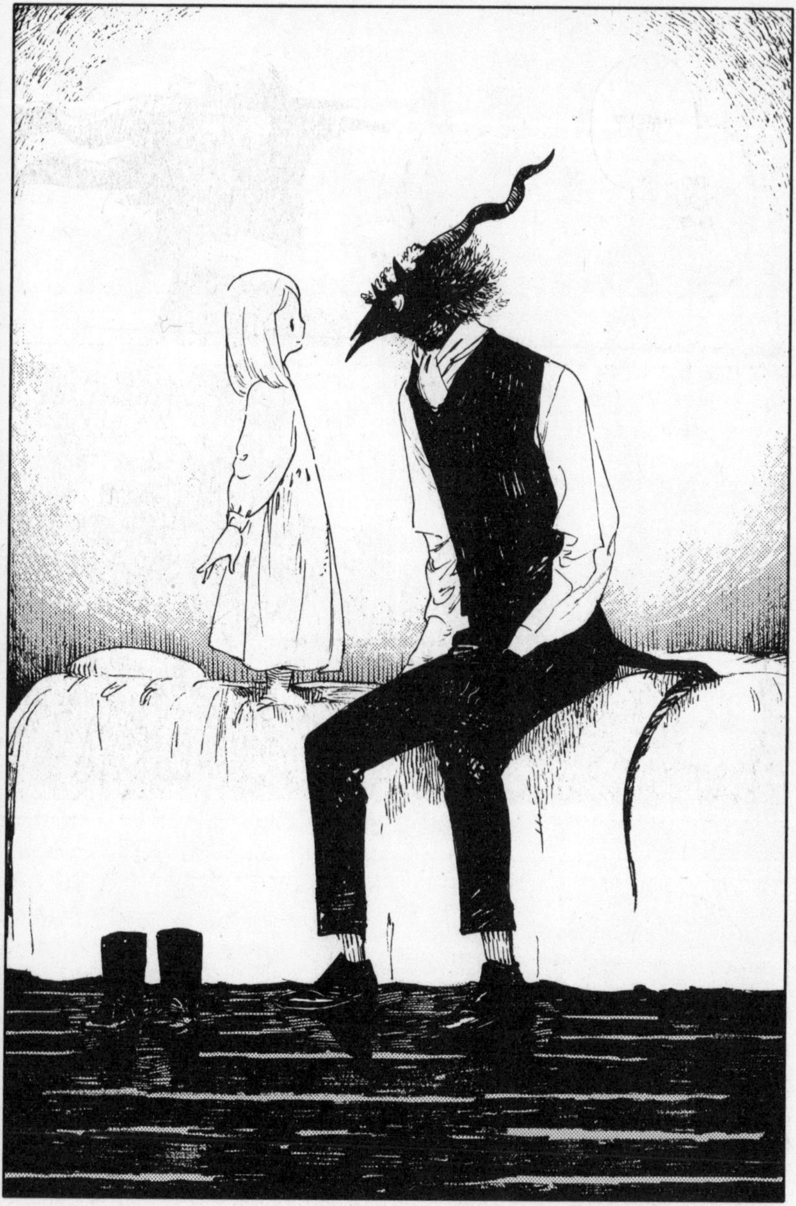

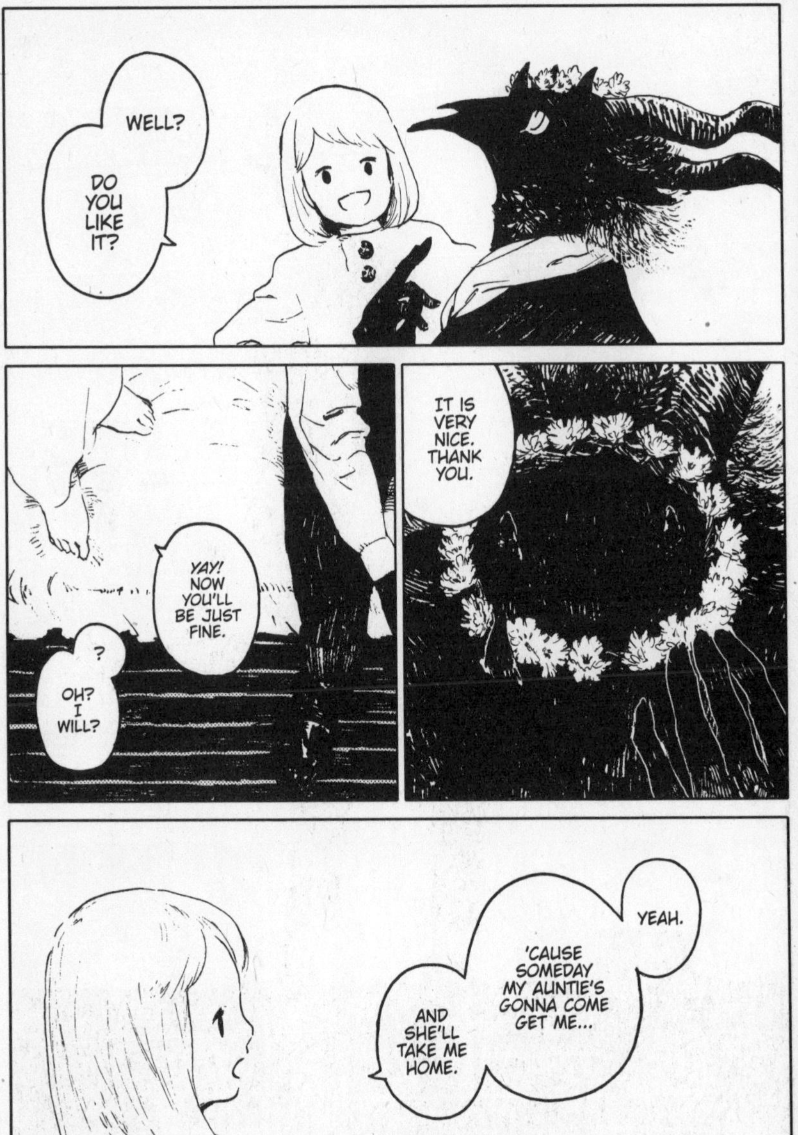
WELL?
DO YOU LIKE IT?
IT IS VERY NICE. THANK YOU.
YAY! NOW YOU'LL BE JUST FINE.
?
OH? I WILL?
YEAH.
'CAUSE SOMEDAY MY AUNTIE'S GONNA COME GET ME...
AND SHE'LL TAKE ME HOME.

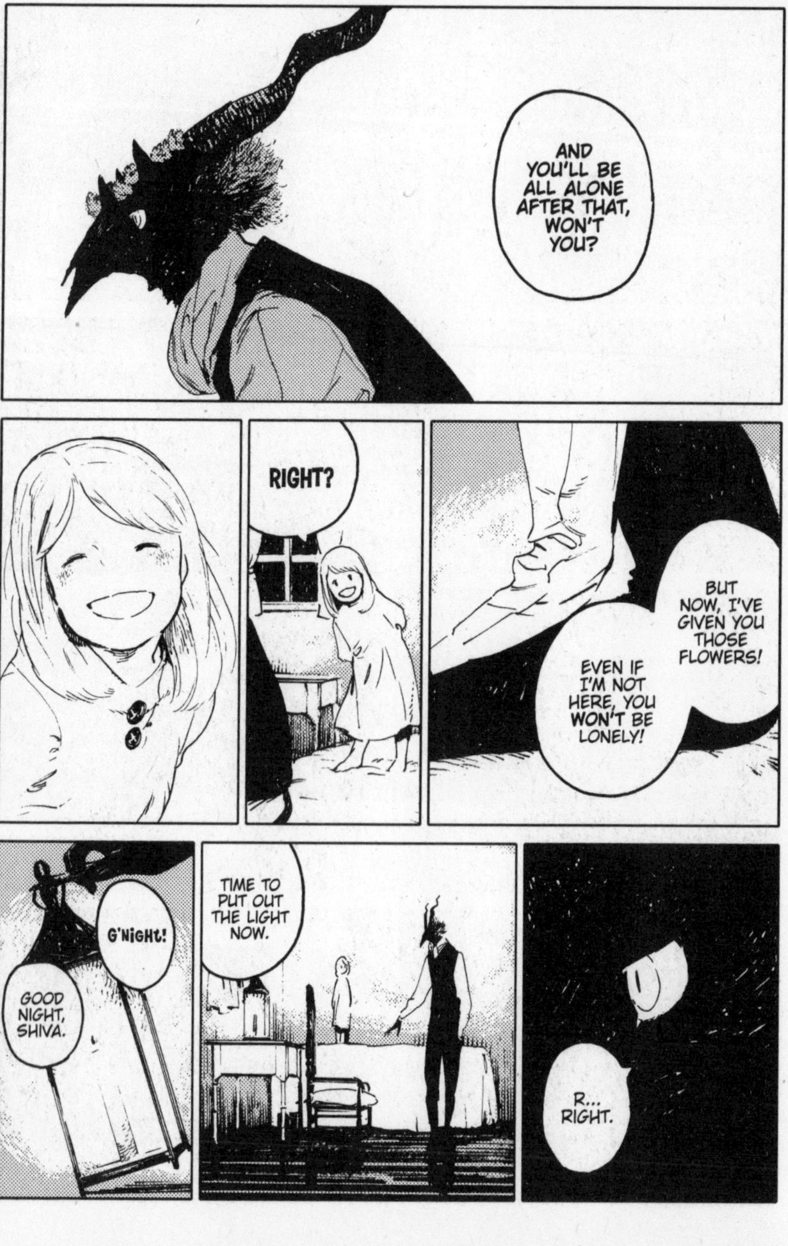
AND YOU'LL BE ALL ALONE AFTER THAT, WON'T YOU?
BUT NOW, I'VE GIVEN YOU THOSE FLOWERS!
EVEN IF I'M NOT HERE, YOU WON'T BE LONELY!
RIGHT?
R... RIGHT.
TIME TO PUT OUT THE LIGHT NOW.
G'NIGHT!
GOOD NIGHT, SHIVA.

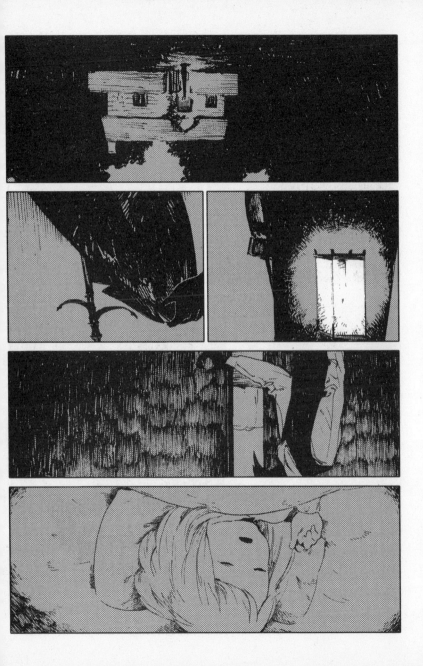

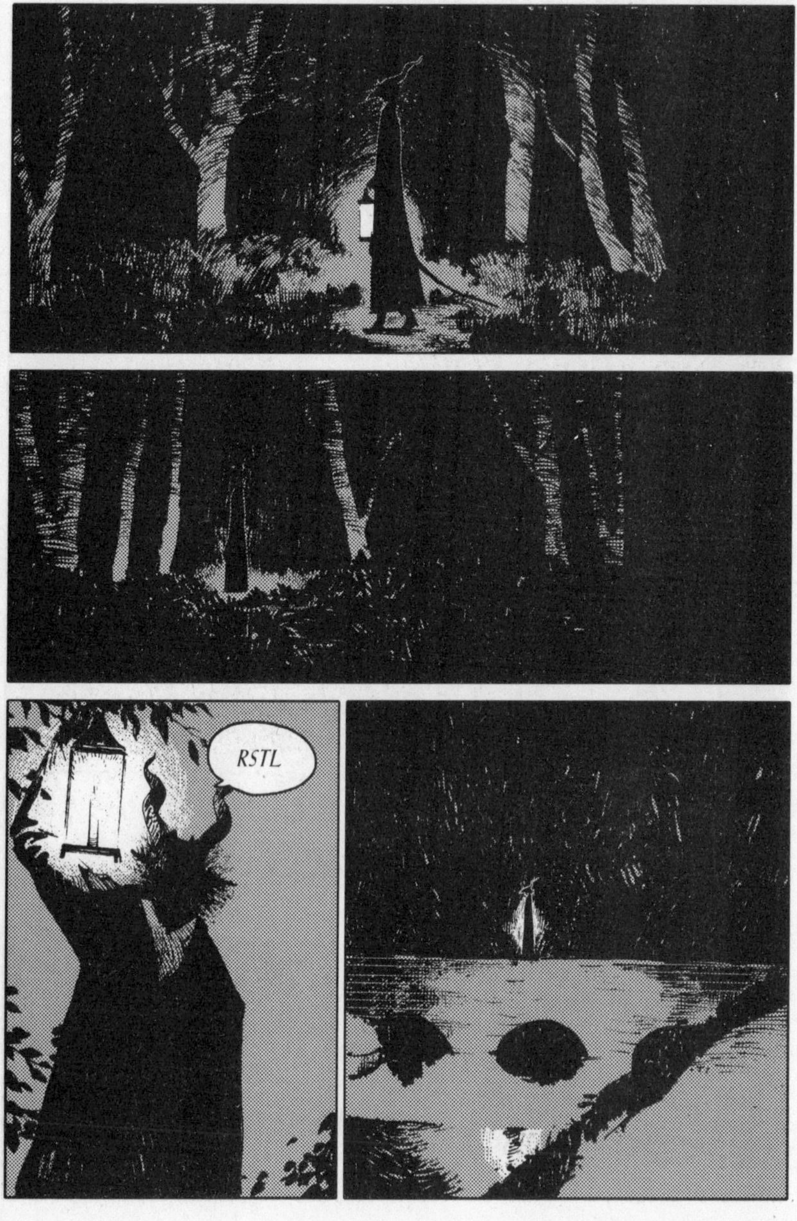
RSTL

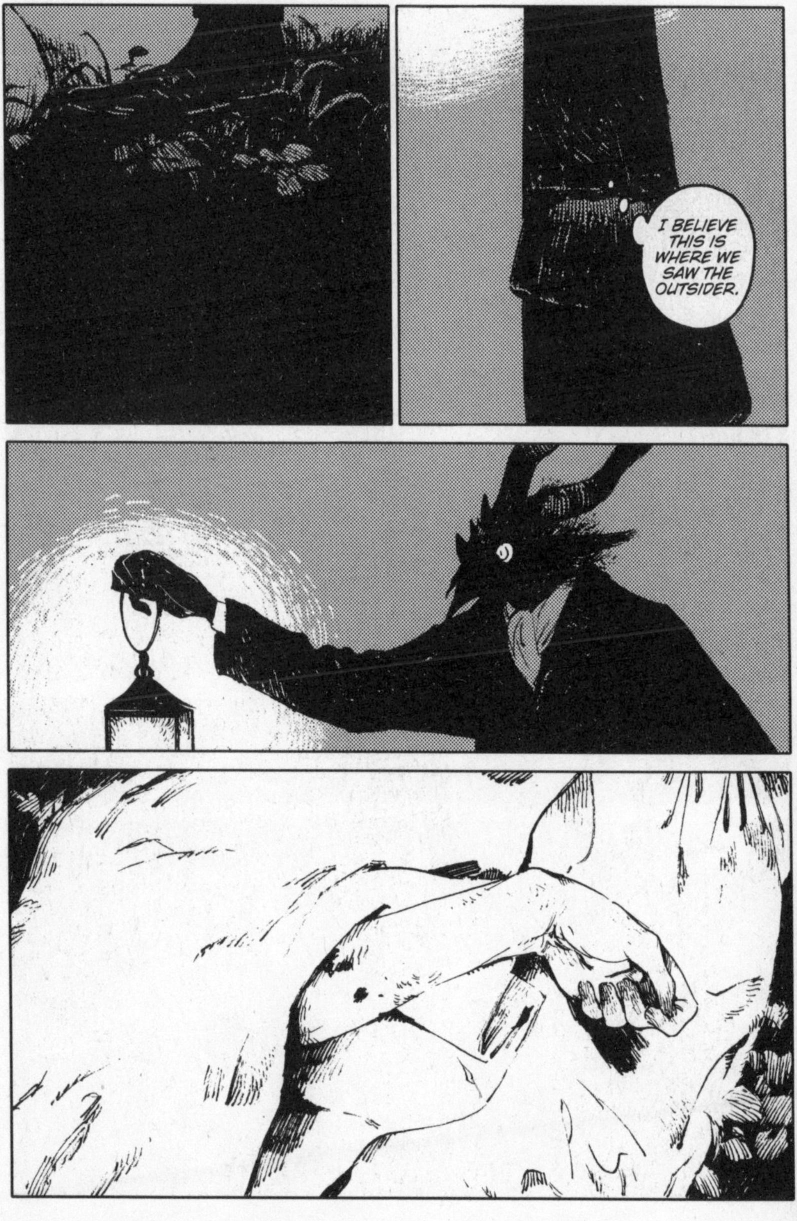
I BELIEVE THIS IS WHERE WE SAW THE OUTSIDER.

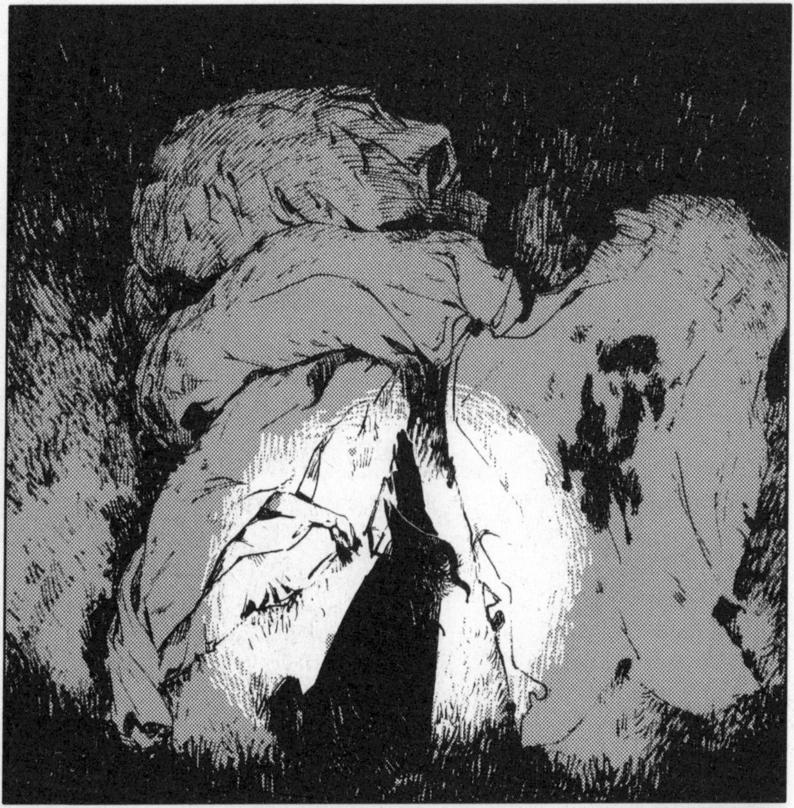
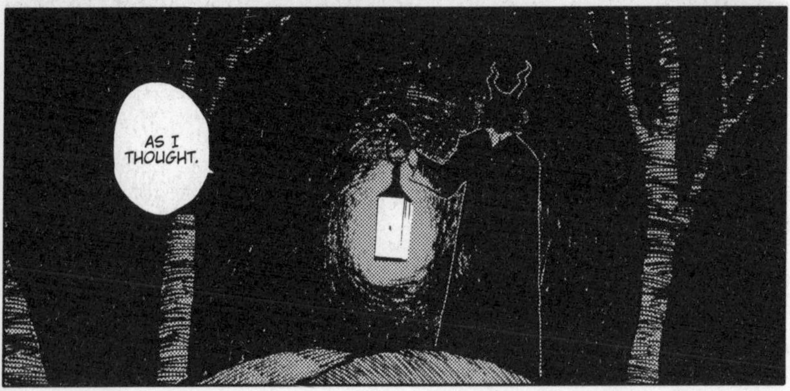
AS I THOUGHT.

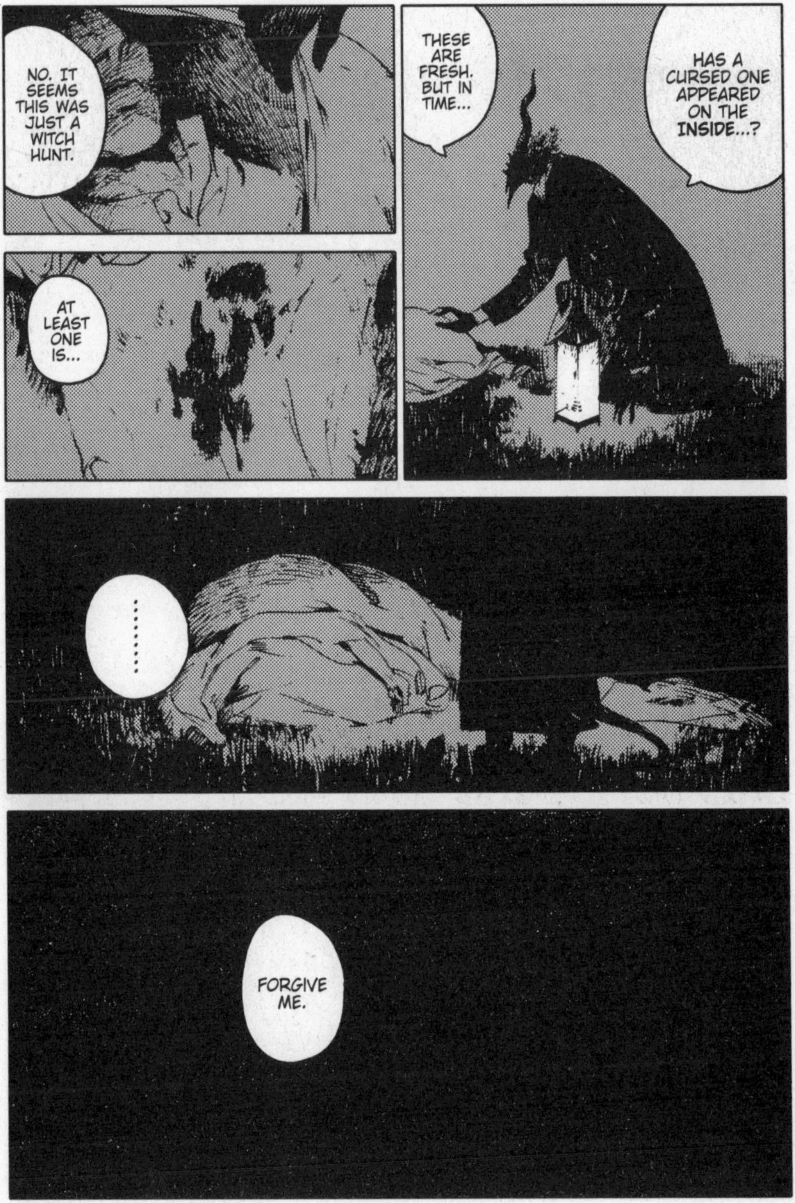
HAS A CURSED ONE APPEARED ON THE INSIDE...?
THESE ARE FRESH. BUT IN TIME...
NO. IT SEEMS THIS WAS JUST A WITCH HUNT.
AT LEAST ONE IS...
....
FORGIVE ME.

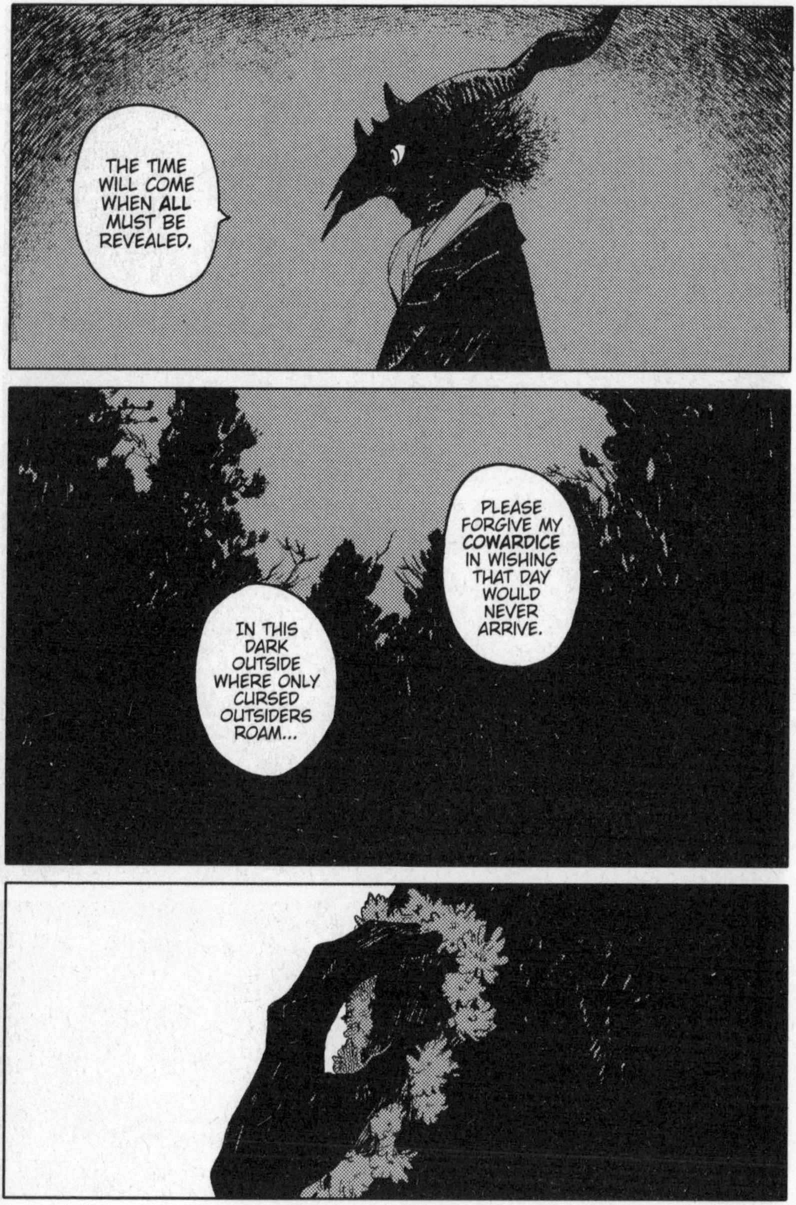
THE TIME WILL COME WHEN ALL MUST BE REVEALED.
PLEASE FORGIVE MY COWARDICE IN WISHING THAT DAY WOULD NEVER ARRIVE.
IN THIS DARK OUTSIDE WHERE ONLY CURSED OUTSIDERS ROAM...

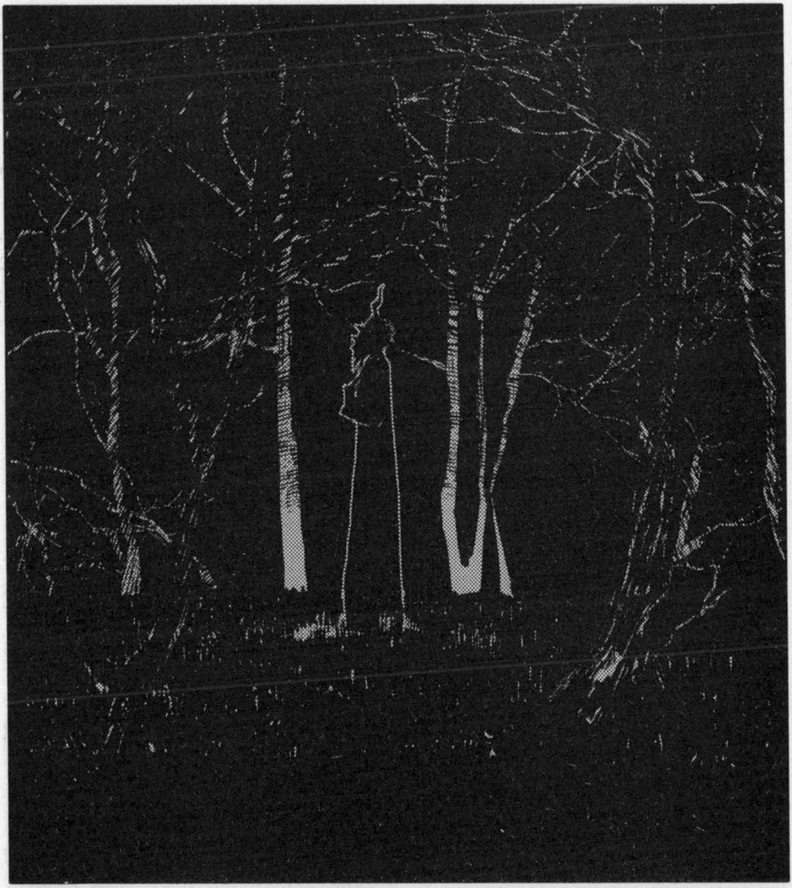

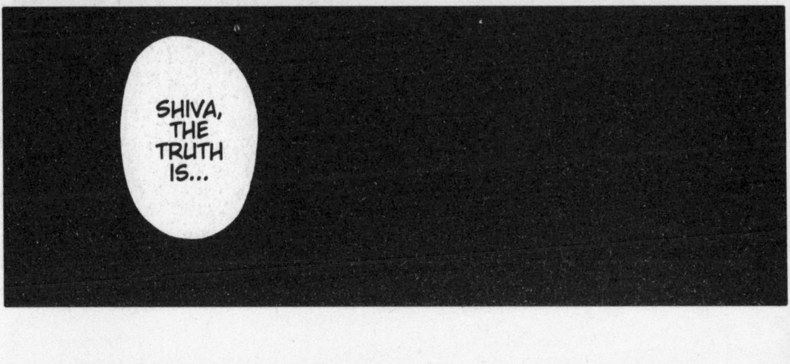
SHIVA, THE TRUTH IS...

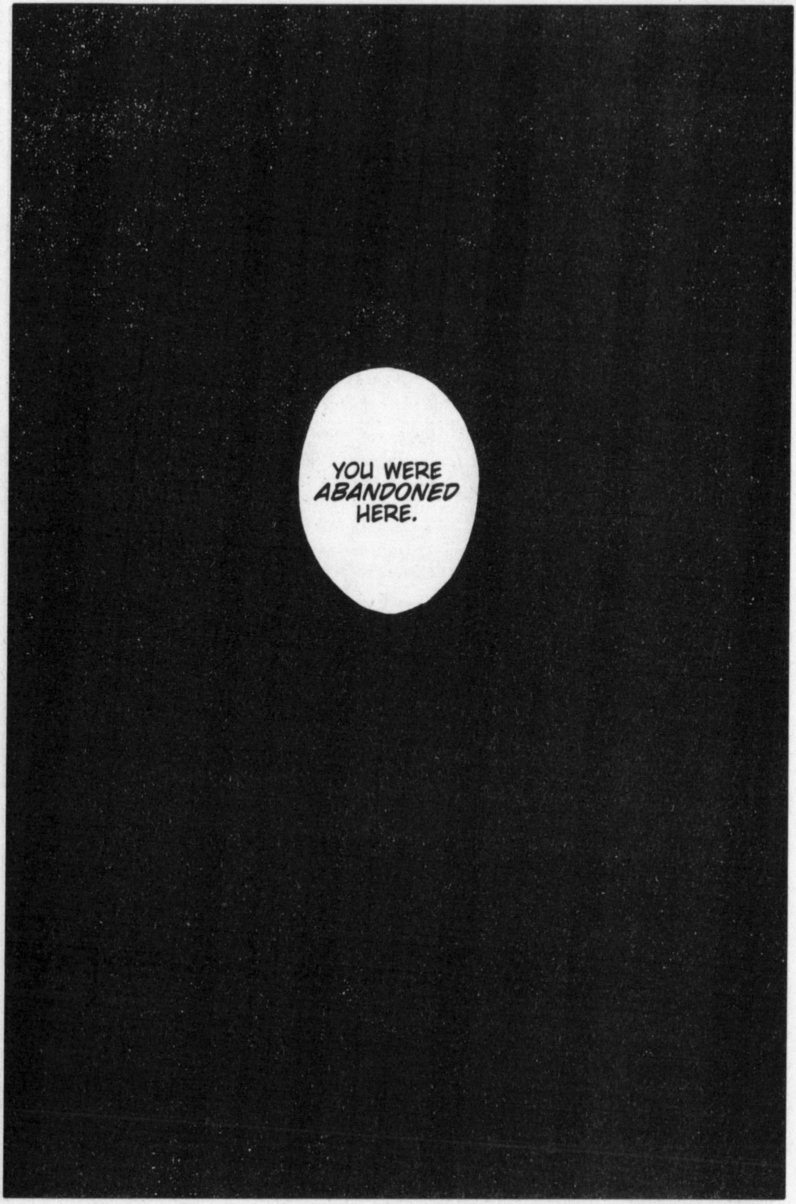
YOU WERE ABANDONED HERE.

Chapter 2

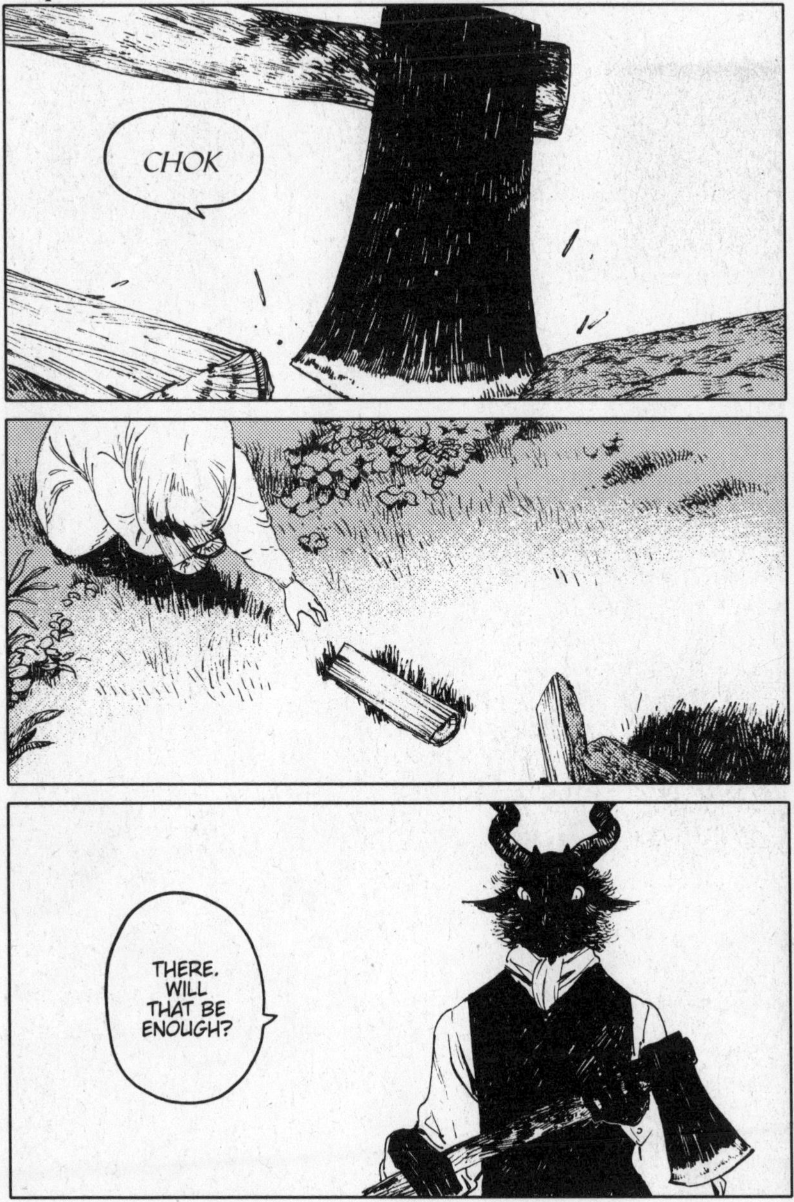
CHOK
THERE. WILL THAT BE ENOUGH?

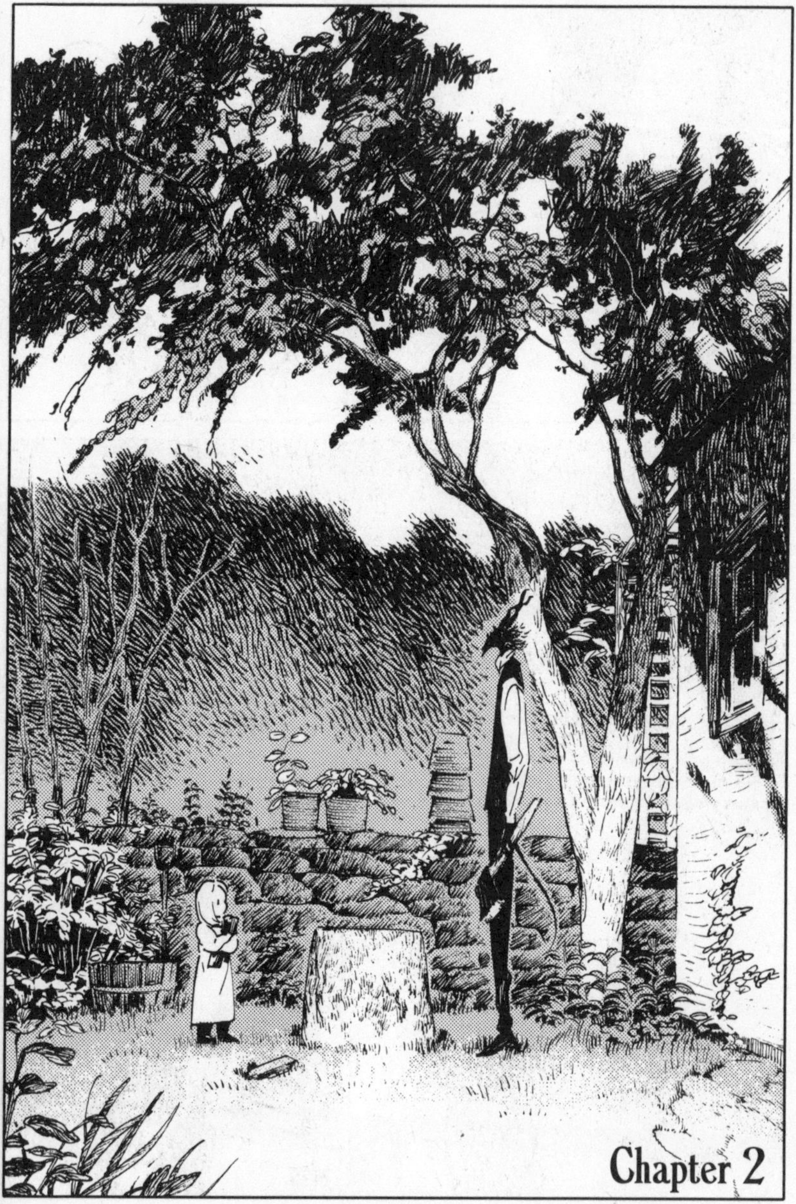
Chapter 2

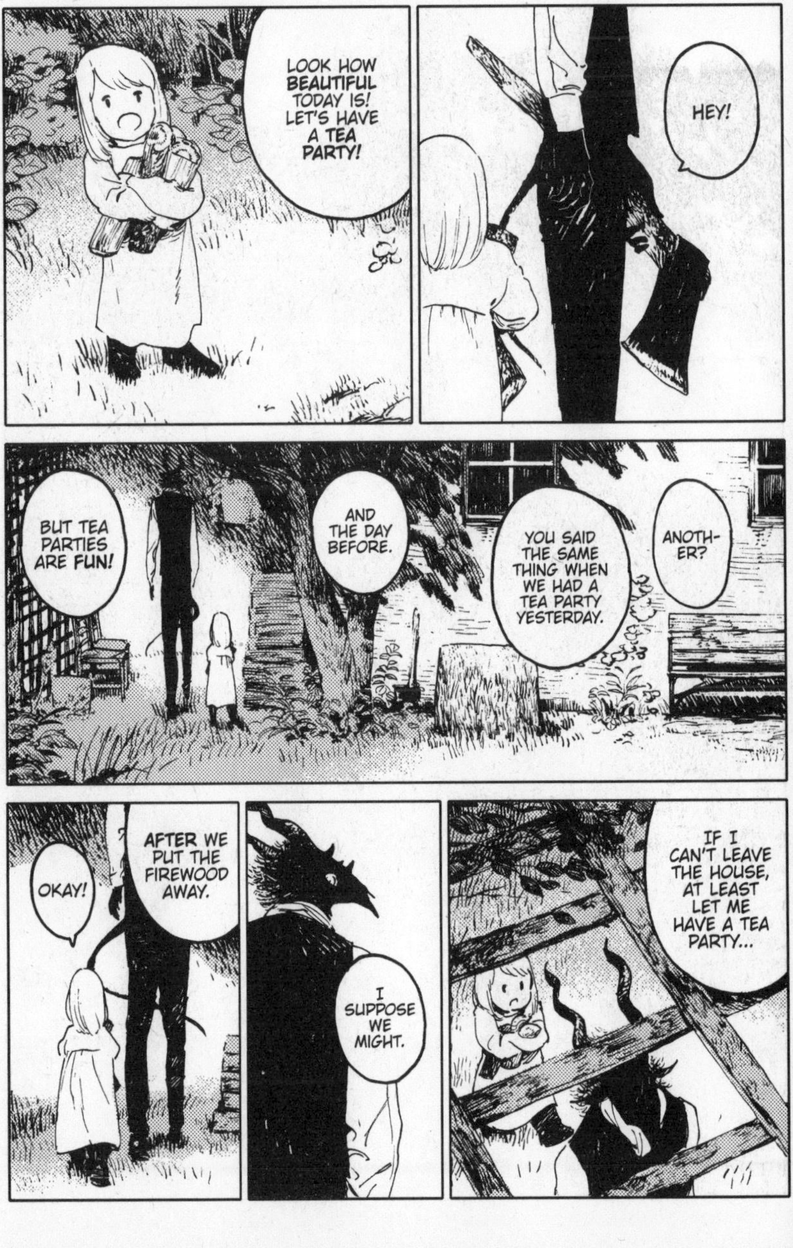
HEY!
LOOK HOW BEAUTIFUL TODAY IS! LET'S HAVE A TEA PARTY!
ANOTHER?
YOU SAID THE SAME THING WHEN WE HAD A TEA PARTY YESTERDAY.
AND THE DAY BEFORE.
BUT TEA PARTIES ARE FUN!
IF I CAN'T LEAVE THE HOUSE, AT LEAST LET ME HAVE A TEA PARTY...
I SUPPOSE WE MIGHT.
AFTER WE PUT THE FIREWOOD AWAY.
OKAY!

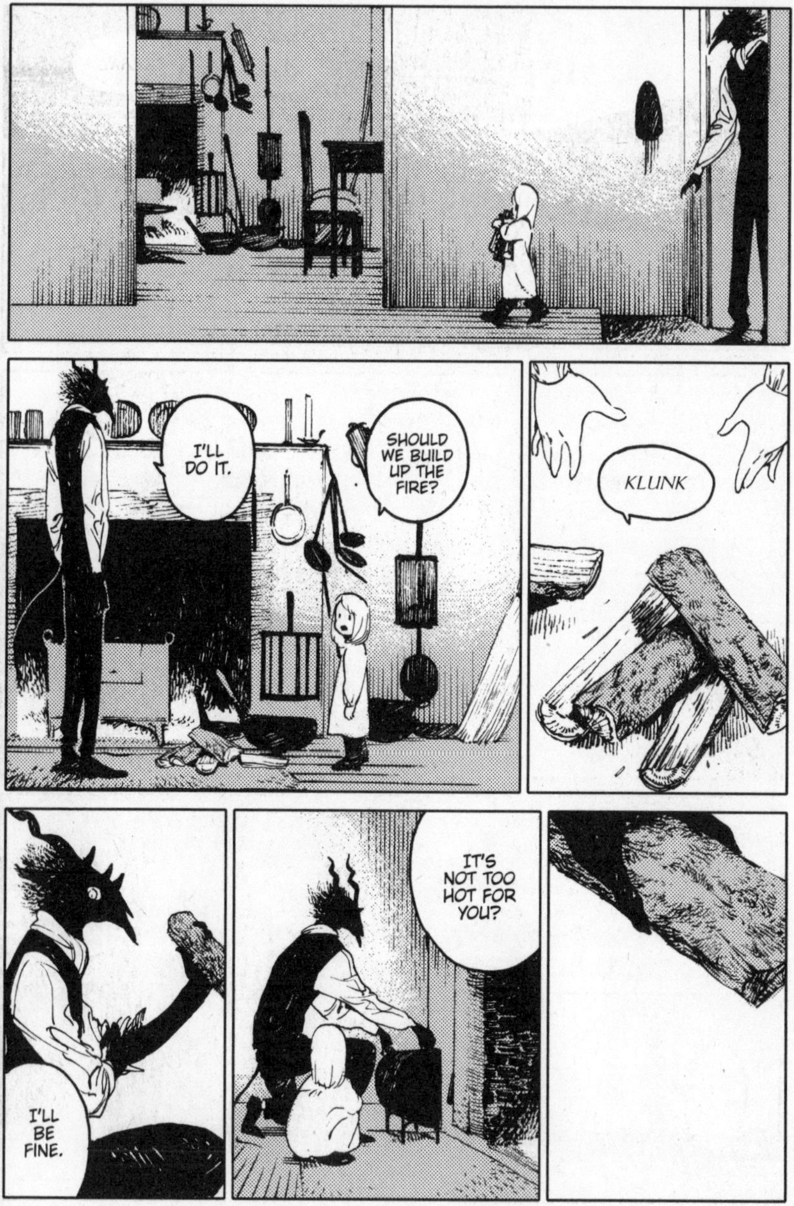
KLUNK
SHOULD WE BUILD UP THE FIRE?
I'LL DO IT.
IT'S NOT TOO HOT FOR YOU?
I'LL BE FINE.

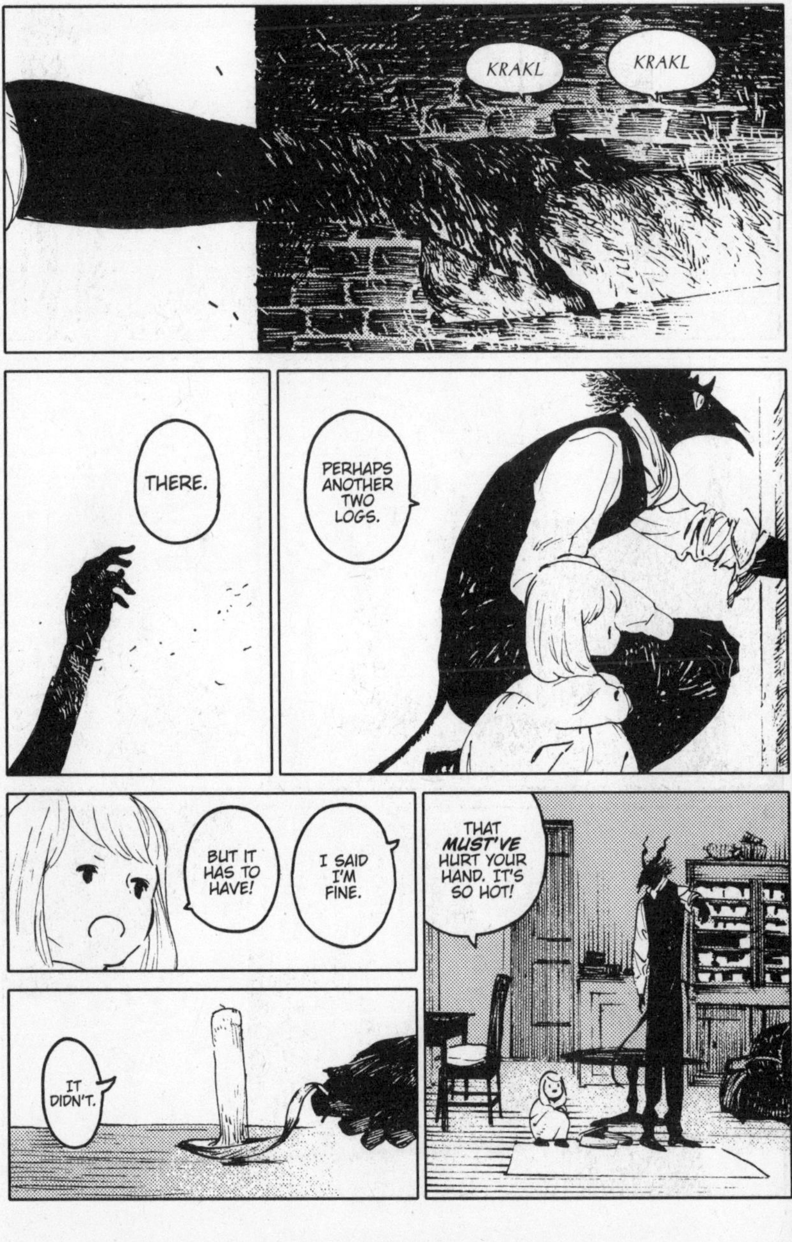
KRAKL
KRAKL
PERHAPS ANOTHER TWO LOGS.
THERE.
THAT *MUST'VE* HURT YOUR HAND. IT'S SO HOT!
I SAID I'M FINE.
BUT IT HAS TO HAVE!
IT DIDN'T.

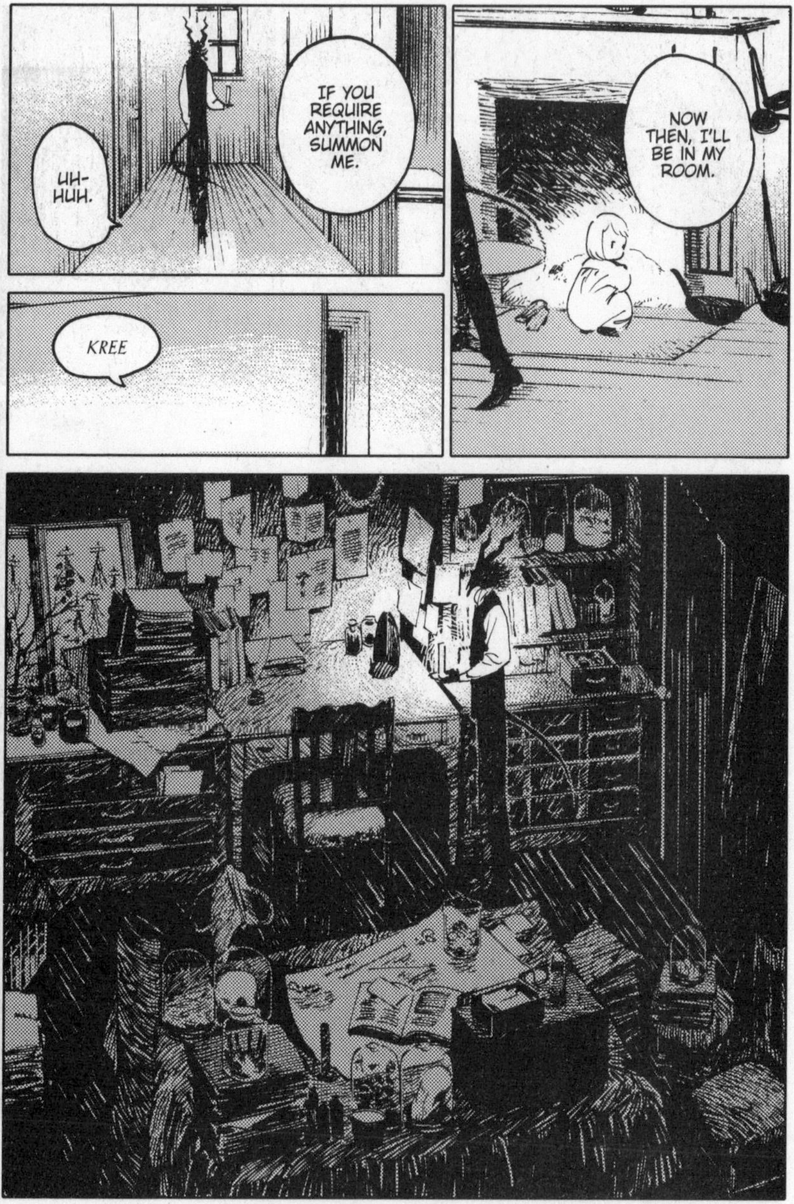
NOW THEN, I'LL BE IN MY ROOM.
IF YOU REQUIRE ANYTHING, SUMMON ME.
UH-HUH.
KREE

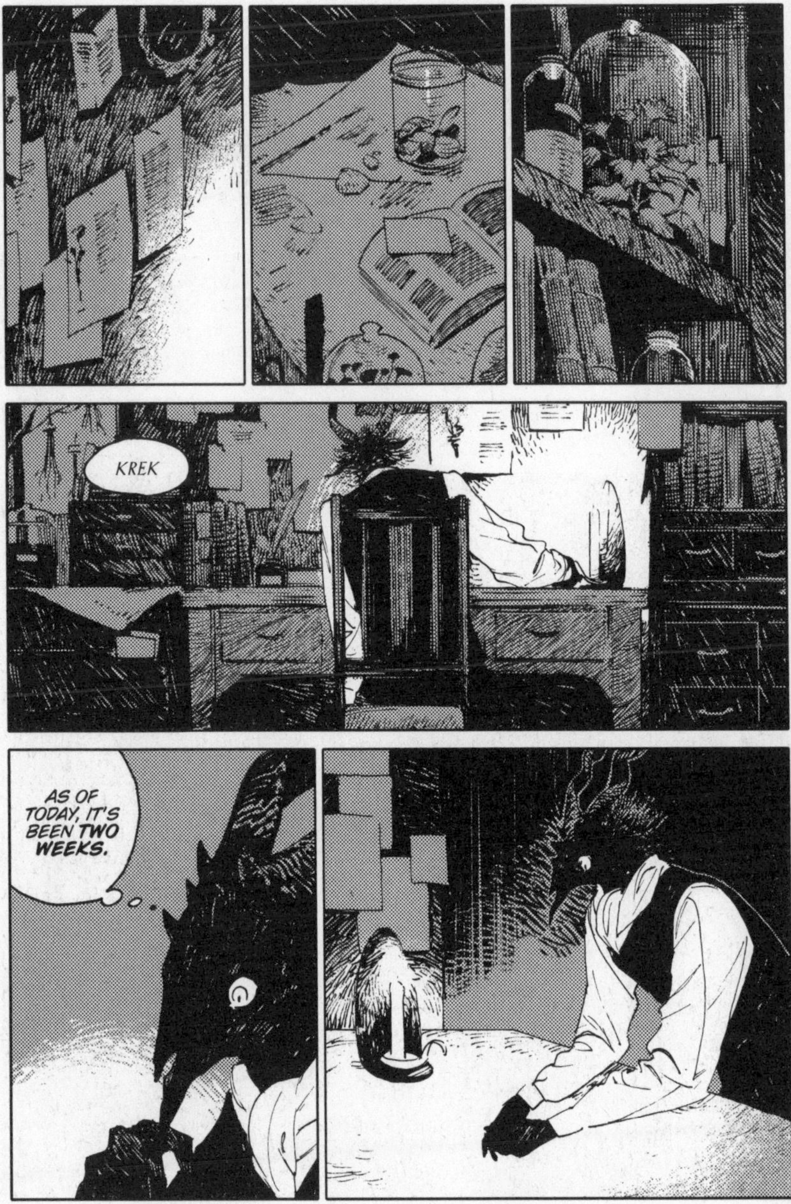
KREK
AS OF TODAY, IT'S BEEN TWO WEEKS.

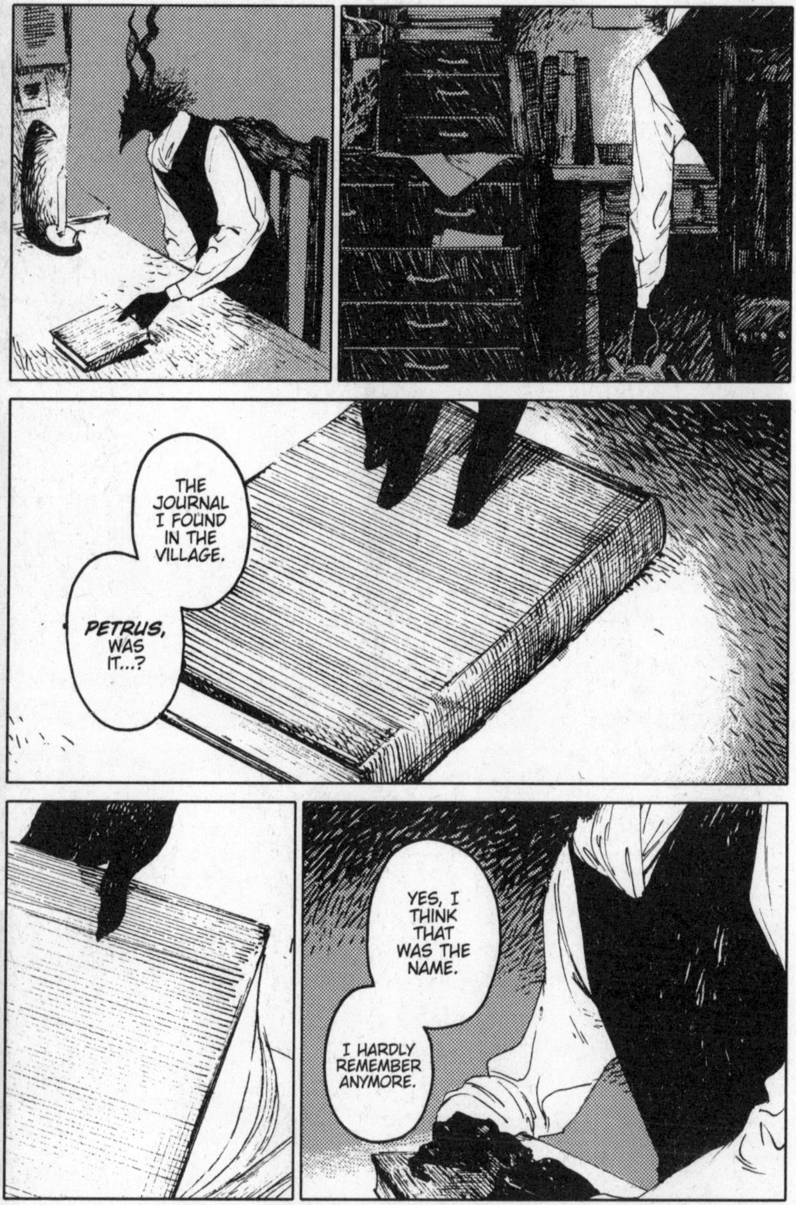
THE JOURNAL I FOUND IN THE VILLAGE.
PETRUS, WAS IT...?
YES, I THINK THAT WAS THE NAME.
I HARDLY REMEMBER ANYMORE.

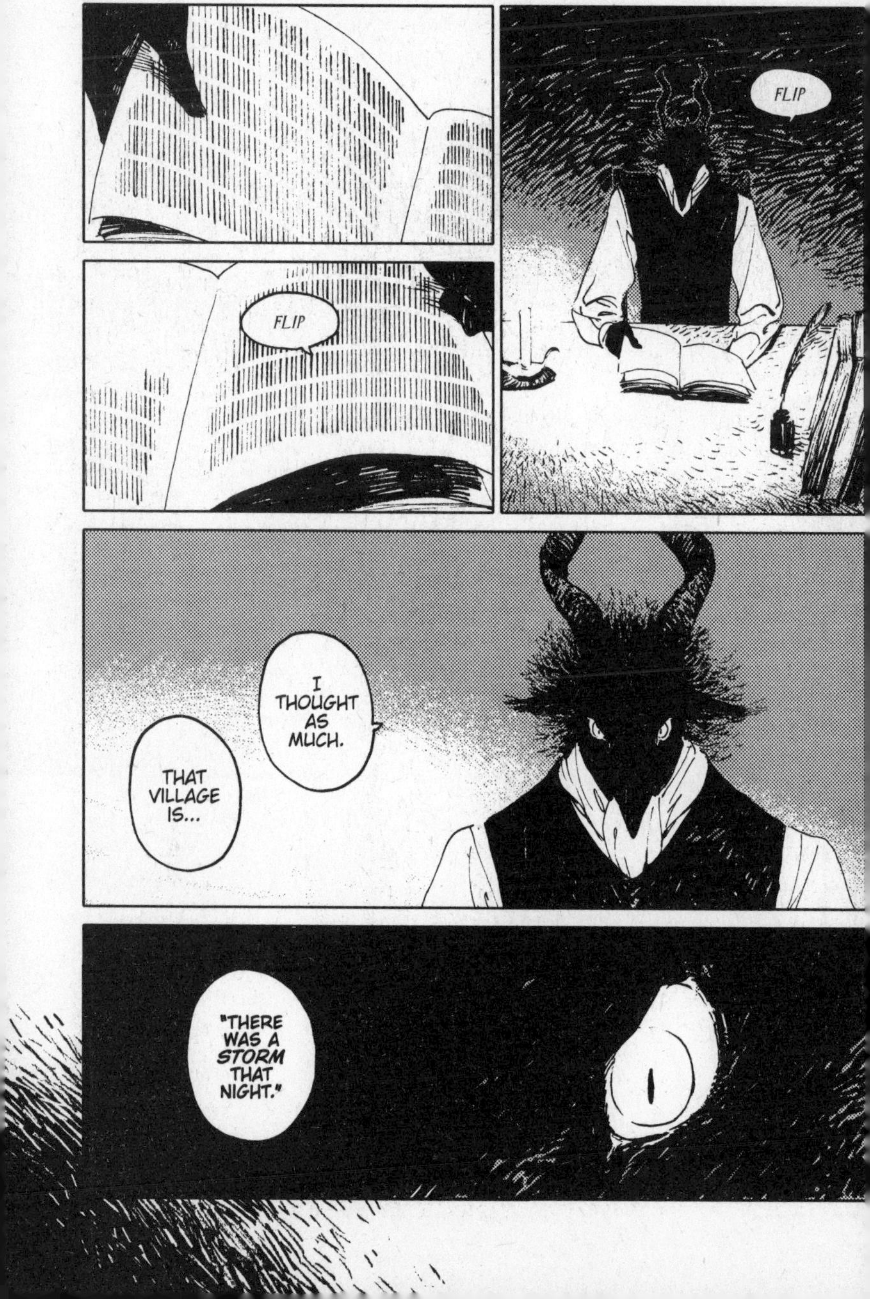
FLIP
FLIP
I THOUGHT AS MUCH.
THAT VILLAGE IS...
"THERE WAS A *STORM* THAT NIGHT."

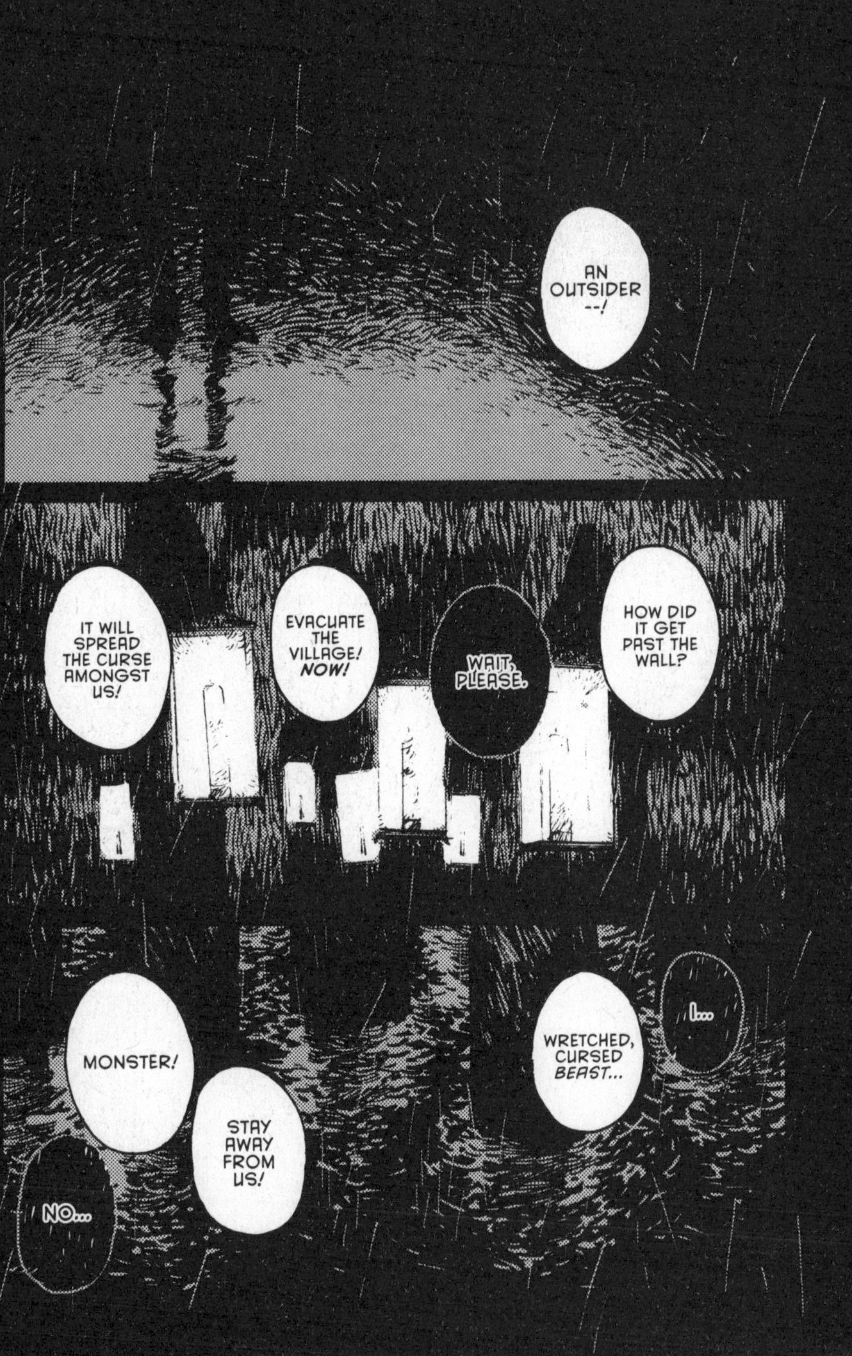
AN OUTSIDER --!
HOW DID IT GET PAST THE WALL?
WAIT, PLEASE.
EVACUATE THE VILLAGE! *NOW!*
IT WILL SPREAD THE CURSE AMONGST US!
I...
WRETCHED, CURSED *BEAST...*
MONSTER!
STAY AWAY FROM US!
NO...

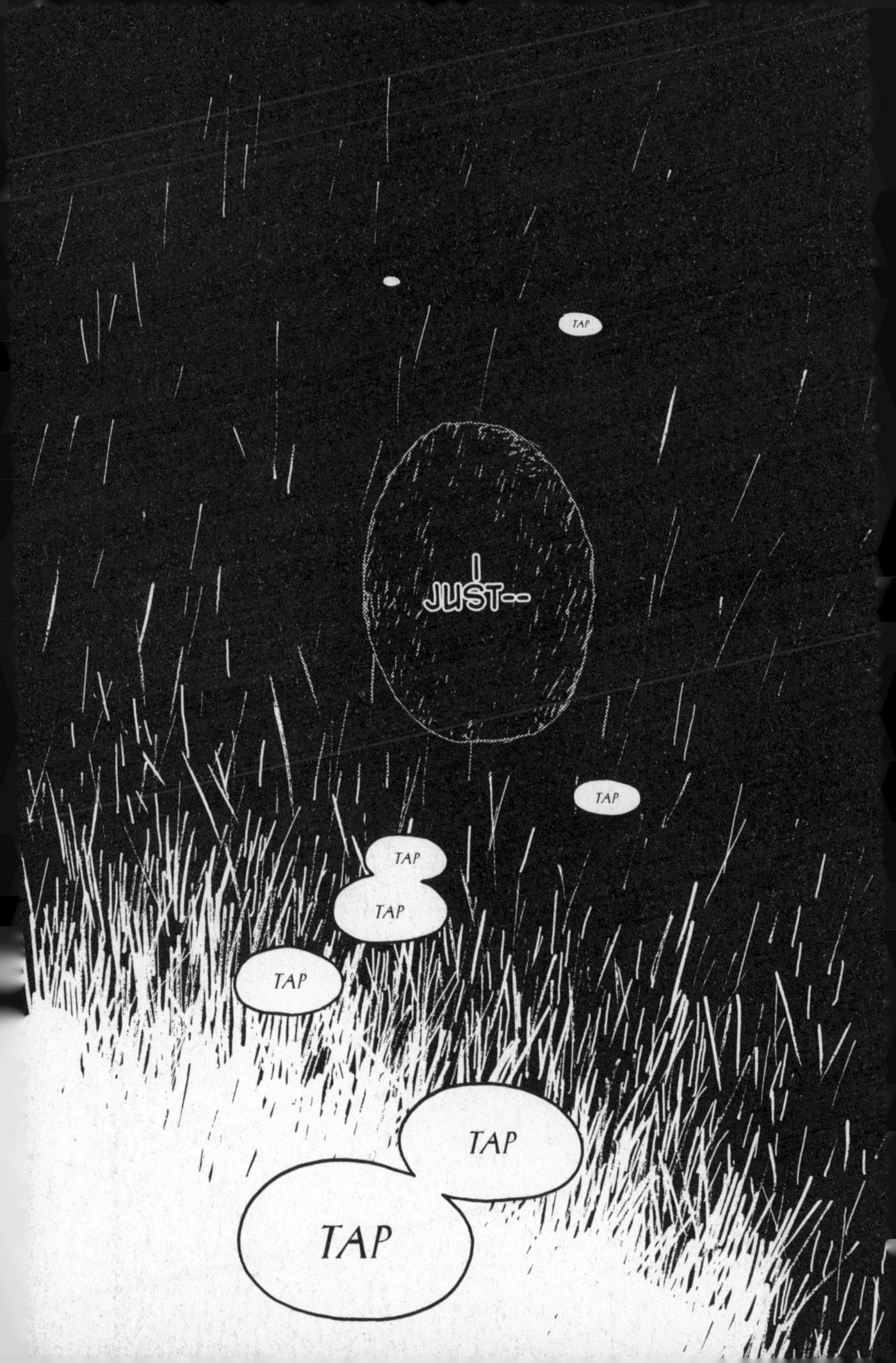
TAP
I JUST--
TAP
TAP
TAP
TAP
TAP
TAP

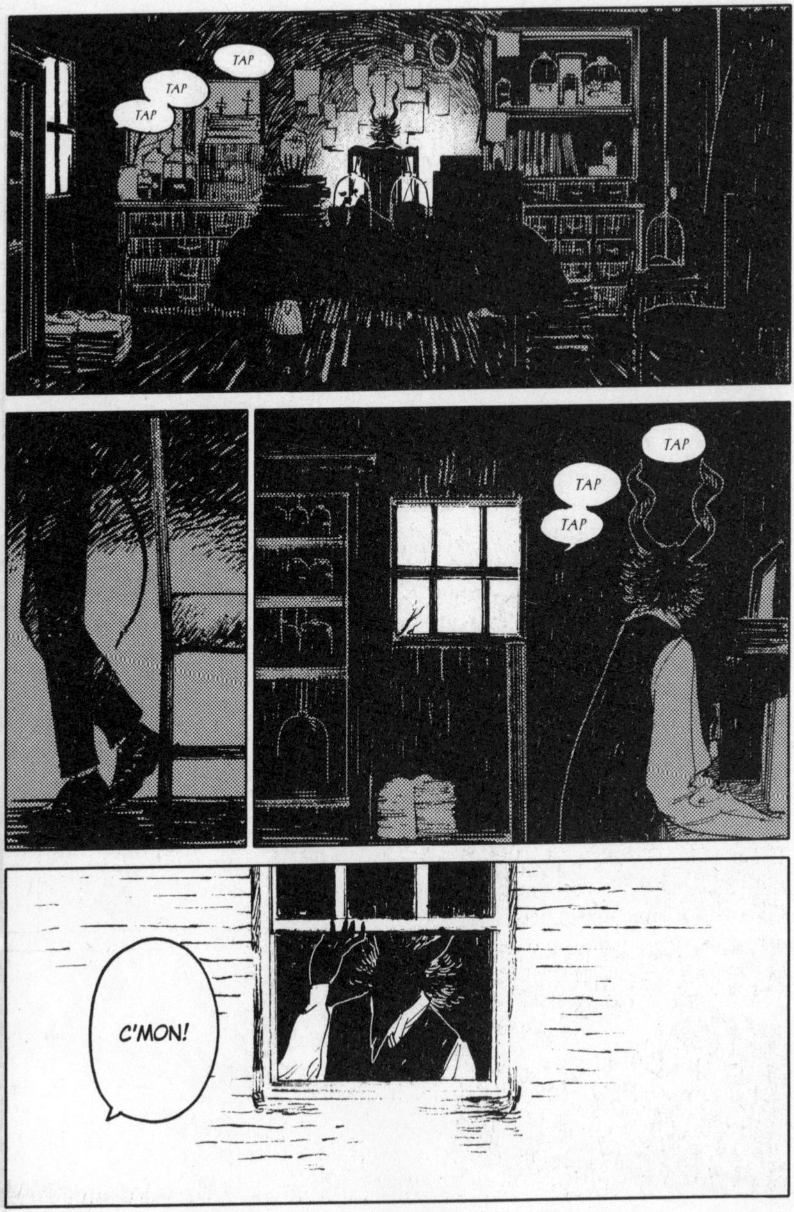
TAP
TAP
TAP
TAP
TAP
TAP
C'MON!

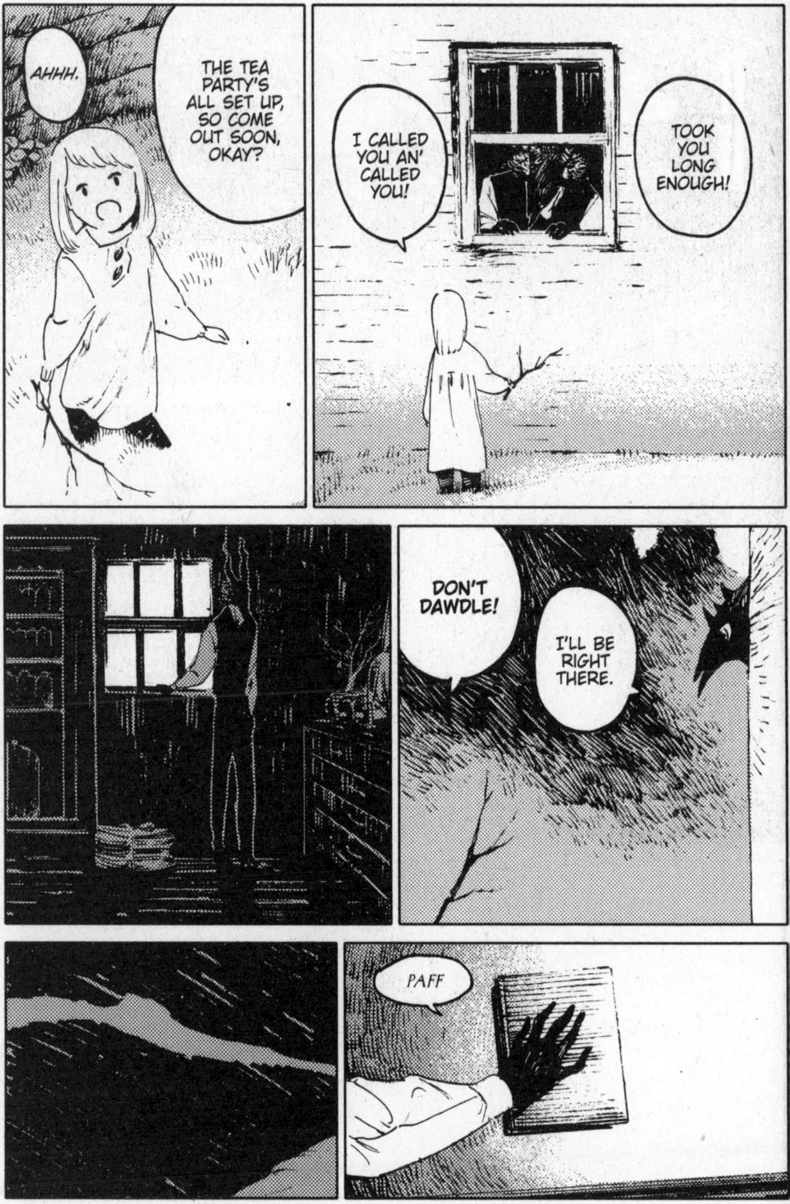
TOOK YOU LONG ENOUGH!
I CALLED YOU AN' CALLED YOU!
THE TEA PARTY'S ALL SET UP, SO COME OUT SOON, OKAY?
AHHH.
I'LL BE RIGHT THERE.
DON'T DAWDLE!
PAFF

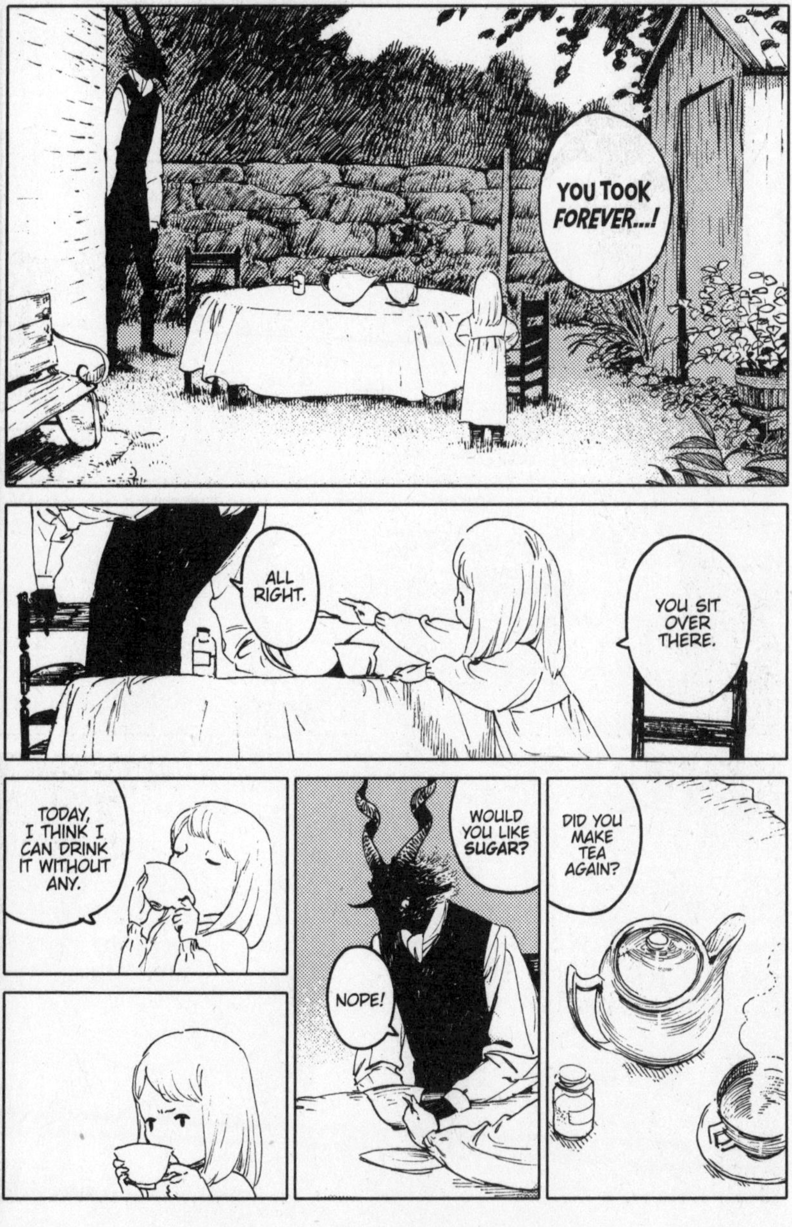
YOU TOOK FOREVER...!
YOU SIT OVER THERE.
ALL RIGHT.
DID YOU MAKE TEA AGAIN?
WOULD YOU LIKE SUGAR?
NOPE!
TODAY, I THINK I CAN DRINK IT WITHOUT ANY.

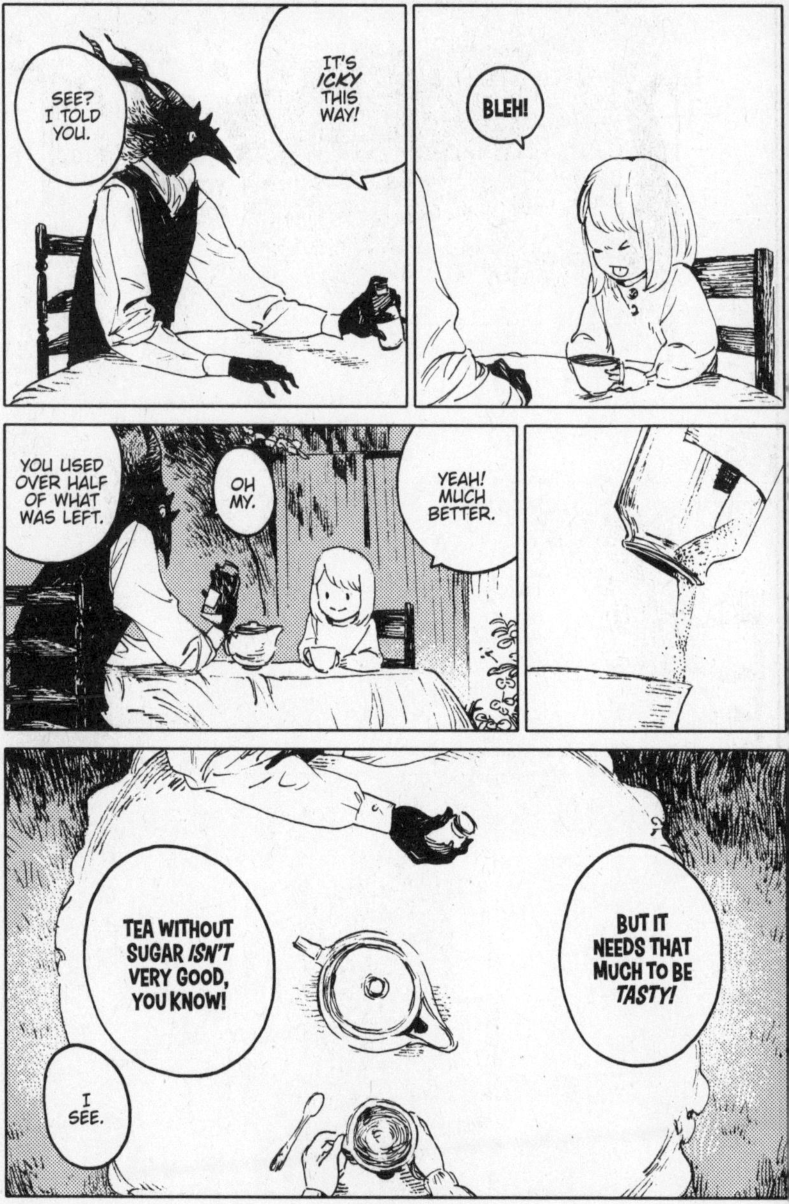
BLEH!
IT'S *ICKY* THIS WAY!
SEE? I TOLD YOU.
YEAH! MUCH BETTER.
OH MY.
YOU USED OVER HALF OF WHAT WAS LEFT.
BUT IT NEEDS THAT MUCH TO BE *TASTY!*
TEA WITHOUT SUGAR *ISN'T* VERY GOOD, YOU KNOW!
I SEE.

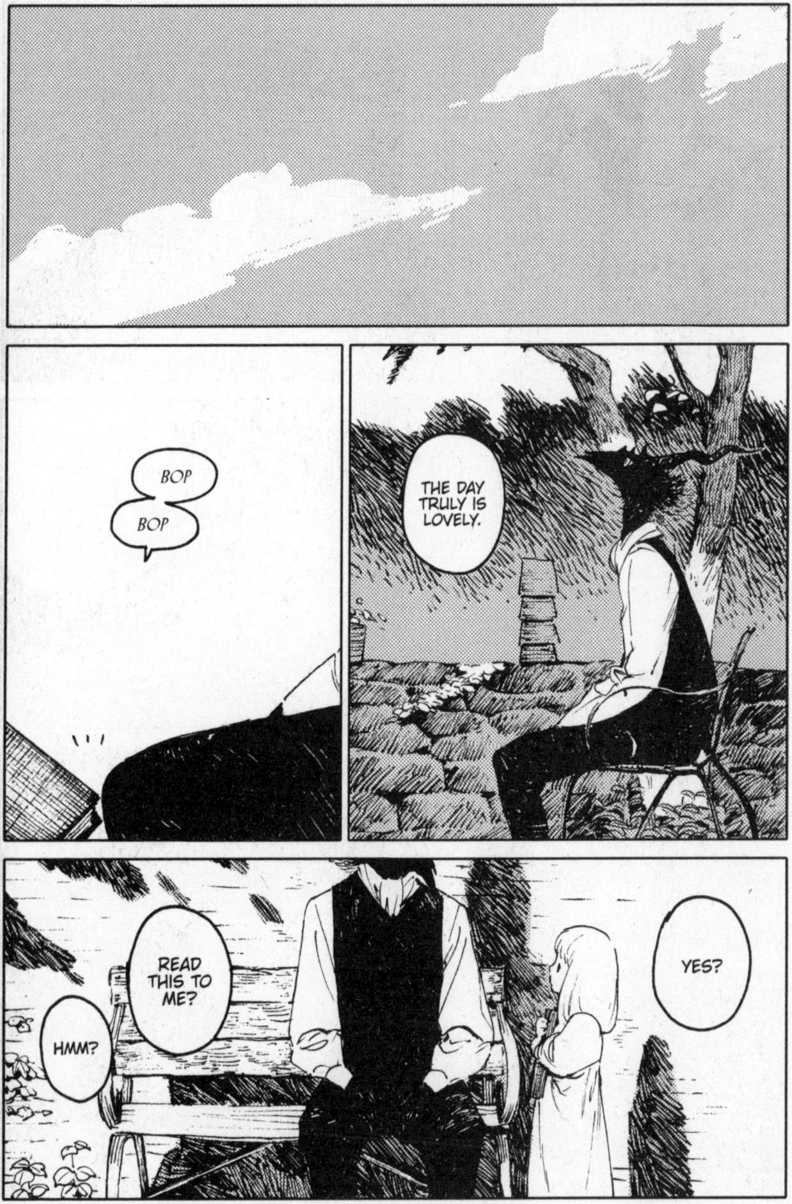
THE DAY TRULY IS LOVELY.
BOP
BOP
YES?
READ THIS TO ME?
HMM?

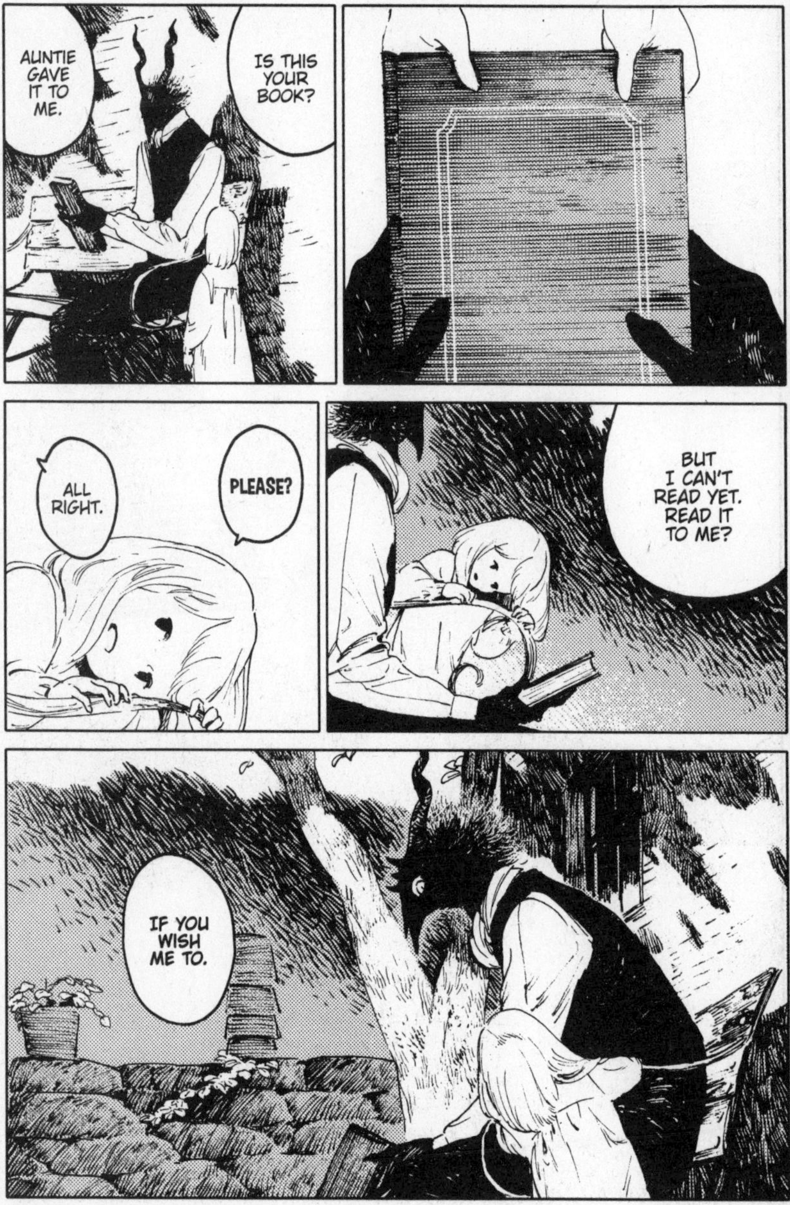
IS THIS YOUR BOOK?
AUNTIE GAVE IT TO ME.
BUT I CAN'T READ YET. READ IT TO ME?
PLEASE?
ALL RIGHT.
IF YOU WISH ME TO.

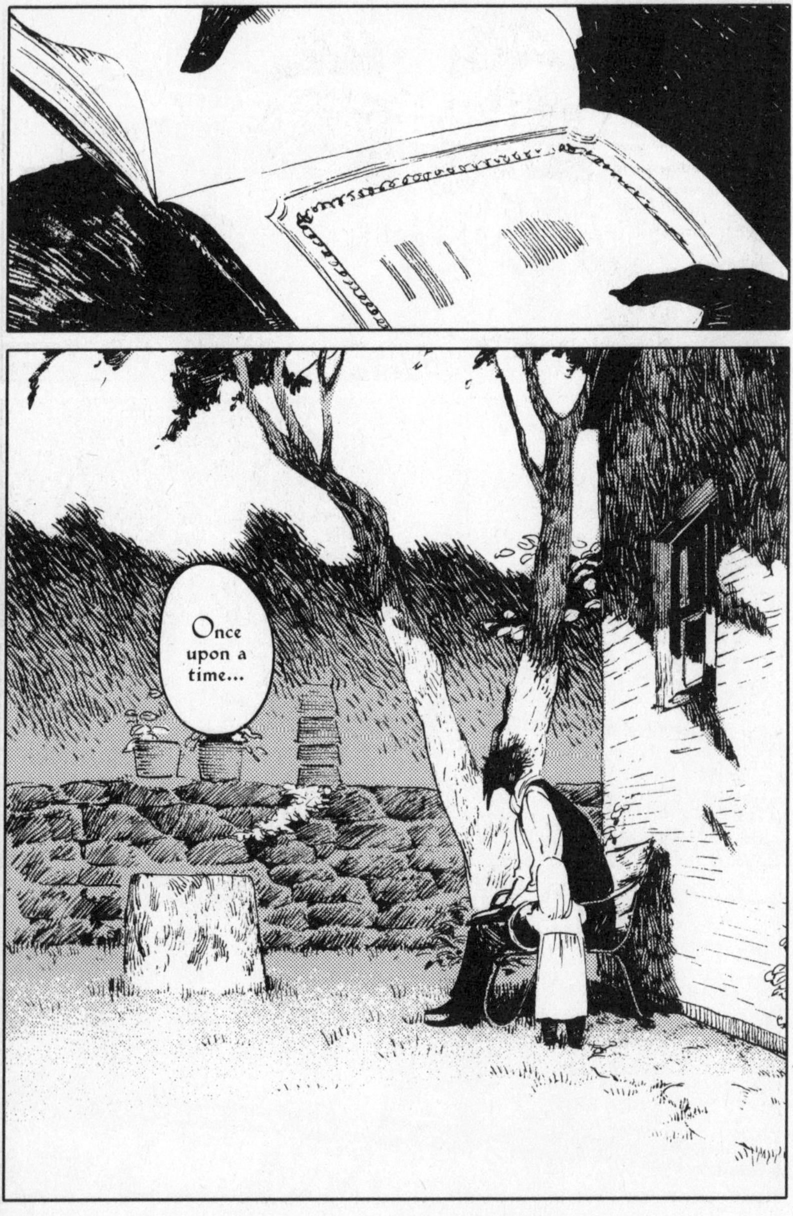
Once upon a time...

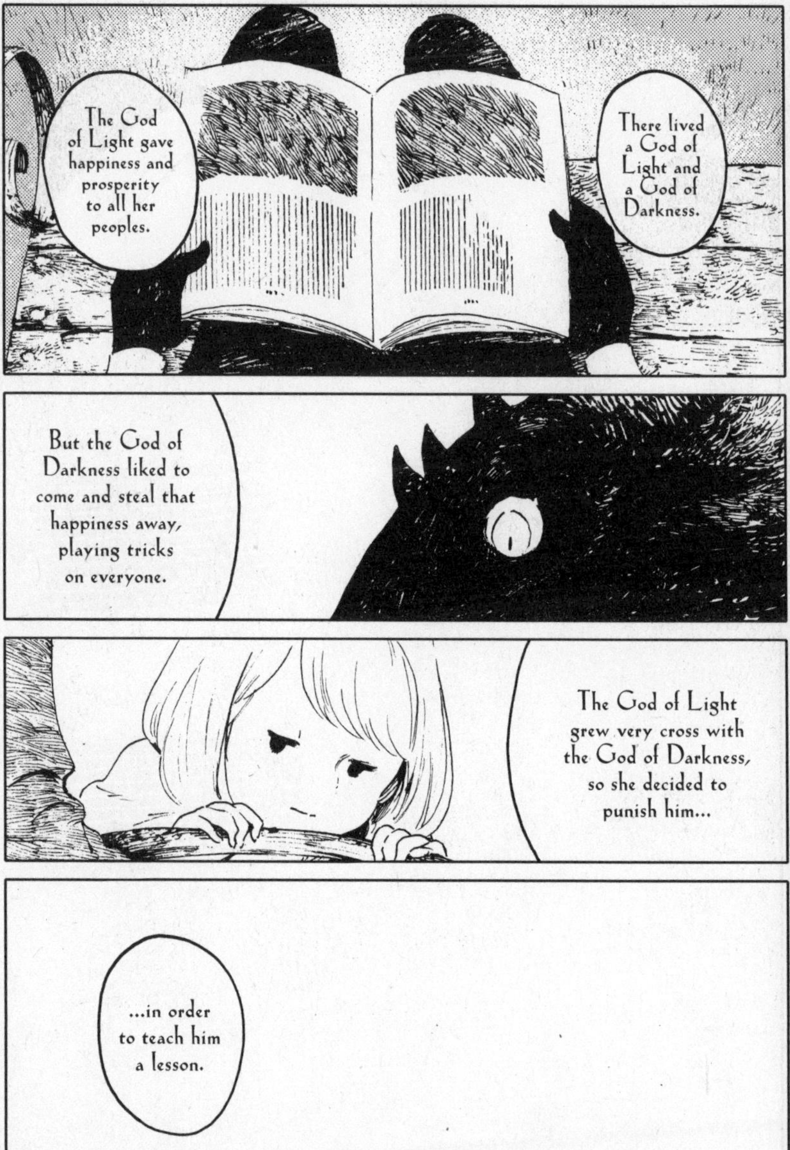
There lived a God of Light and a God of Darkness.
The God of Light gave happiness and prosperity to all her peoples.
But the God of Darkness liked to come and steal that happiness away, playing tricks on everyone.
The God of Light grew very cross with the God of Darkness, so she decided to punish him...
...in order to teach him a lesson.

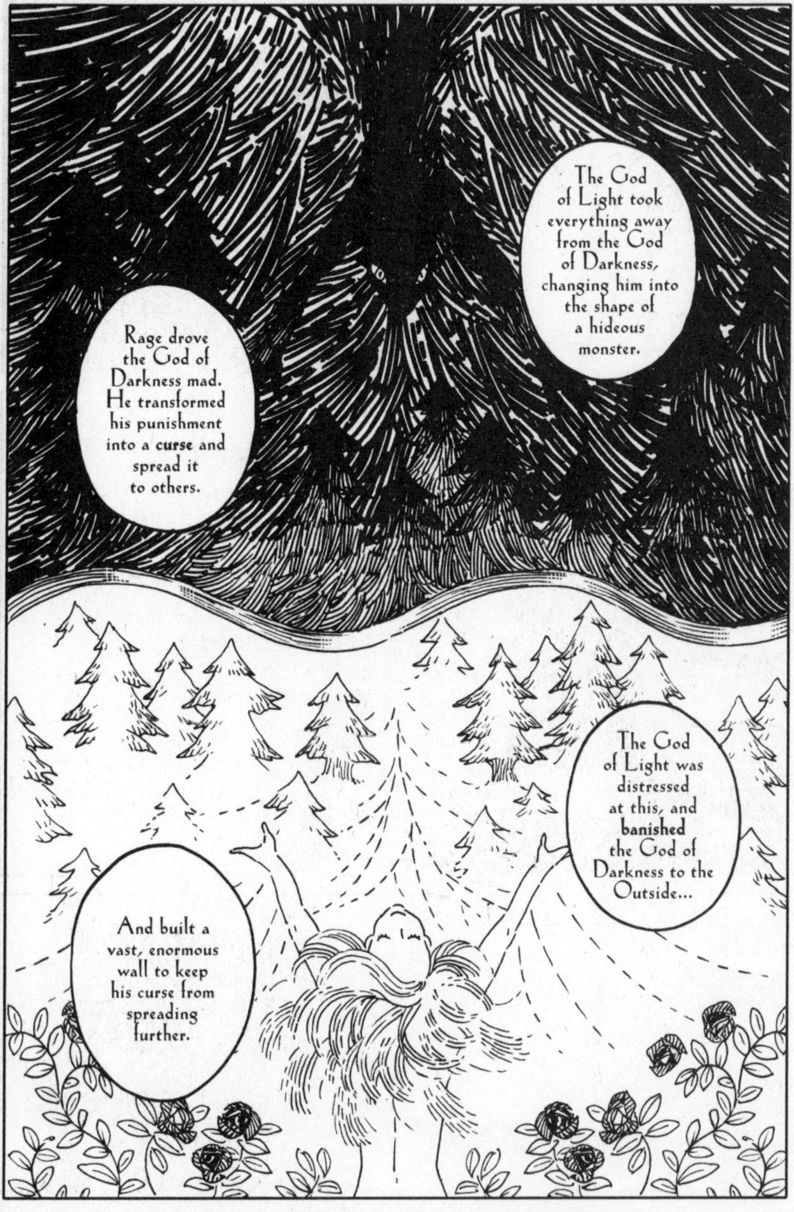
The God of Light took everything away from the God of Darkness, changing him into the shape of a hideous monster.
Rage drove the God of Darkness mad. He transformed his punishment into a **curse** and spread it to others.
The God of Light was distressed at this, and **banished** the God of Darkness to the Outside...
And built a vast, enormous wall to keep his curse from spreading further.

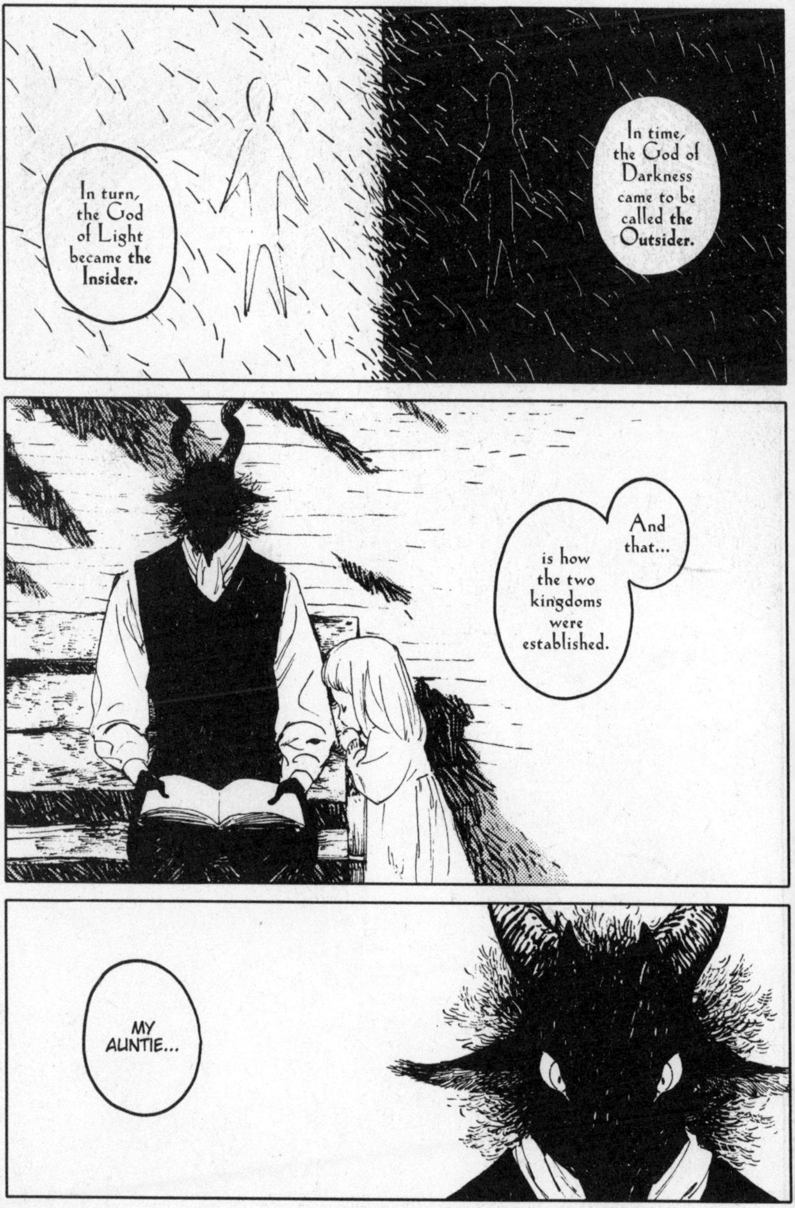
In time, the God of Darkness came to be called the Outsider.
In turn, the God of Light became the Insider.
And that...
is how the two kingdoms were established.
MY AUNTIE...

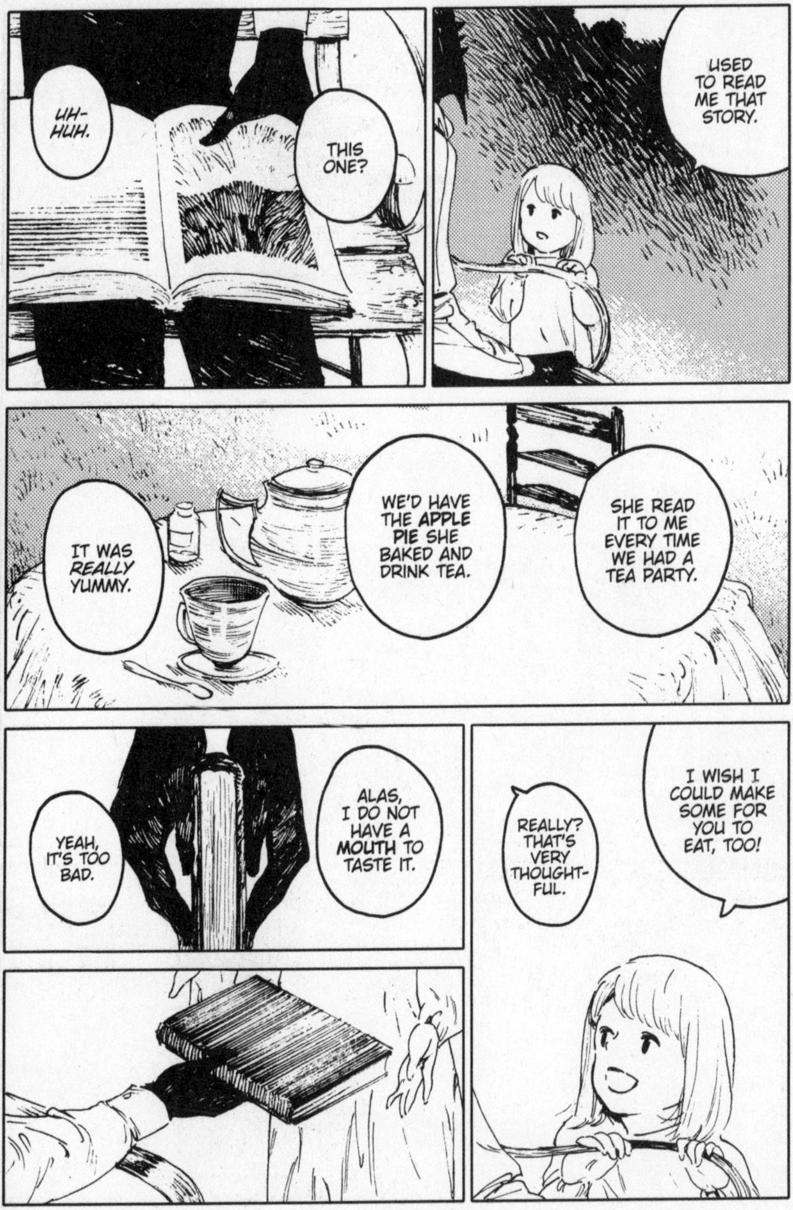
USED TO READ ME THAT STORY.
THIS ONE?
UH-HUH.
SHE READ IT TO ME EVERY TIME WE HAD A TEA PARTY.
WE'D HAVE THE APPLE PIE SHE BAKED AND DRINK TEA.
IT WAS REALLY YUMMY.
I WISH I COULD MAKE SOME FOR YOU TO EAT, TOO!
REALLY? THAT'S VERY THOUGHT-FUL.
ALAS, I DO NOT HAVE A MOUTH TO TASTE IT.
YEAH, IT'S TOO BAD.

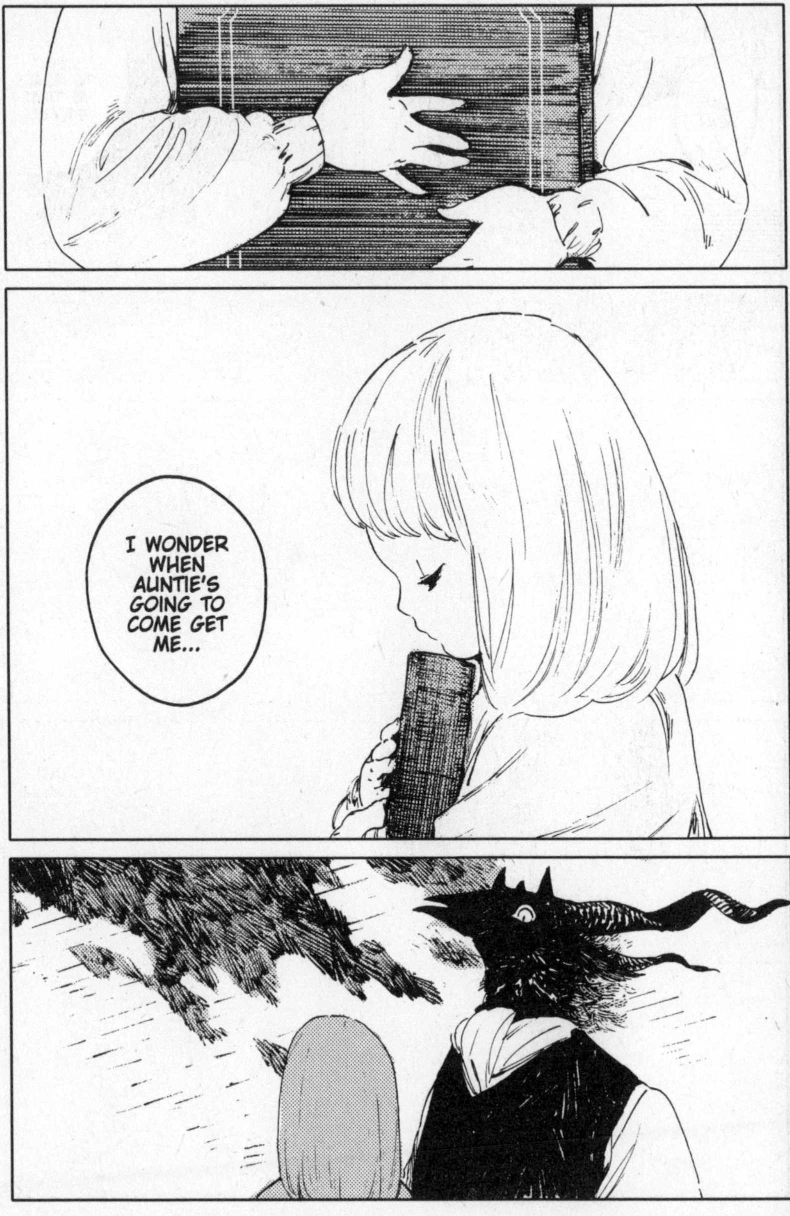
I WONDER WHEN AUNTIE'S GOING TO COME GET ME...

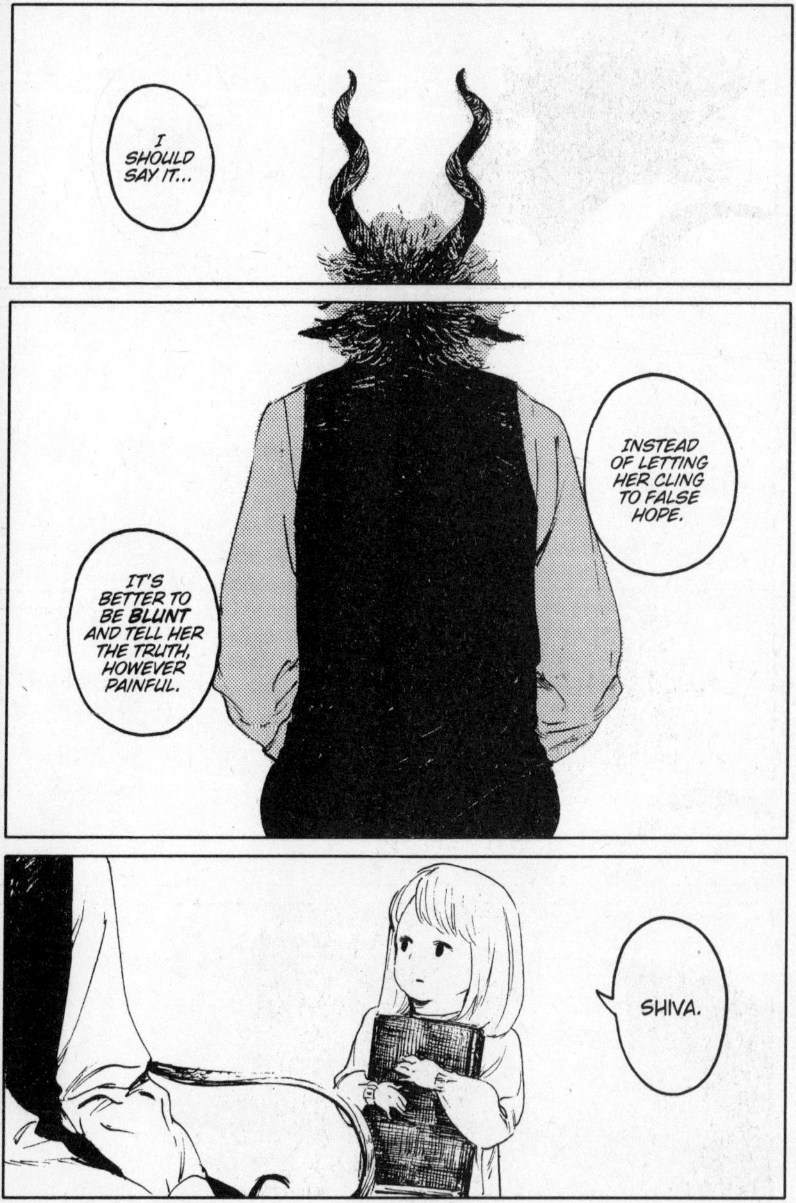
I SHOULD SAY IT...
INSTEAD OF LETTING HER CLING TO FALSE HOPE.
IT'S BETTER TO BE **BLUNT** AND TELL HER THE TRUTH, HOWEVER PAINFUL.
SHIVA.

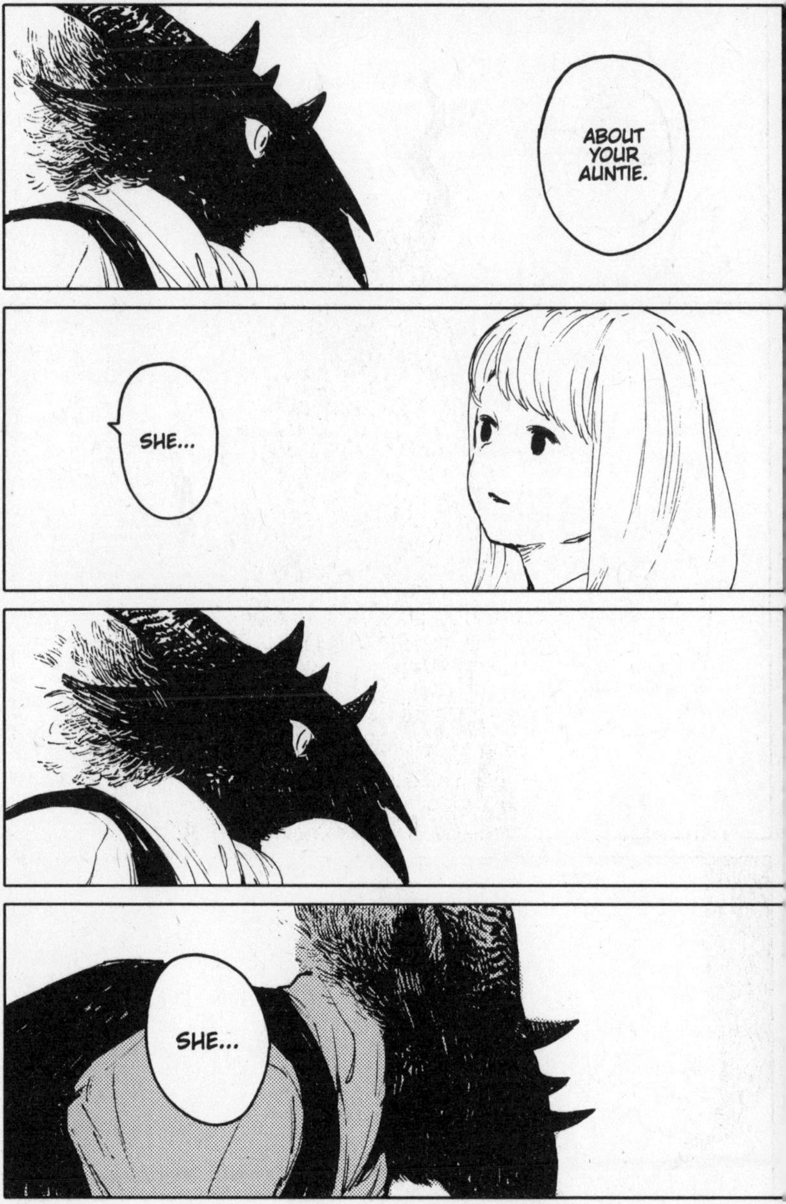
ABOUT YOUR AUNTIE.
SHE...
SHE...

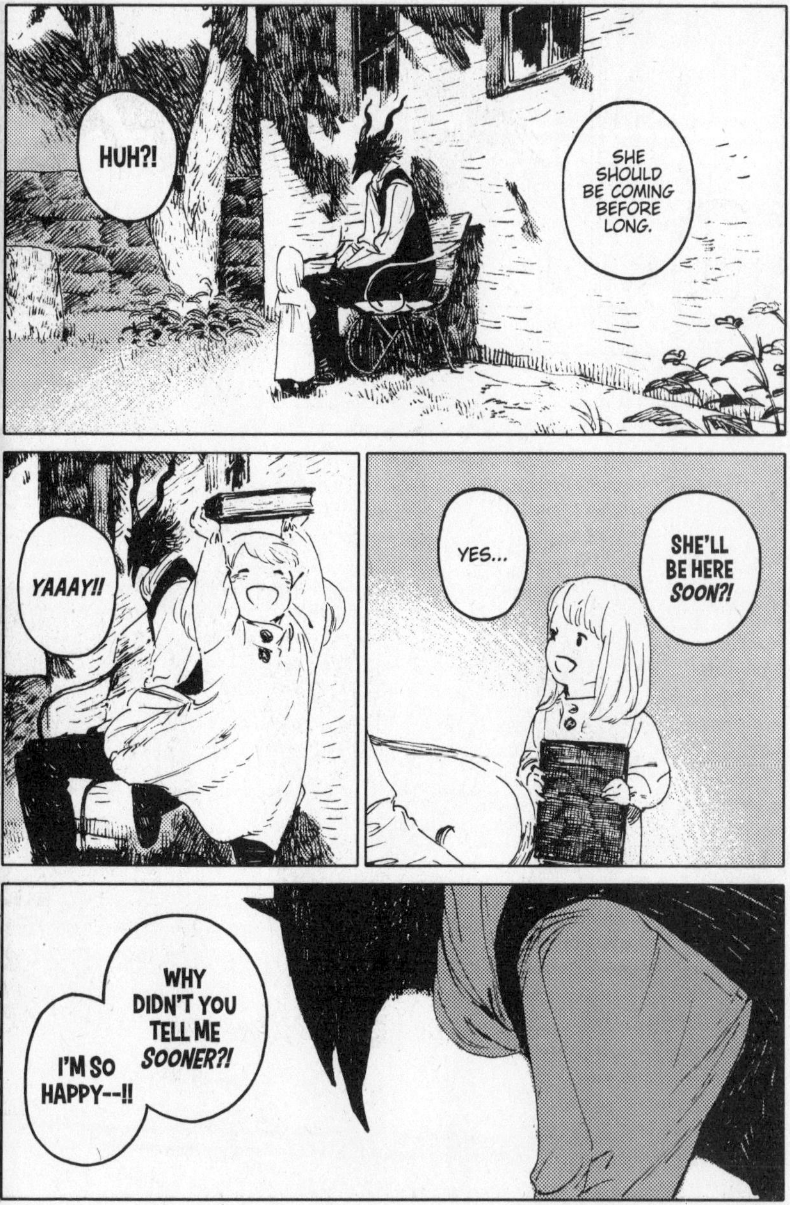
SHE SHOULD BE COMING BEFORE LONG.
HUH?!
SHE'LL BE HERE SOON?!
YES...
YAAAY!!
WHY DIDN'T YOU TELL ME SOONER?!
I'M SO HAPPY--!!

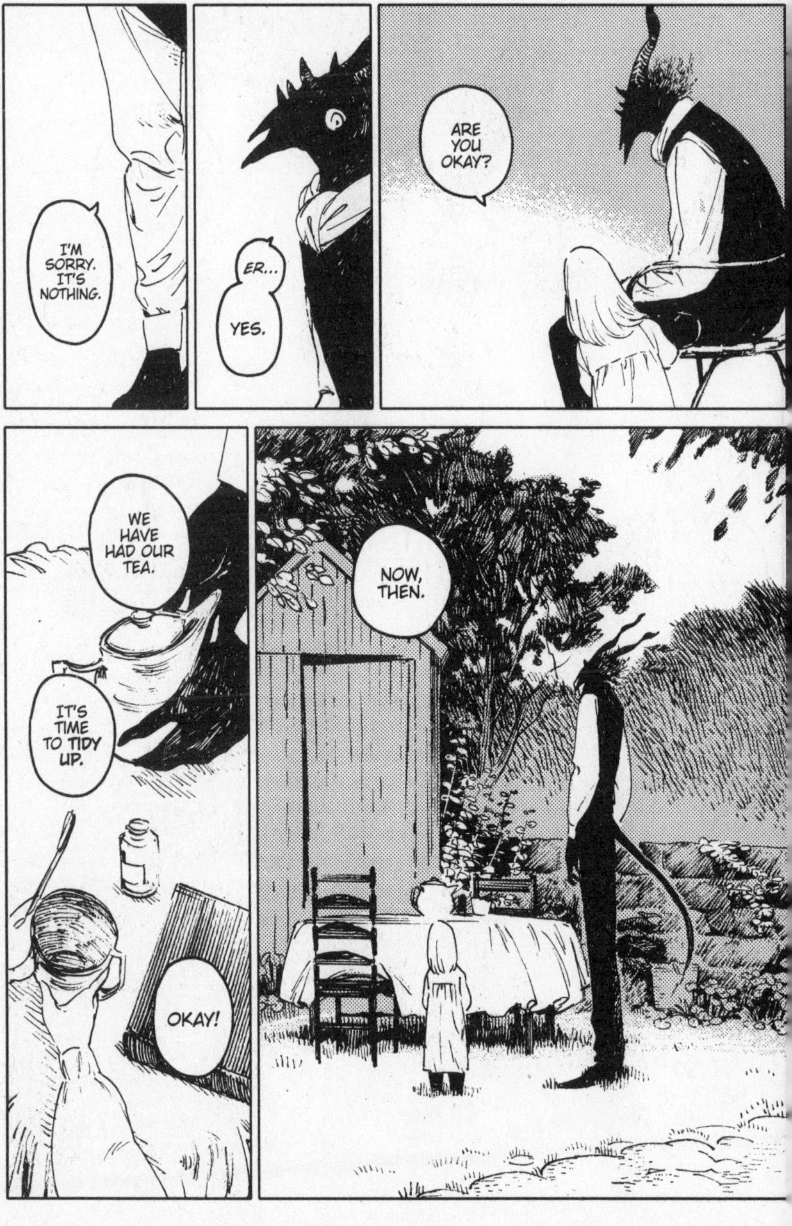
ARE YOU OKAY?
ER...
YES.
I'M SORRY. IT'S NOTHING.
NOW, THEN.
WE HAVE HAD OUR TEA.
IT'S TIME TO TIDY UP.
OKAY!

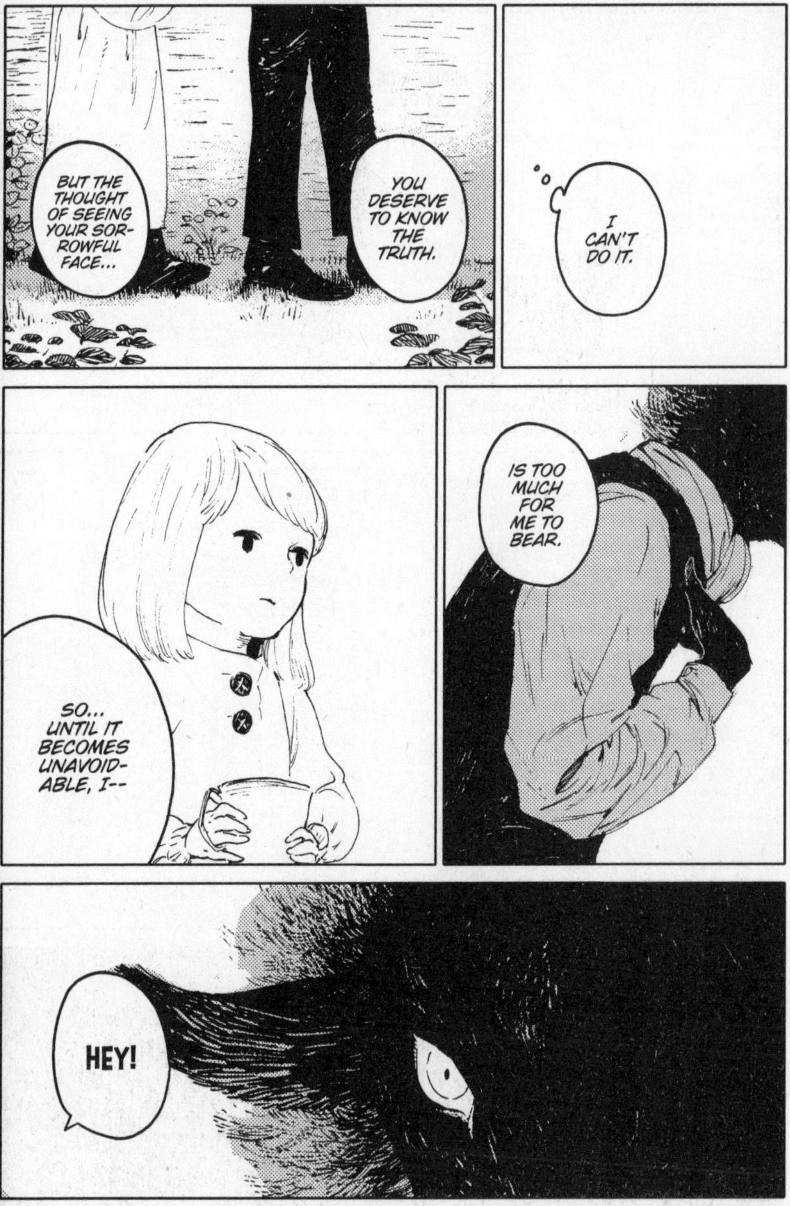
I CAN'T DO IT.
YOU DESERVE TO KNOW THE TRUTH.
BUT THE THOUGHT OF SEEING YOUR SOR-ROWFUL FACE...
IS TOO MUCH FOR ME TO BEAR.
SO... UNTIL IT BECOMES UNAVOID-ABLE, I--
HEY!

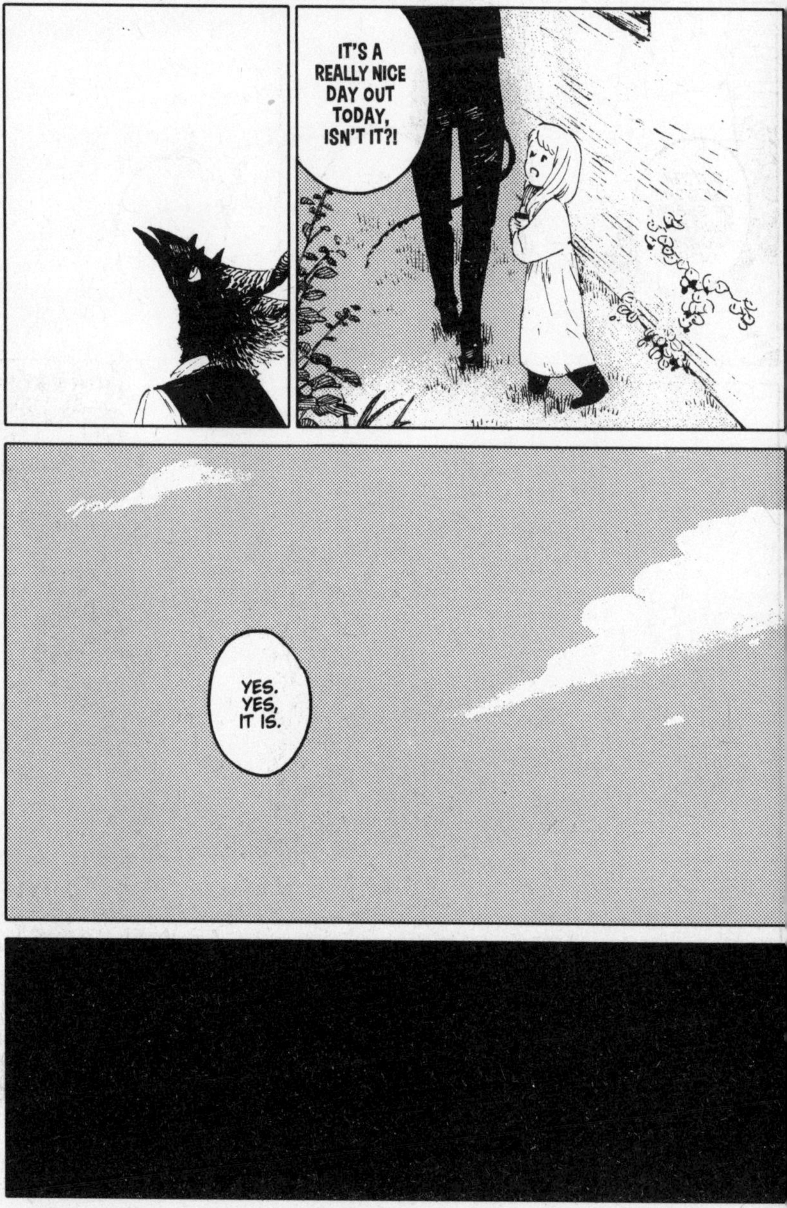
IT'S A REALLY NICE DAY OUT TODAY, ISN'T IT?!
YES. YES, IT IS.

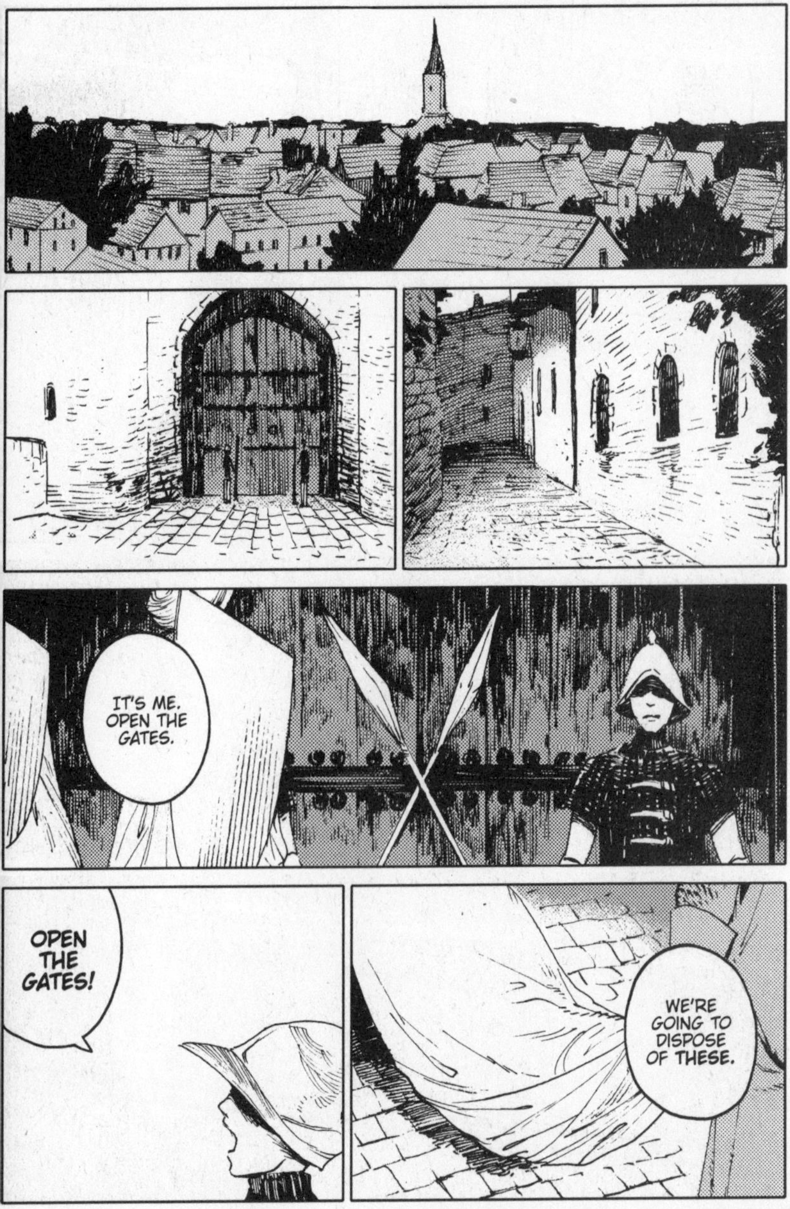
IT'S ME. OPEN THE GATES.
WE'RE GOING TO DISPOSE OF THESE.
OPEN THE GATES!

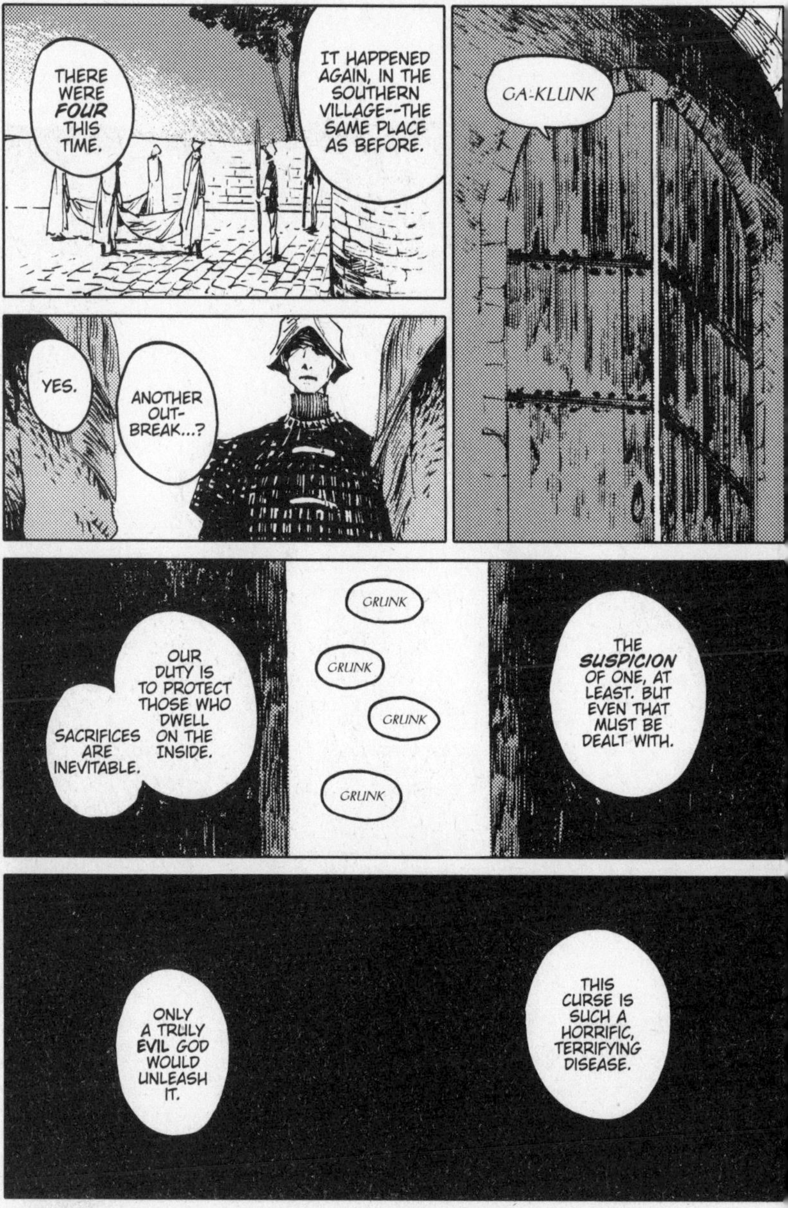
GA-KLUNK
IT HAPPENED AGAIN, IN THE SOUTHERN VILLAGE--THE SAME PLACE AS BEFORE.
THERE WERE **FOUR** THIS TIME.
ANOTHER OUT-BREAK...?
YES.
THE **SUSPICION** OF ONE, AT LEAST. BUT EVEN THAT MUST BE DEALT WITH.
GRUNK
GRUNK
GRUNK
GRUNK
OUR DUTY IS TO PROTECT THOSE WHO DWELL ON THE INSIDE.
SACRIFICES ARE INEVITABLE.
THIS CURSE IS SUCH A HORRIFIC, TERRIFYING DISEASE.
ONLY A TRULY EVIL GOD WOULD UNLEASH IT.

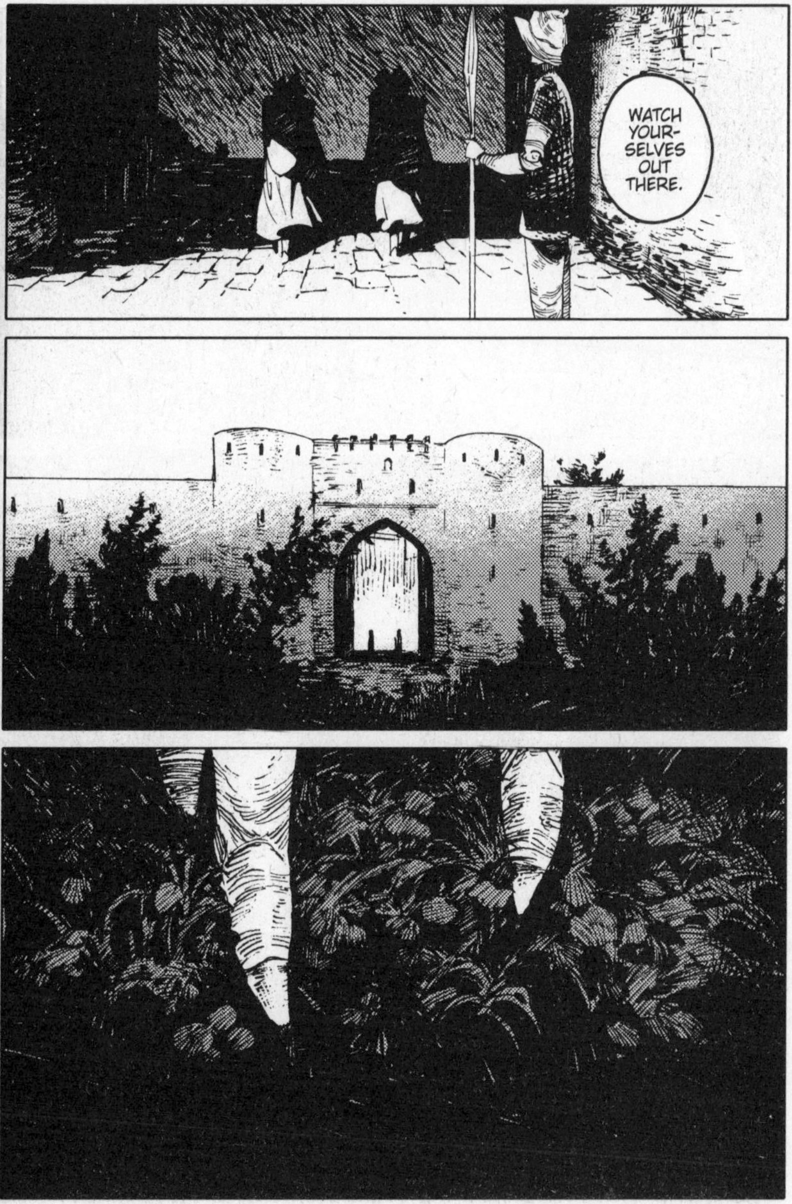
WATCH YOUR-SELVES OUT THERE.

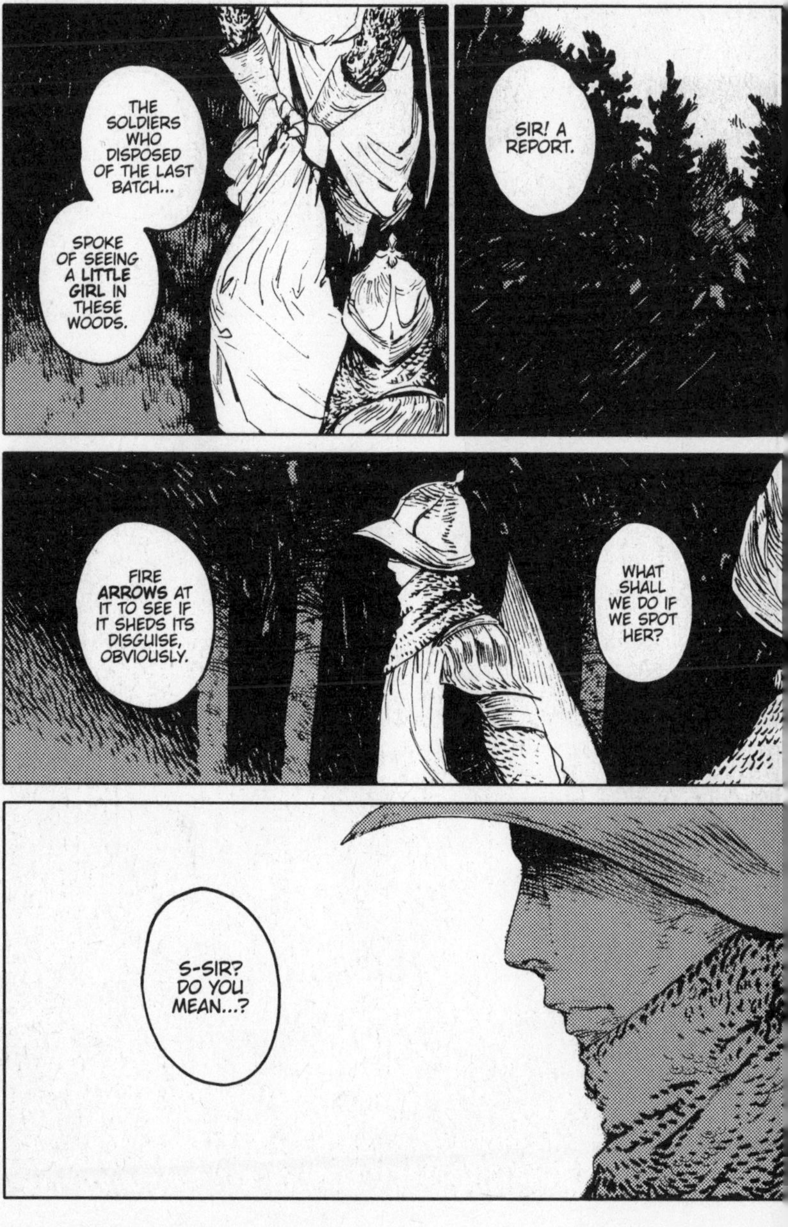
SIR! A REPORT.
THE SOLDIERS WHO DISPOSED OF THE LAST BATCH...
SPOKE OF SEEING A LITTLE GIRL IN THESE WOODS.
WHAT SHALL WE DO IF WE SPOT HER?
FIRE ARROWS AT IT TO SEE IF IT SHEDS ITS DISGUISE, OBVIOUSLY.
S-SIR? DO YOU MEAN...?

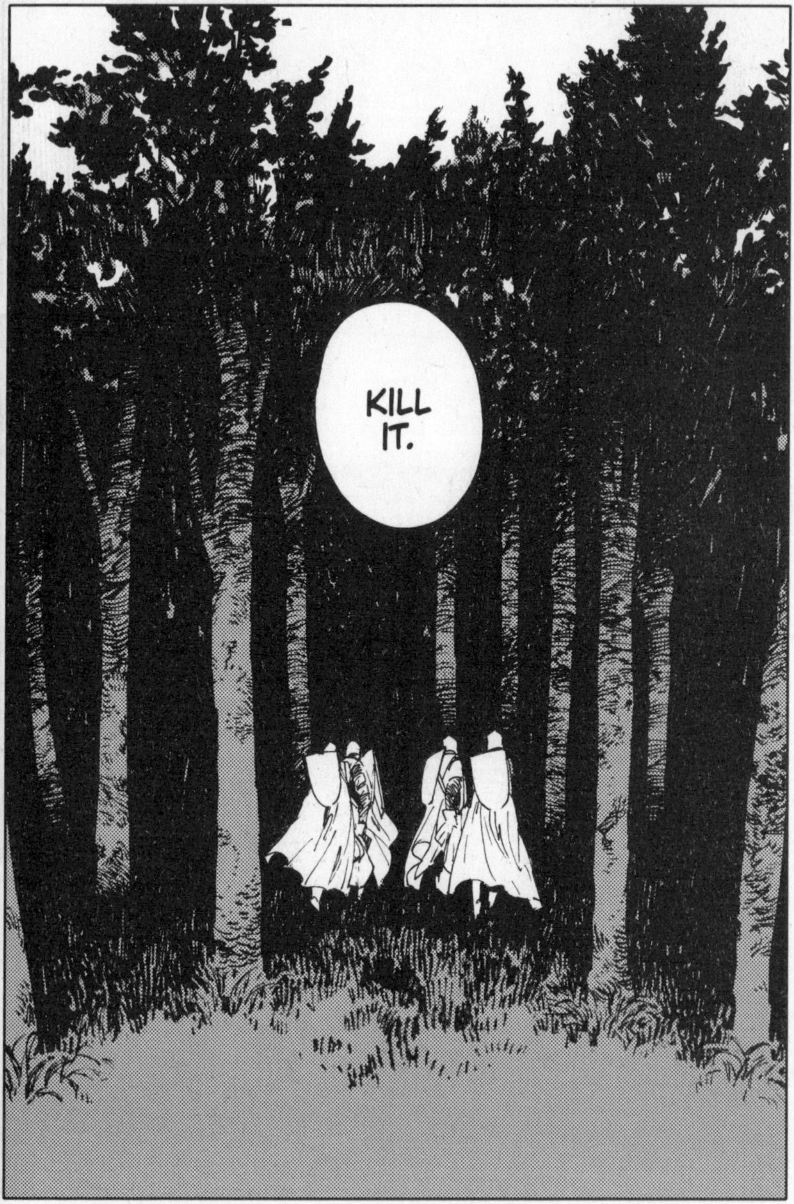
KILL IT.

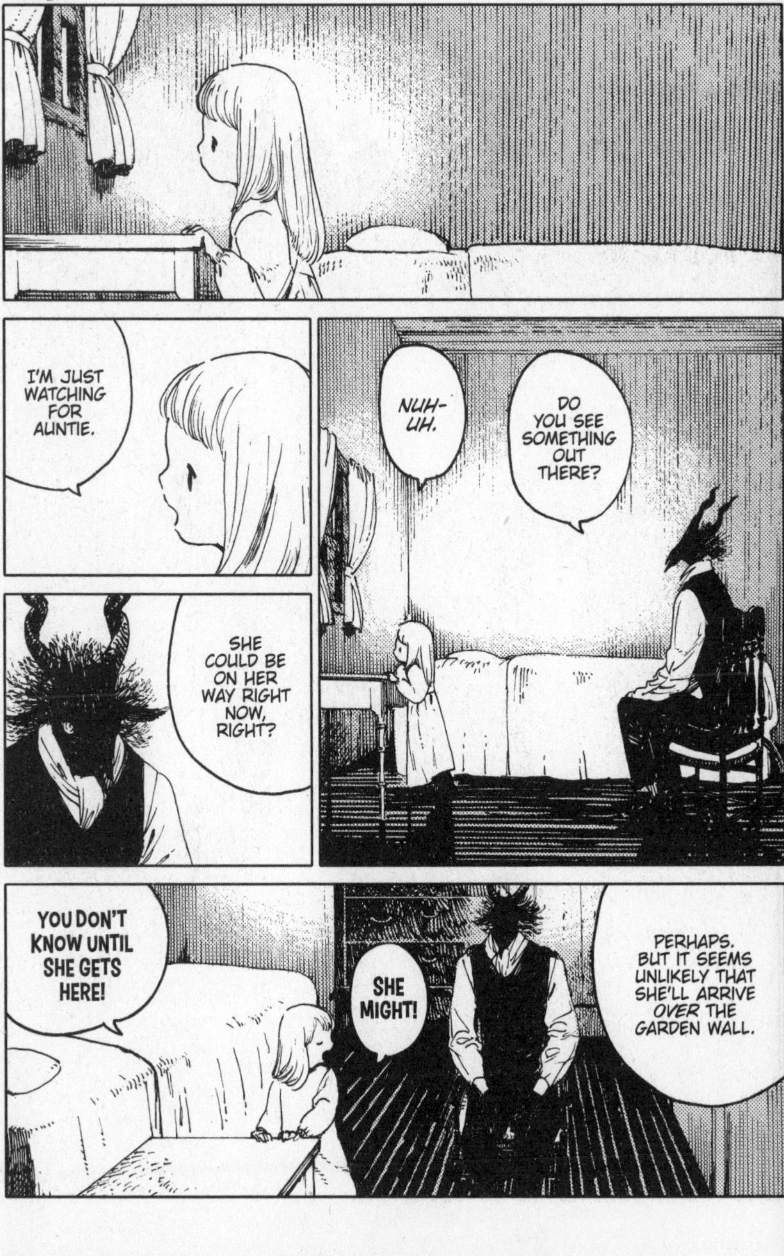
DO YOU SEE SOMETHING OUT THERE?
NUH-UH.
I'M JUST WATCHING FOR AUNTIE.
SHE COULD BE ON HER WAY RIGHT NOW, RIGHT?
PERHAPS. BUT IT SEEMS UNLIKELY THAT SHE'LL ARRIVE OVER THE GARDEN WALL.
SHE MIGHT!
YOU DON'T KNOW UNTIL SHE GETS HERE!

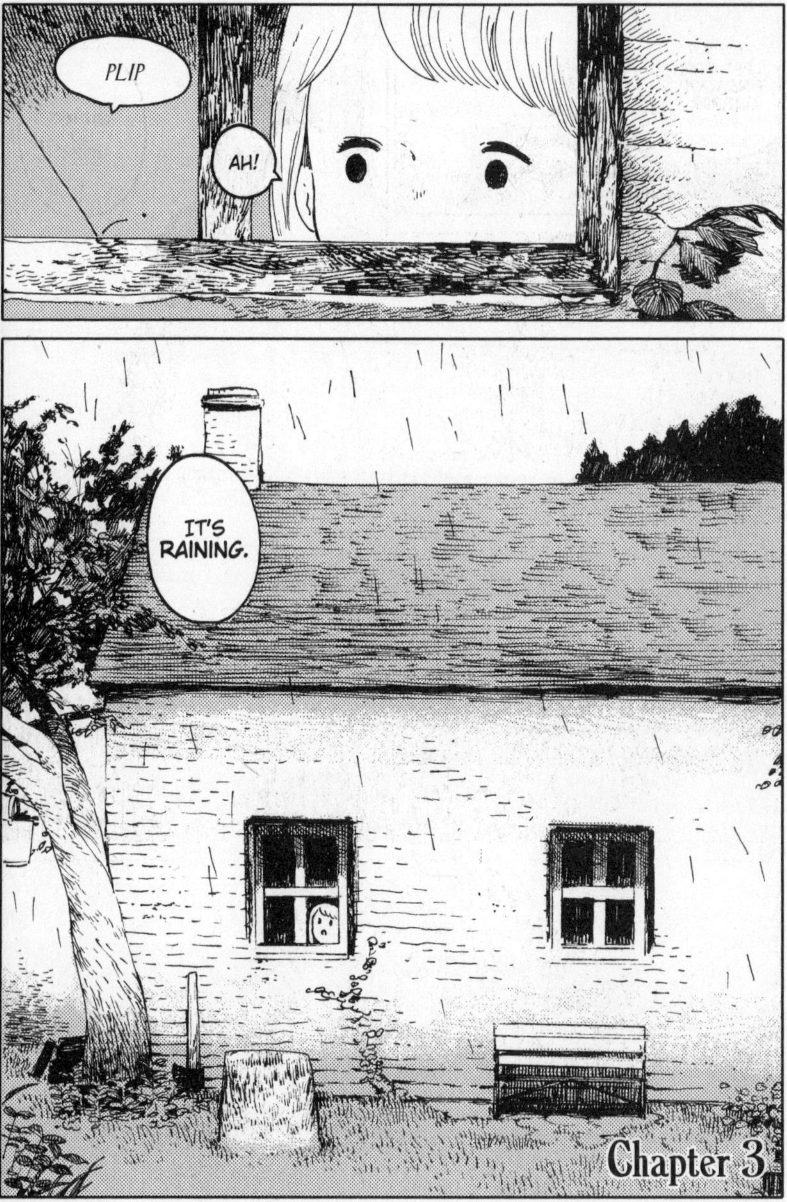
PLIP
AH!
IT'S RAINING.
Chapter 3

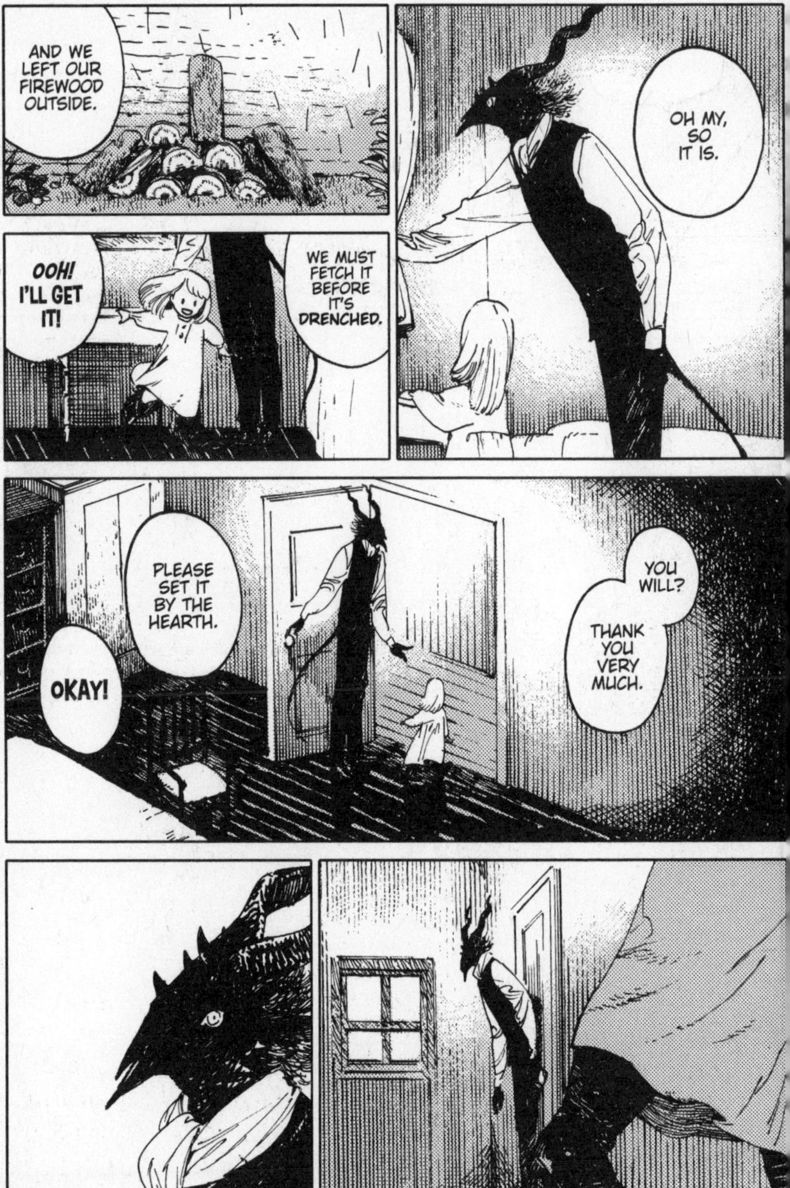
OH MY, SO IT IS.
AND WE LEFT OUR FIREWOOD OUTSIDE.
WE MUST FETCH IT BEFORE IT'S DRENCHED.
OOH! I'LL GET IT!
YOU WILL?
THANK YOU VERY MUCH.
PLEASE SET IT BY THE HEARTH.
OKAY!

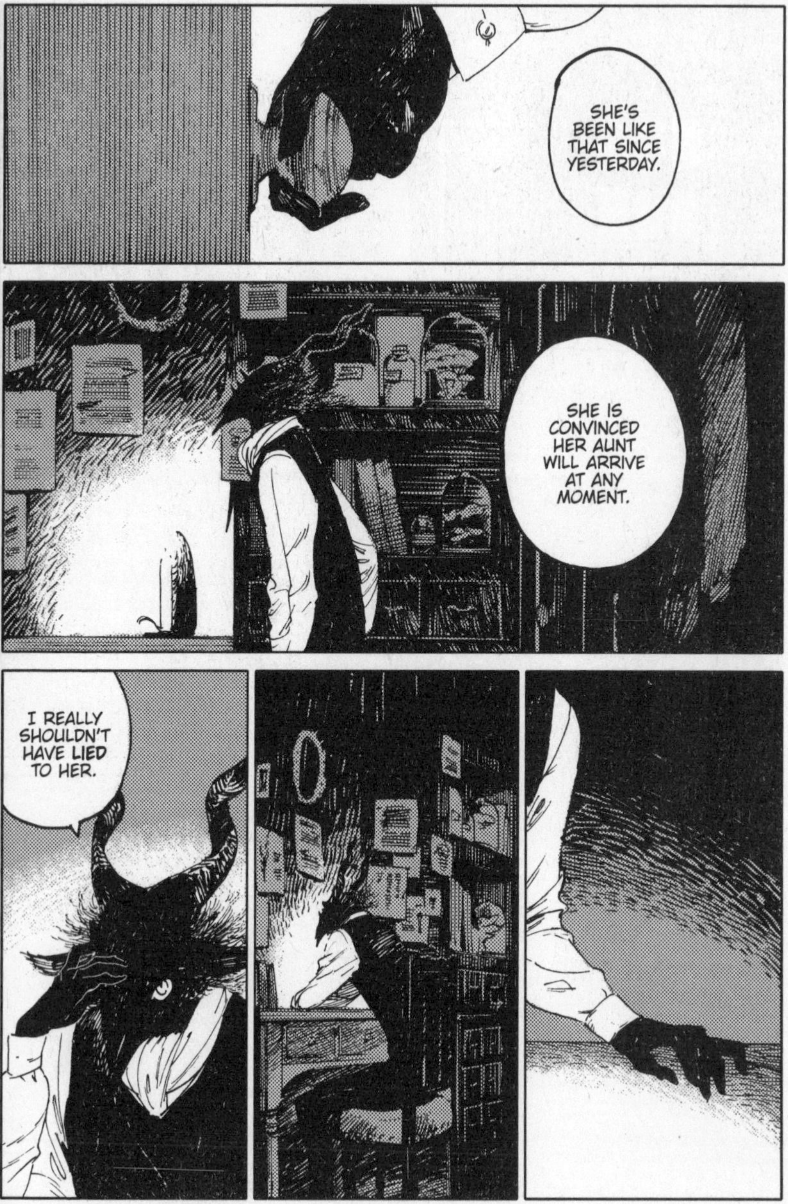
SHE'S BEEN LIKE THAT SINCE YESTERDAY.
SHE IS CONVINCED HER AUNT WILL ARRIVE AT ANY MOMENT.
I REALLY SHOULDN'T HAVE LIED TO HER.

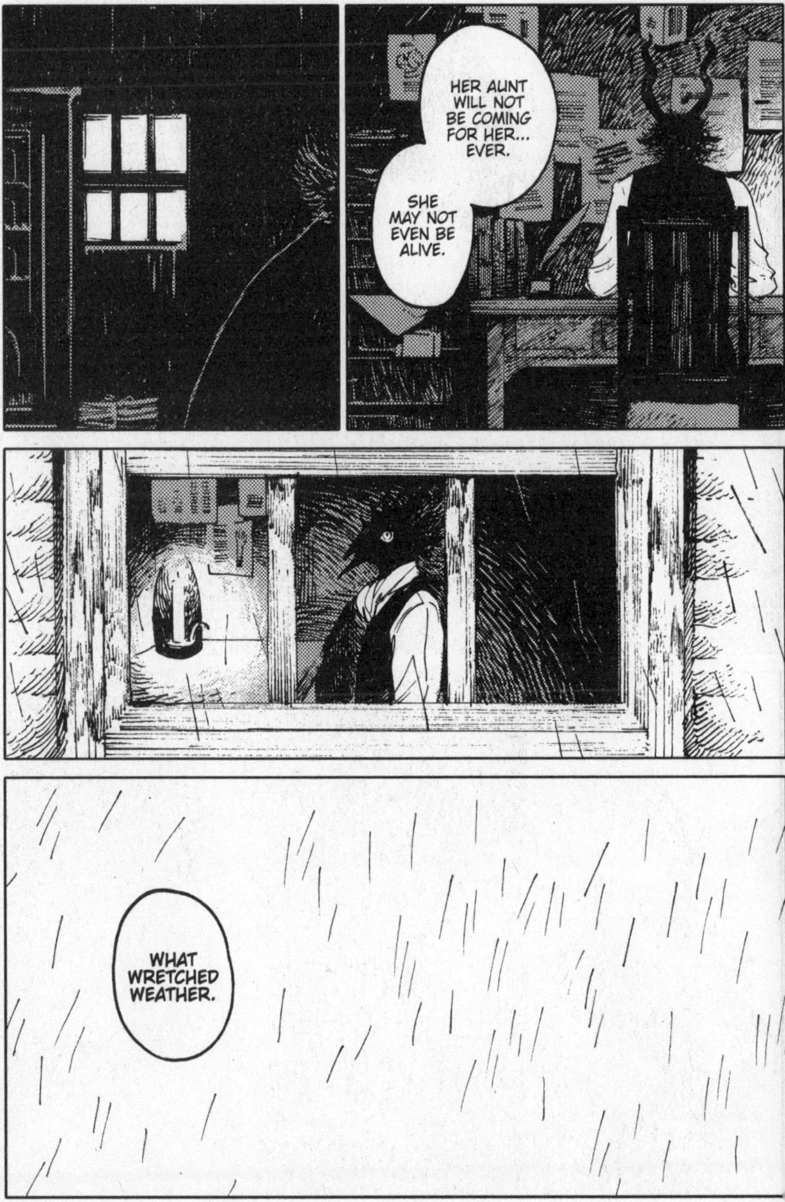
HER AUNT WILL NOT BE COMING FOR HER... EVER.
SHE MAY NOT EVEN BE ALIVE.
WHAT WRETCHED WEATHER.

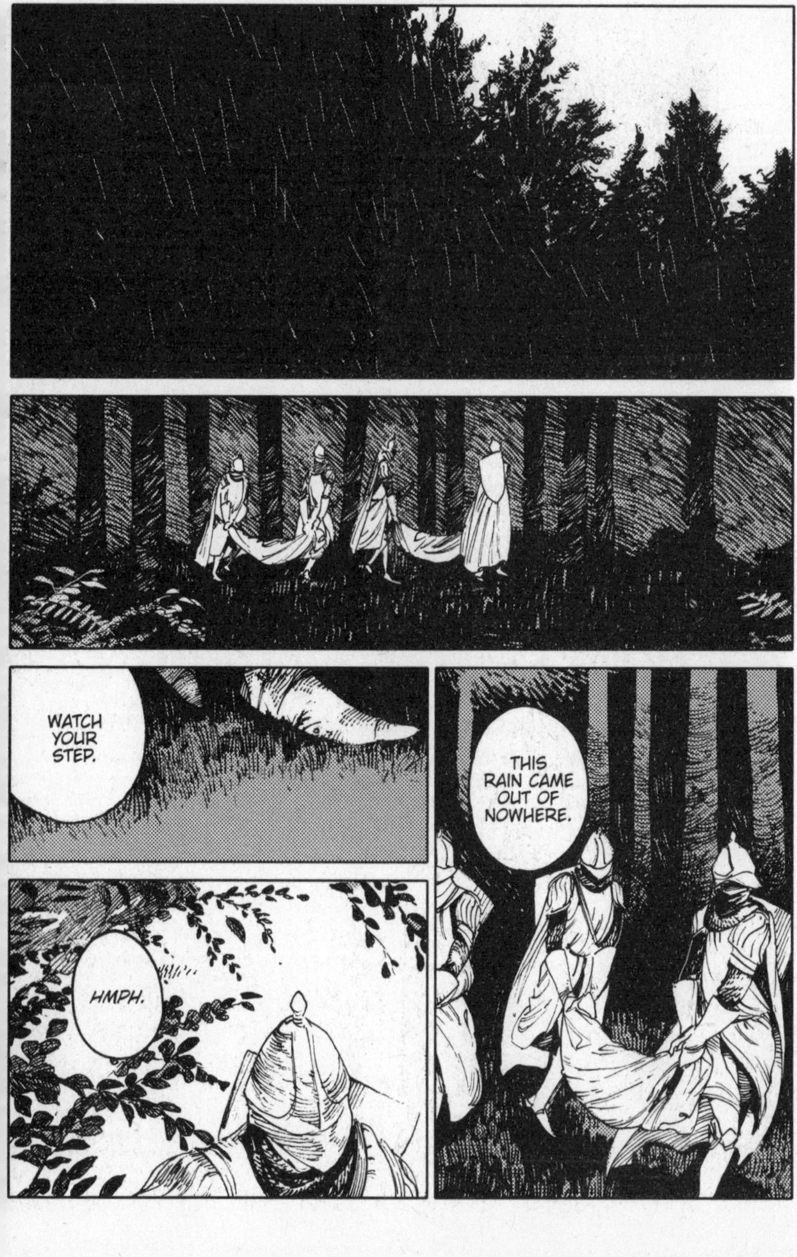
THIS RAIN CAME OUT OF NOWHERE.
WATCH YOUR STEP.
HMPH.

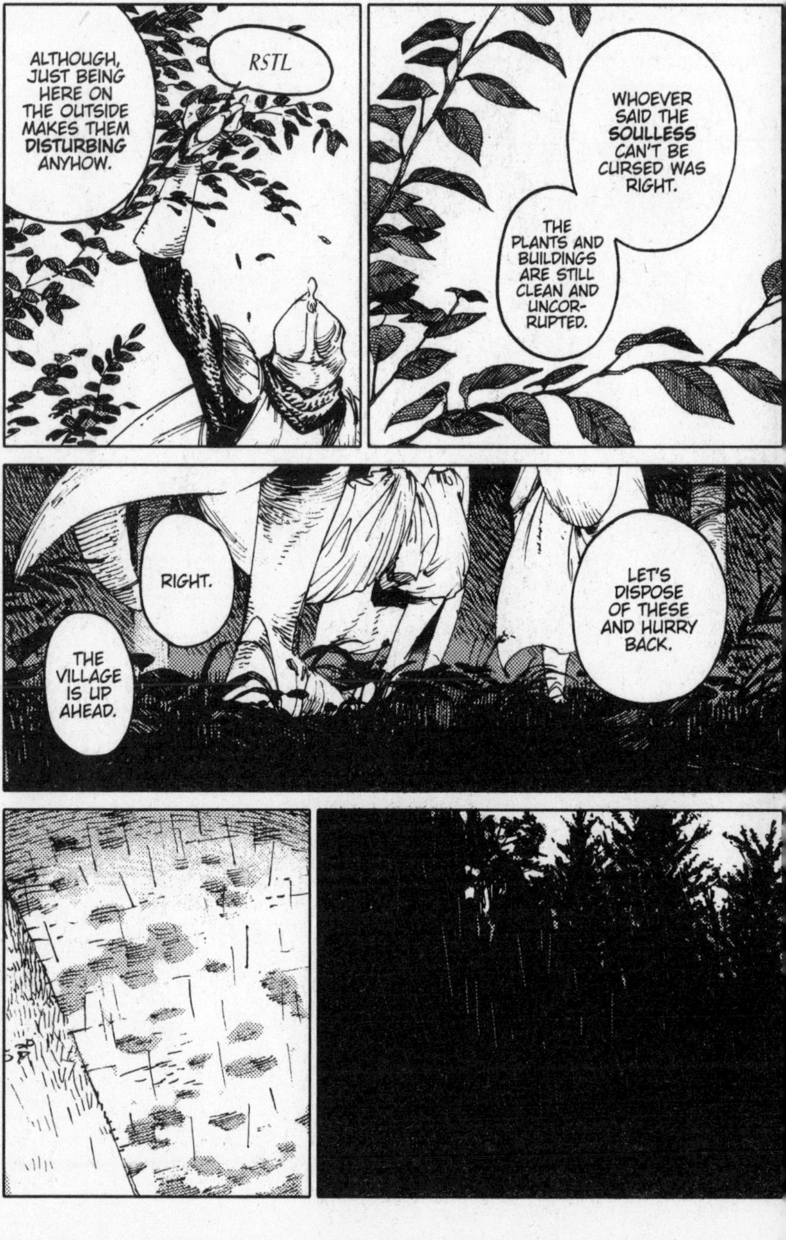
THE PLANTS AND BUILDINGS ARE STILL CLEAN AND UNCORRUPTED.
WHOEVER SAID THE SOULLESS CAN'T BE CURSED WAS RIGHT.
RSTL
ALTHOUGH, JUST BEING HERE ON THE OUTSIDE MAKES THEM DISTURBING ANYHOW.
LET'S DISPOSE OF THESE AND HURRY BACK.
RIGHT.
THE VILLAGE IS UP AHEAD.

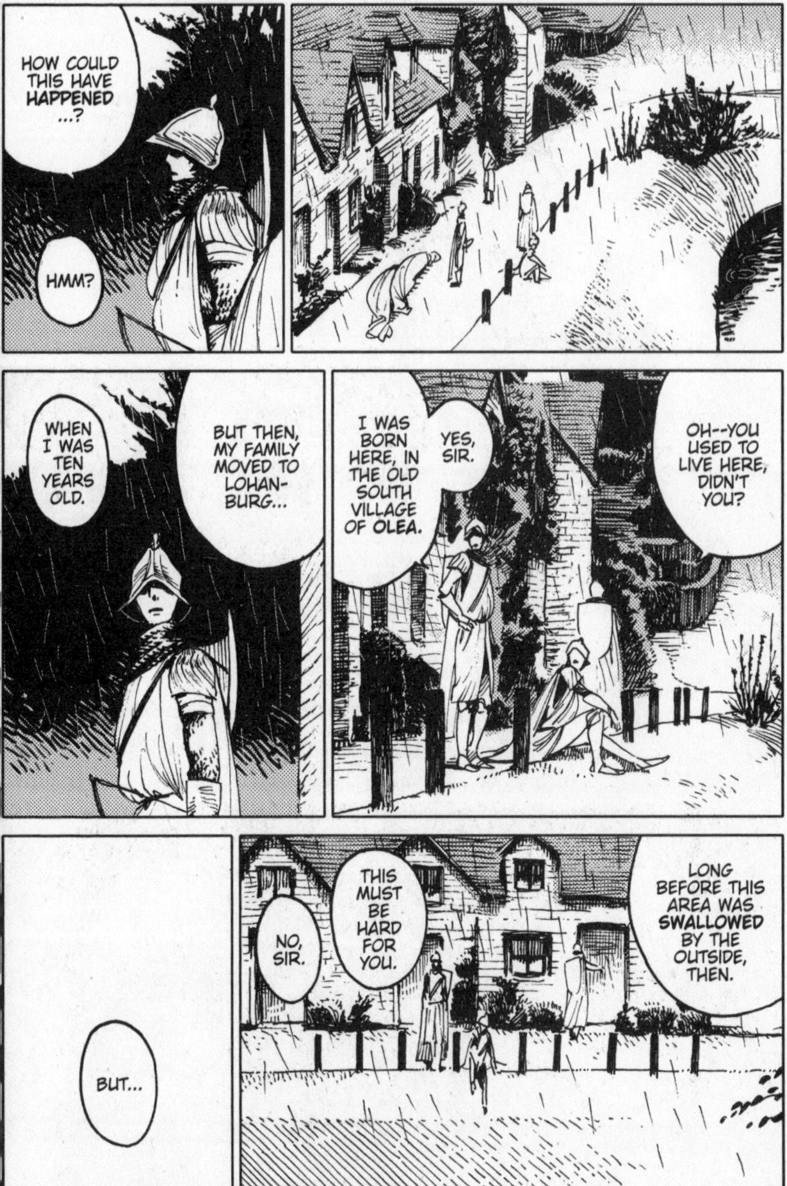
HOW COULD THIS HAVE HAPPENED ...?
HMM?
OH--YOU USED TO LIVE HERE, DIDN'T YOU?
YES, SIR.
I WAS BORN HERE, IN THE OLD SOUTH VILLAGE OF OLEA.
BUT THEN, MY FAMILY MOVED TO LOHANBURG...
WHEN I WAS TEN YEARS OLD.
LONG BEFORE THIS AREA WAS SWALLOWED BY THE OUTSIDE, THEN.
THIS MUST BE HARD FOR YOU.
NO, SIR.
BUT...

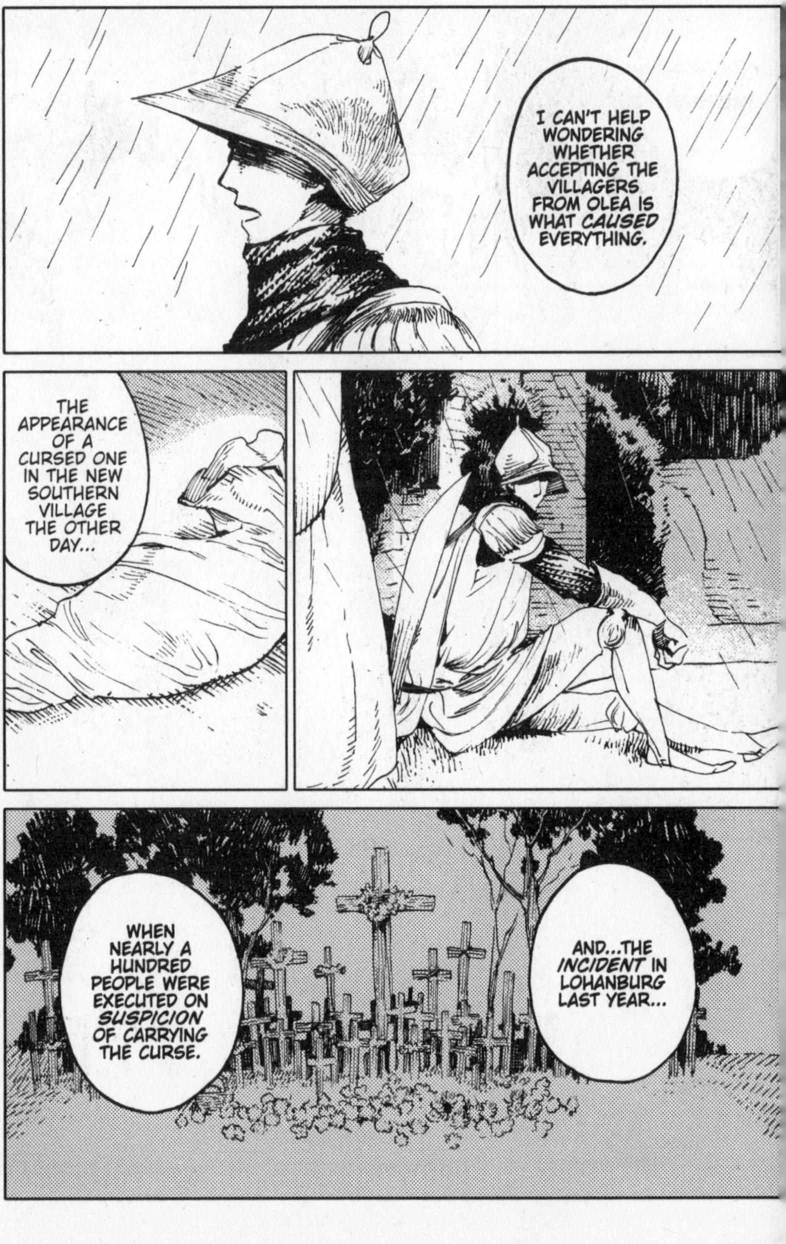
I CAN'T HELP WONDERING WHETHER ACCEPTING THE VILLAGERS FROM OLEA IS WHAT *CAUSED* EVERYTHING.
THE APPEARANCE OF A CURSED ONE IN THE NEW SOUTHERN VILLAGE THE OTHER DAY...
AND...THE *INCIDENT* IN LOHANBURG LAST YEAR...
WHEN NEARLY A HUNDRED PEOPLE WERE EXECUTED ON *SUSPICION* OF CARRYING THE CURSE.

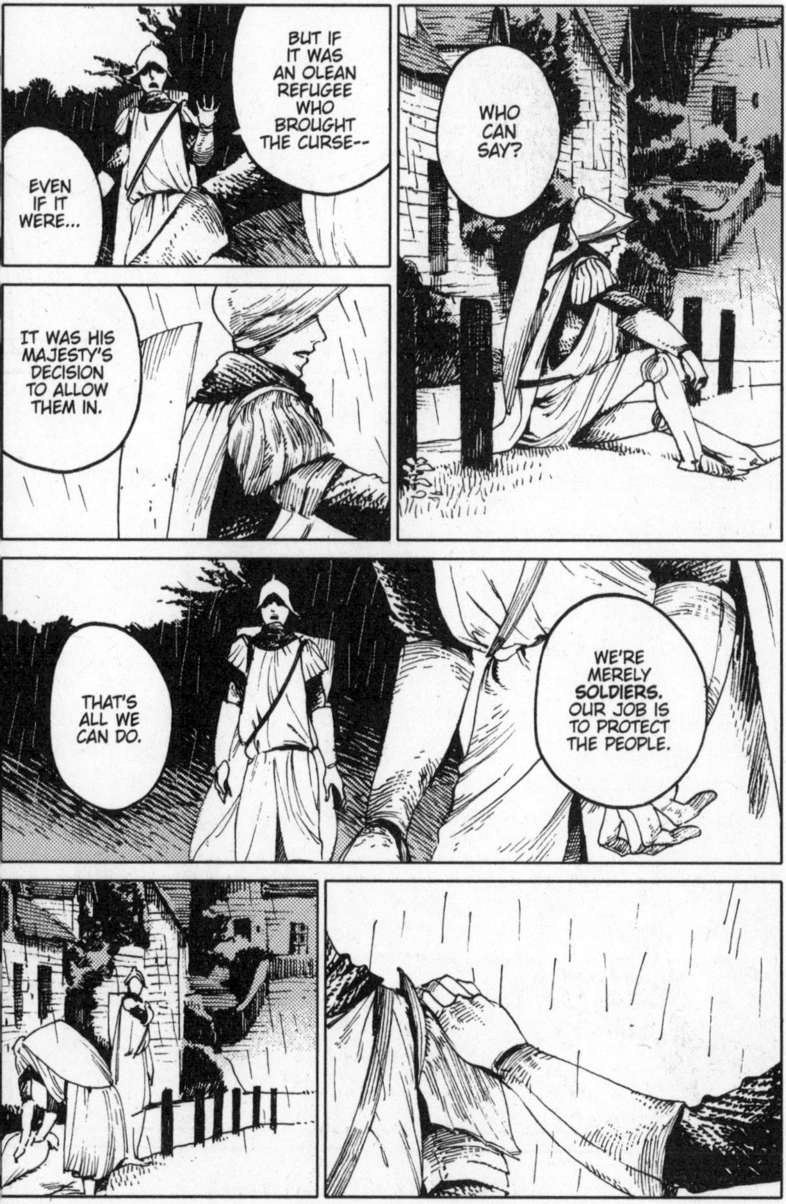
WHO CAN SAY?
BUT IF IT WAS AN OLEAN REFUGEE WHO BROUGHT THE CURSE--
EVEN IF IT WERE...
IT WAS HIS MAJESTY'S DECISION TO ALLOW THEM IN.
WE'RE MERELY SOLDIERS. OUR JOB IS TO PROTECT THE PEOPLE.
THAT'S ALL WE CAN DO.

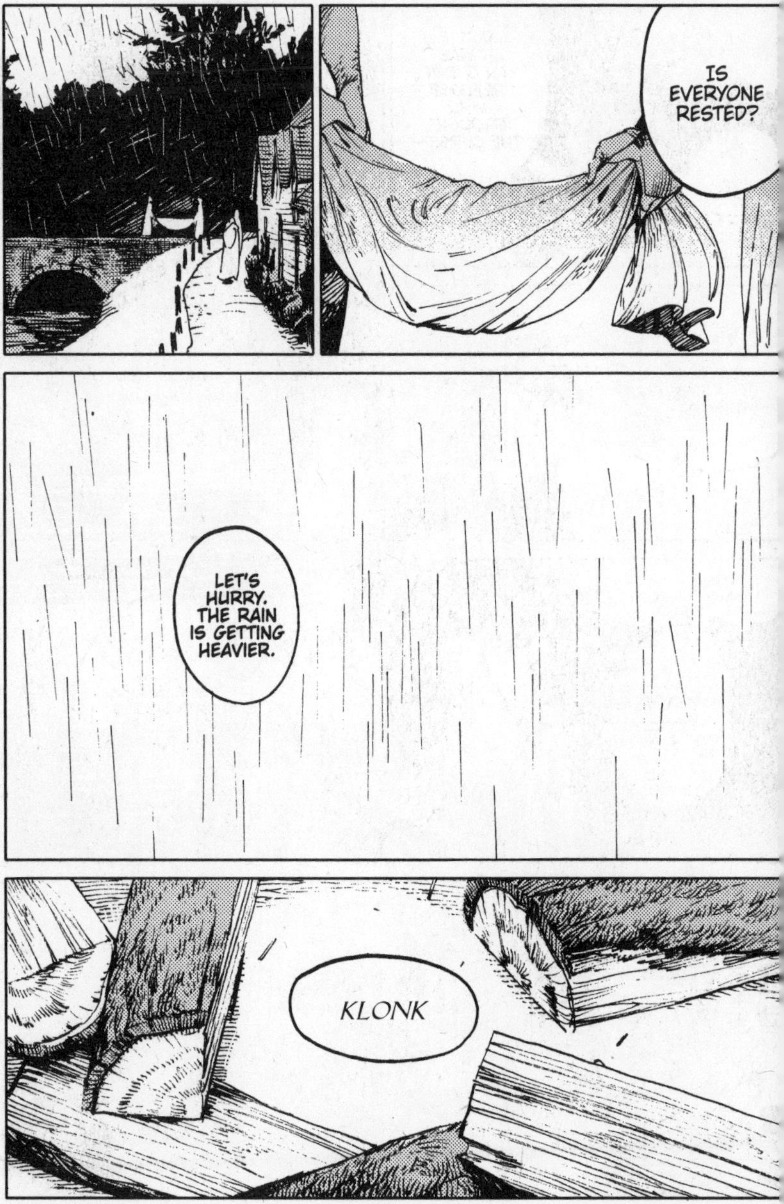
IS EVERYONE RESTED?
LET'S HURRY. THE RAIN IS GETTING HEAVIER.
KLONK

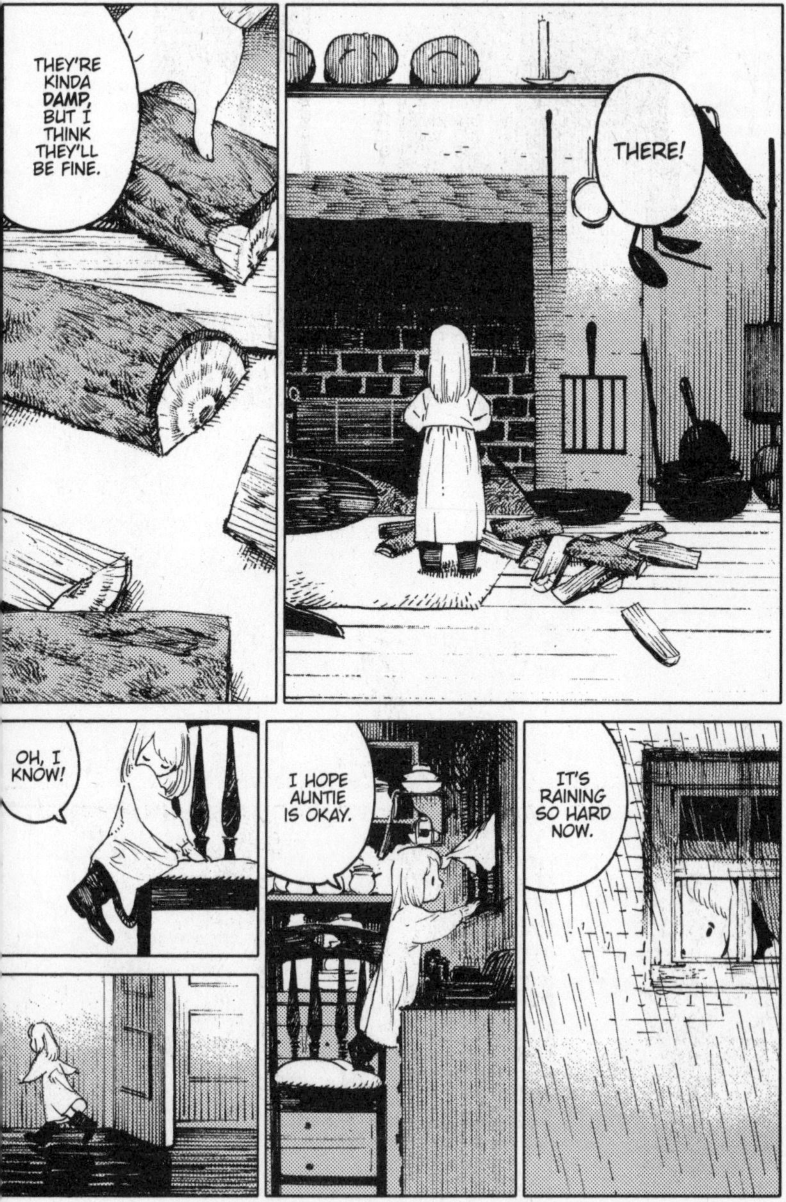
THERE!
THEY'RE KINDA DAMP, BUT I THINK THEY'LL BE FINE.
IT'S RAINING SO HARD NOW.
I HOPE AUNTIE IS OKAY.
OH, I KNOW!

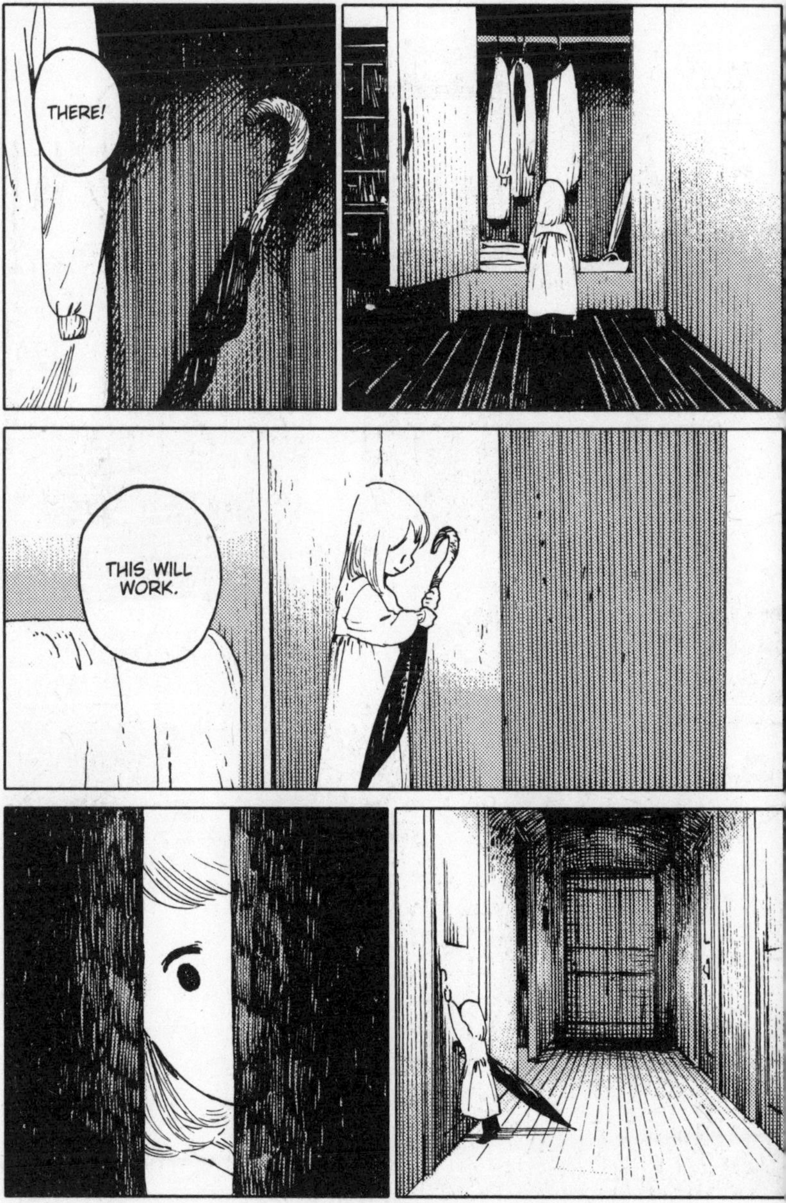
THERE!
THIS WILL WORK.

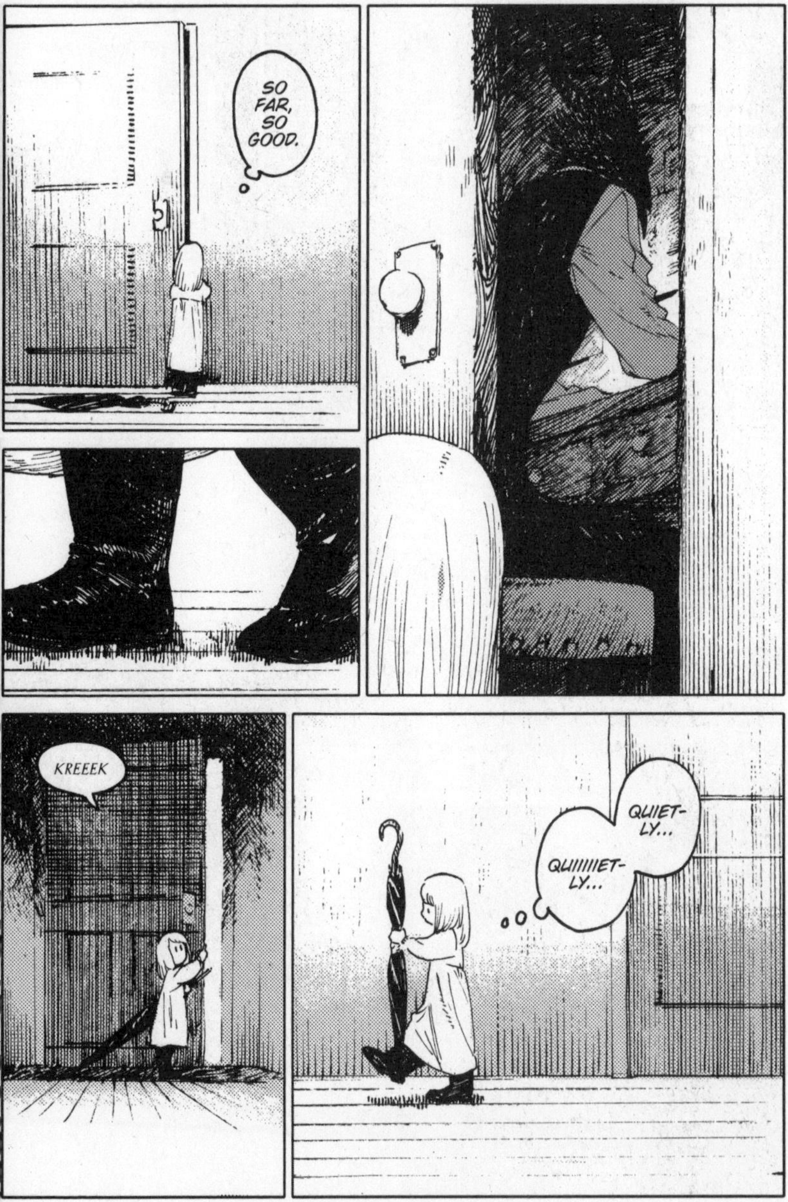
SO FAR, SO GOOD.
QUIET-LY...
QUIIIIIET-LY...
KREEEK

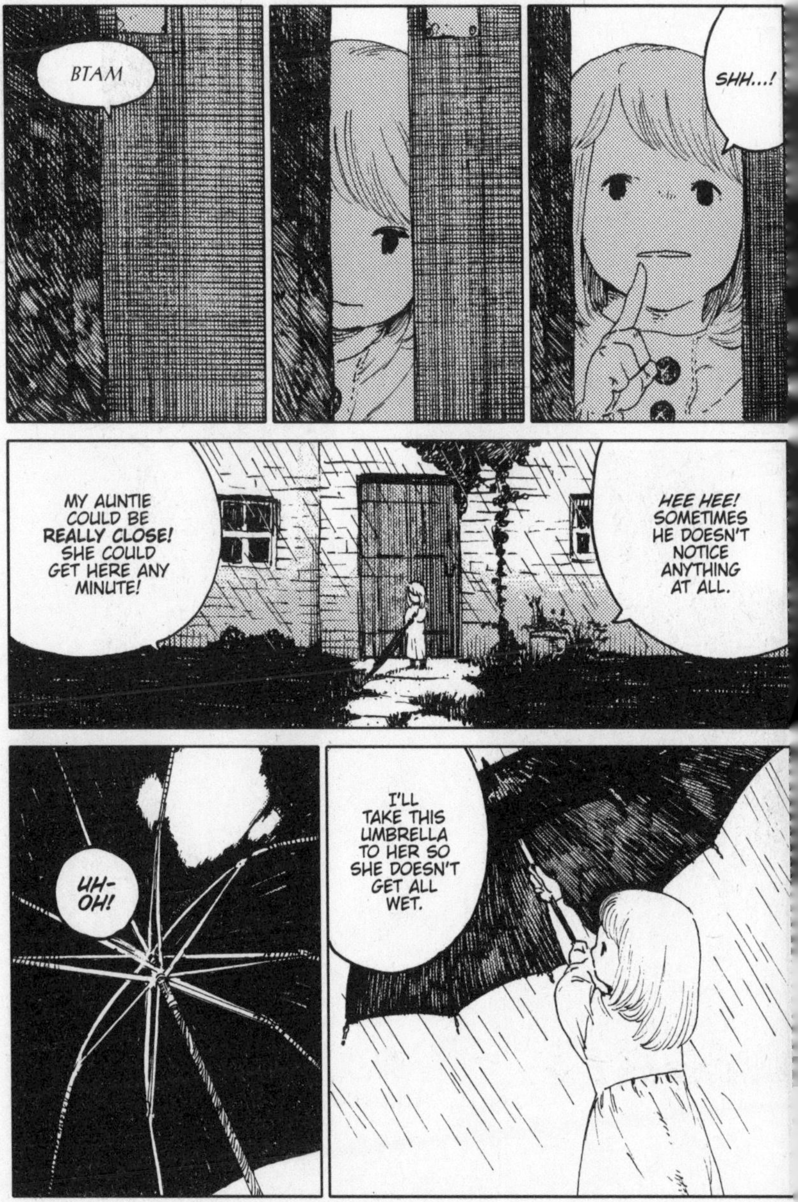
SHH...!
BTAM
HEE HEE! SOMETIMES HE DOESN'T NOTICE ANYTHING AT ALL.
MY AUNTIE COULD BE REALLY CLOSE! SHE COULD GET HERE ANY MINUTE!
I'LL TAKE THIS UMBRELLA TO HER SO SHE DOESN'T GET ALL WET.
UH-OH!

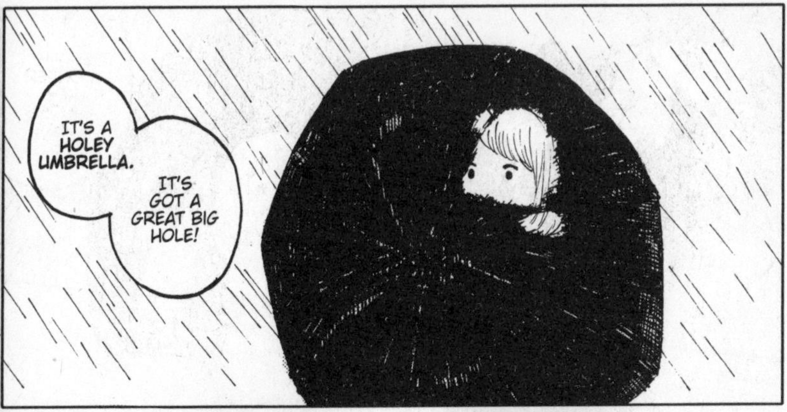
IT'S A HOLEY UMBRELLA.
IT'S GOT A GREAT BIG HOLE!

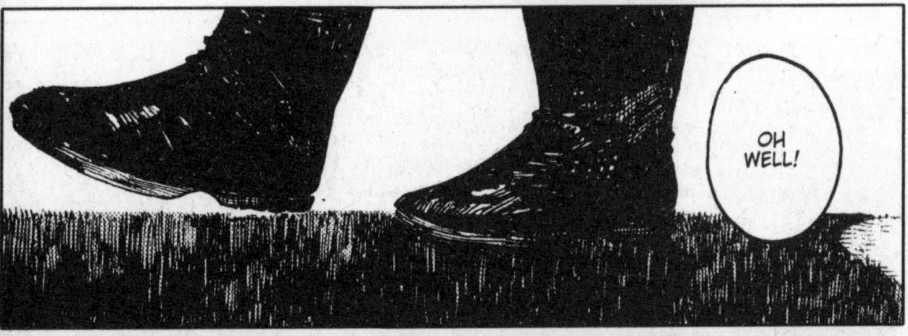
OH WELL!

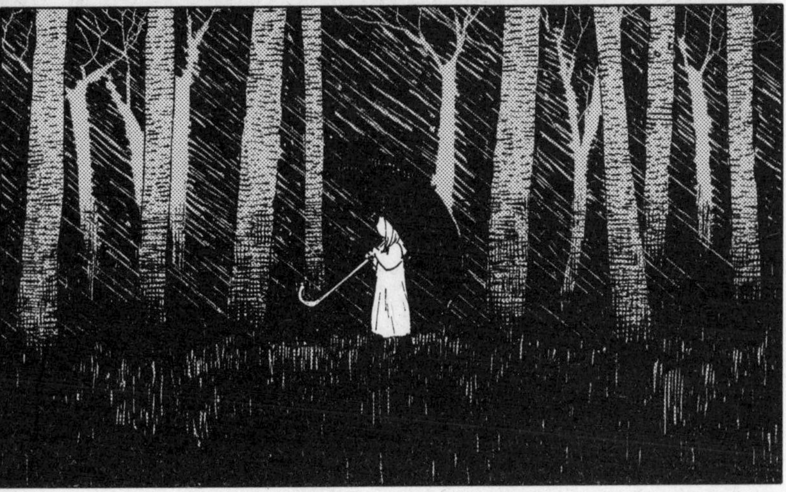

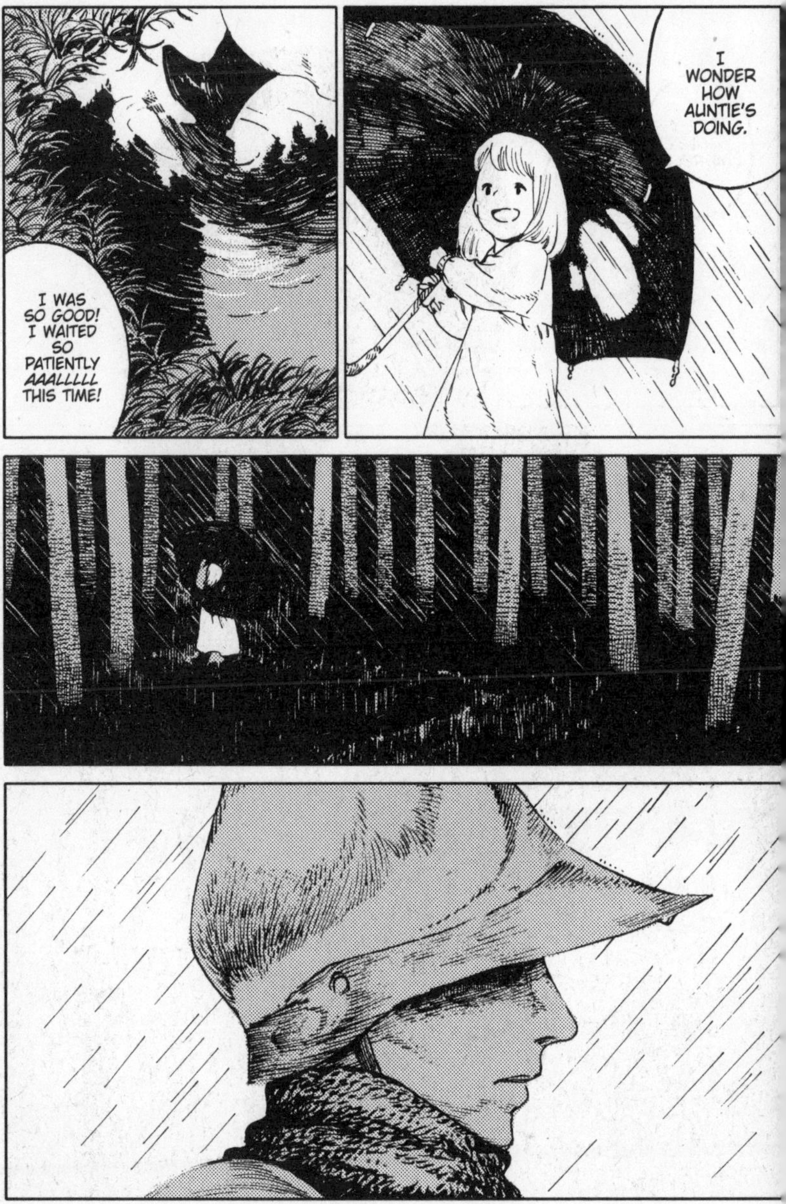
I WONDER HOW AUNTIE'S DOING.
I WAS SO GOOD! I WAITED SO PATIENTLY AAALLLLL THIS TIME!

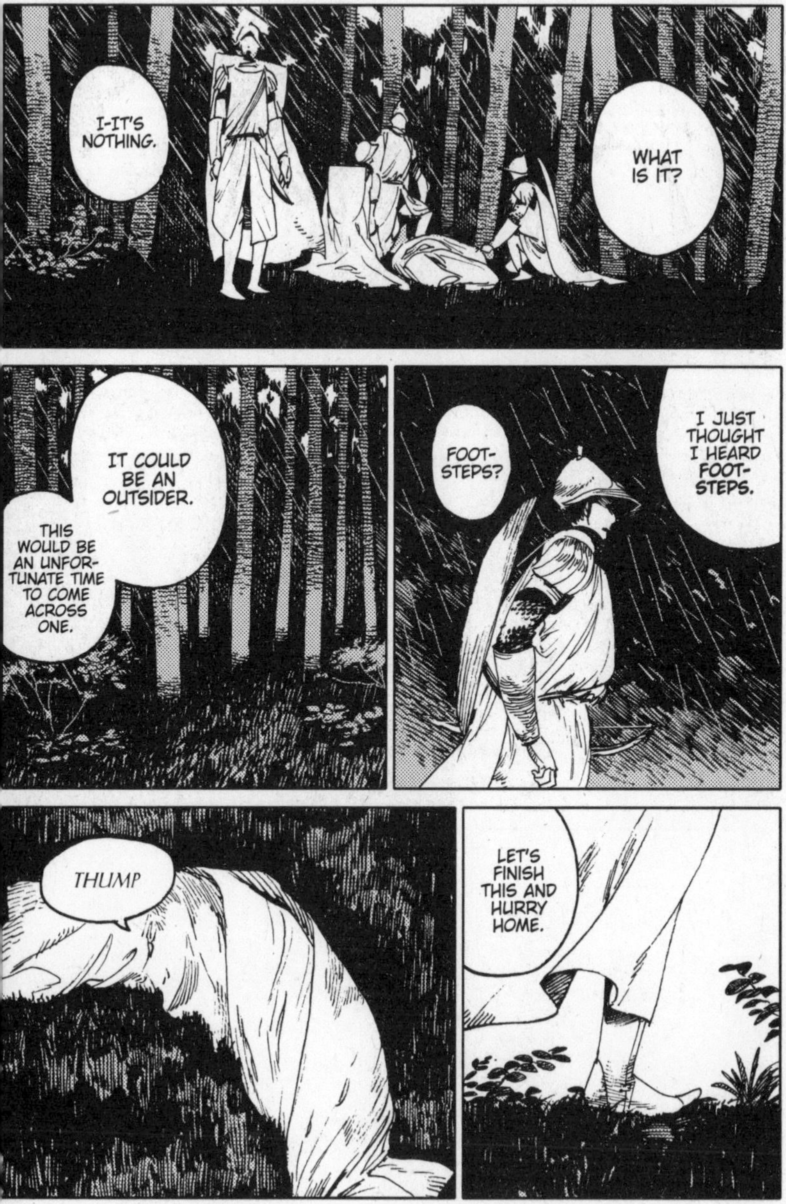
WHAT IS IT?
I-IT'S NOTHING.
I JUST THOUGHT I HEARD FOOT-STEPS.
FOOT-STEPS?
IT COULD BE AN OUTSIDER.
THIS WOULD BE AN UNFOR-TUNATE TIME TO COME ACROSS ONE.
LET'S FINISH THIS AND HURRY HOME.
THUMP

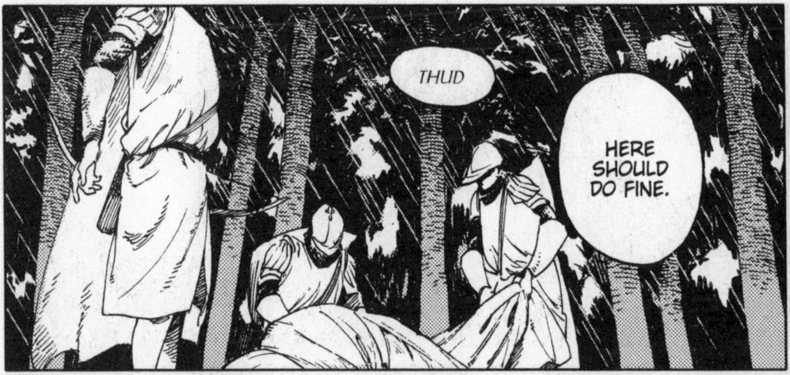
HERE SHOULD DO FINE.
THUD
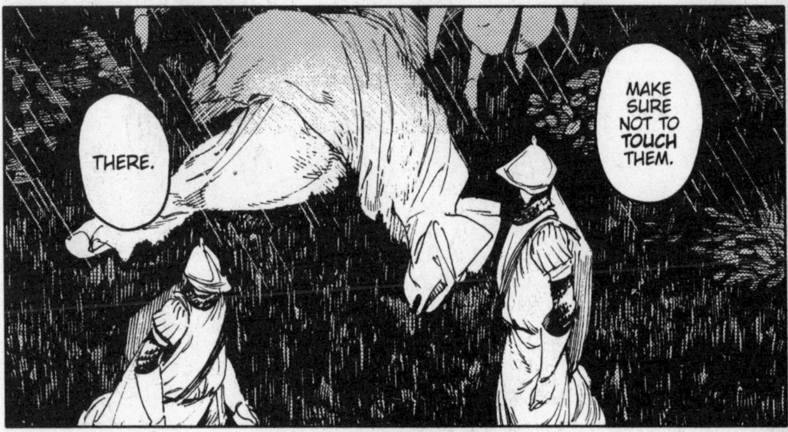
MAKE SURE NOT TO TOUCH THEM.
THERE.
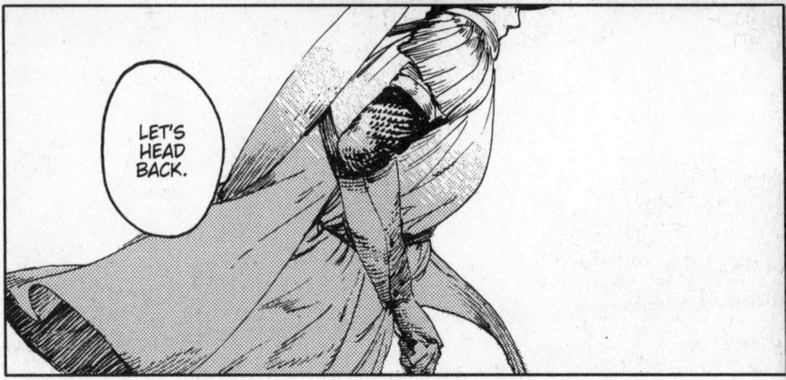
LET'S HEAD BACK.

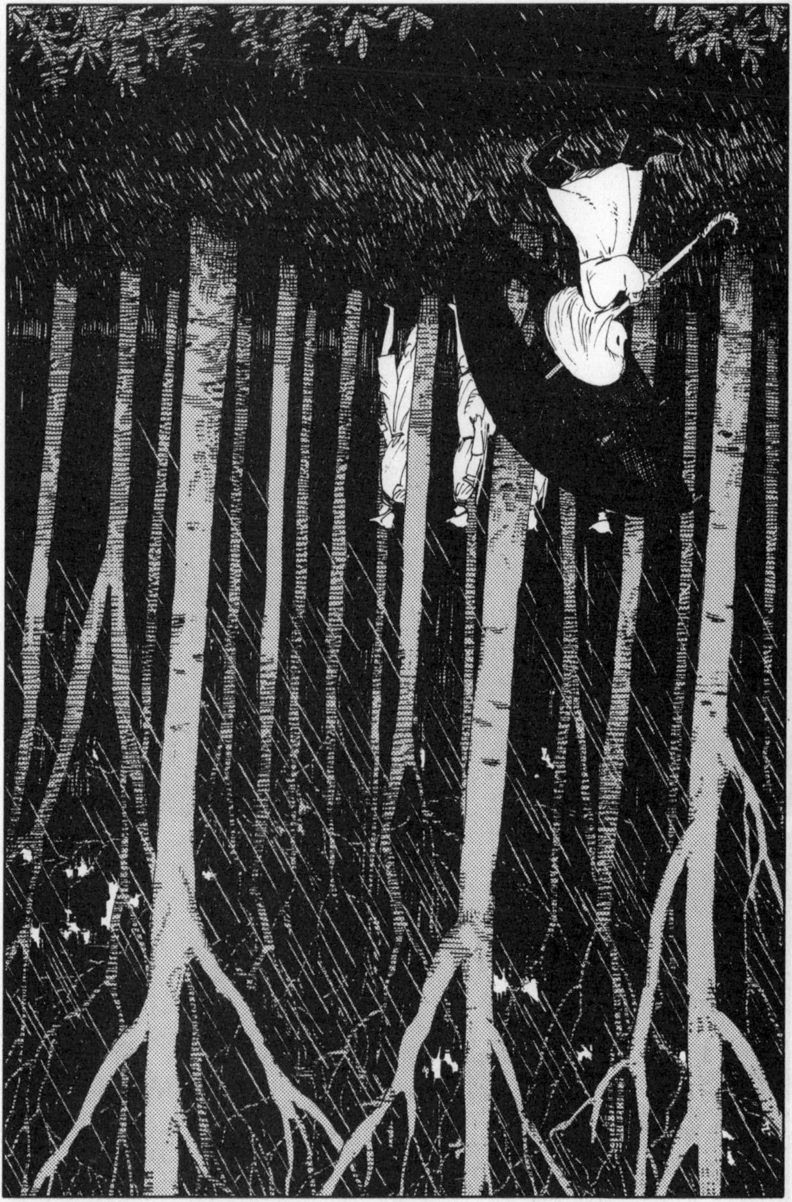

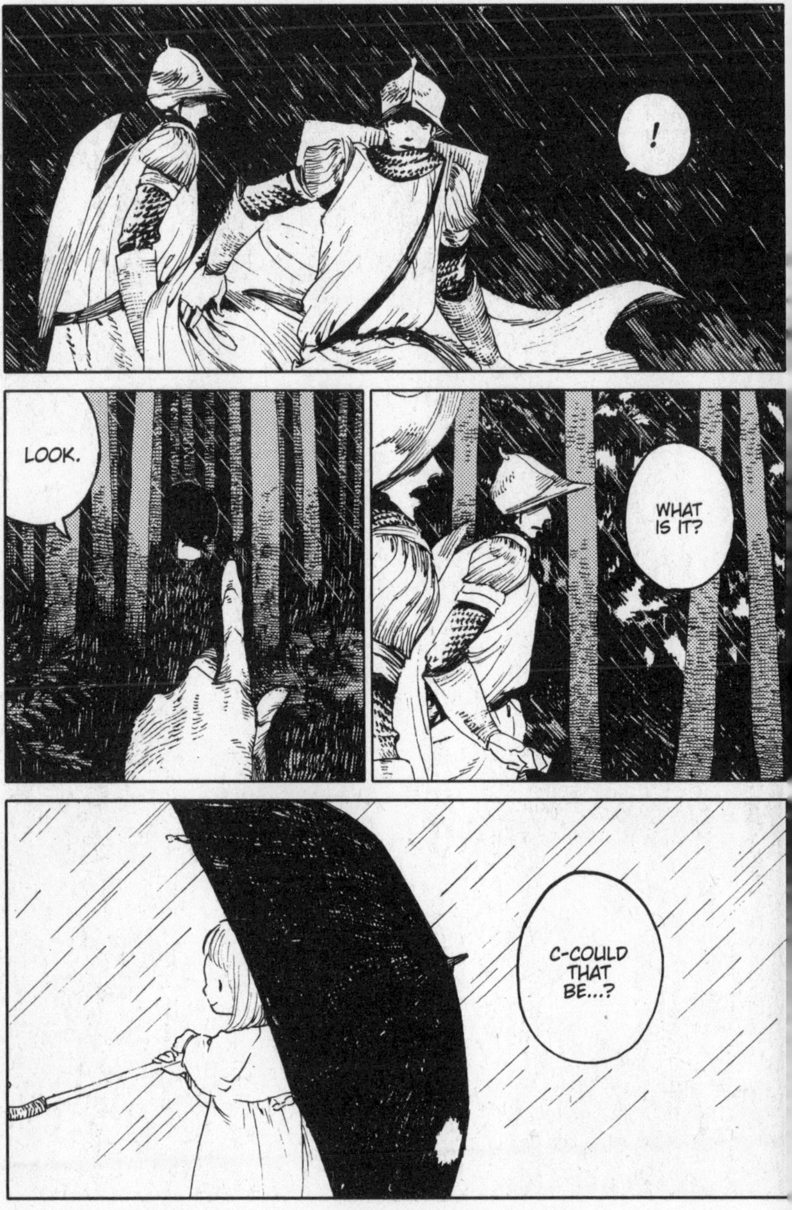
!
WHAT IS IT?
LOOK.
C-COULD THAT BE...?

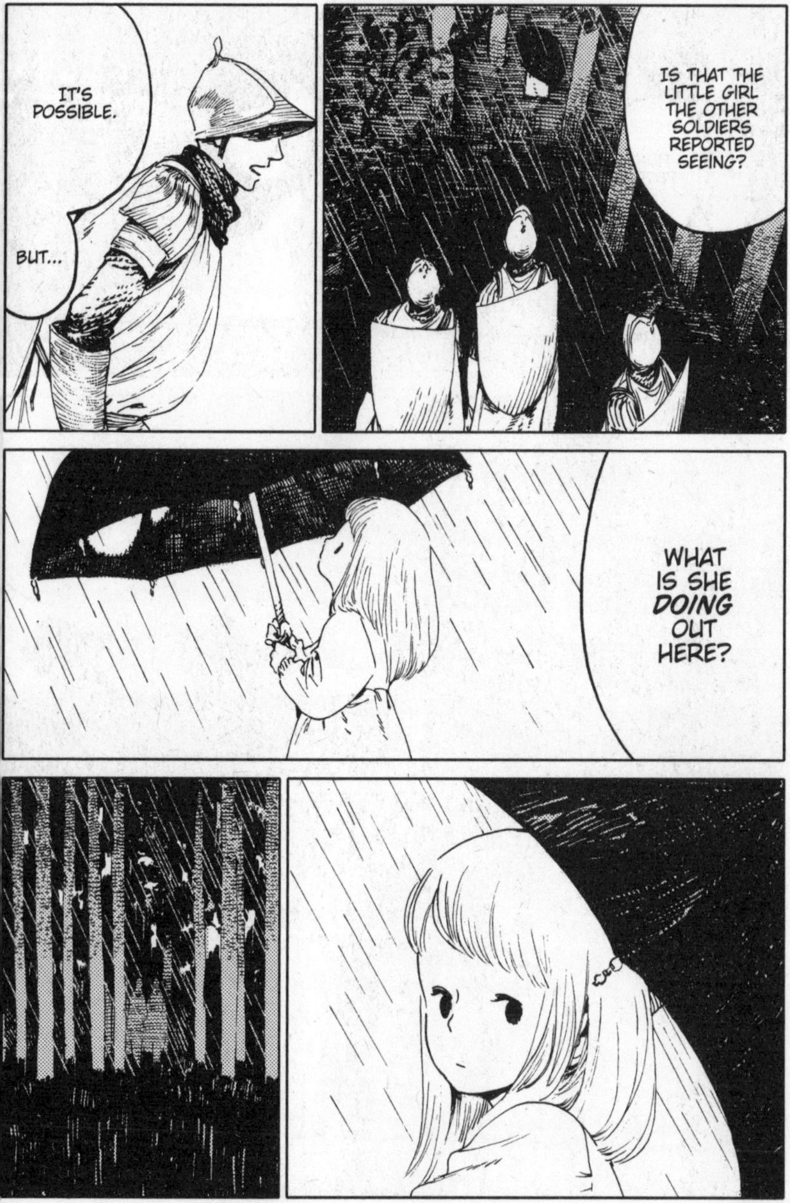
IS THAT THE LITTLE GIRL THE OTHER SOLDIERS REPORTED SEEING?
IT'S POSSIBLE.
BUT...
WHAT IS SHE *DOING* OUT HERE?

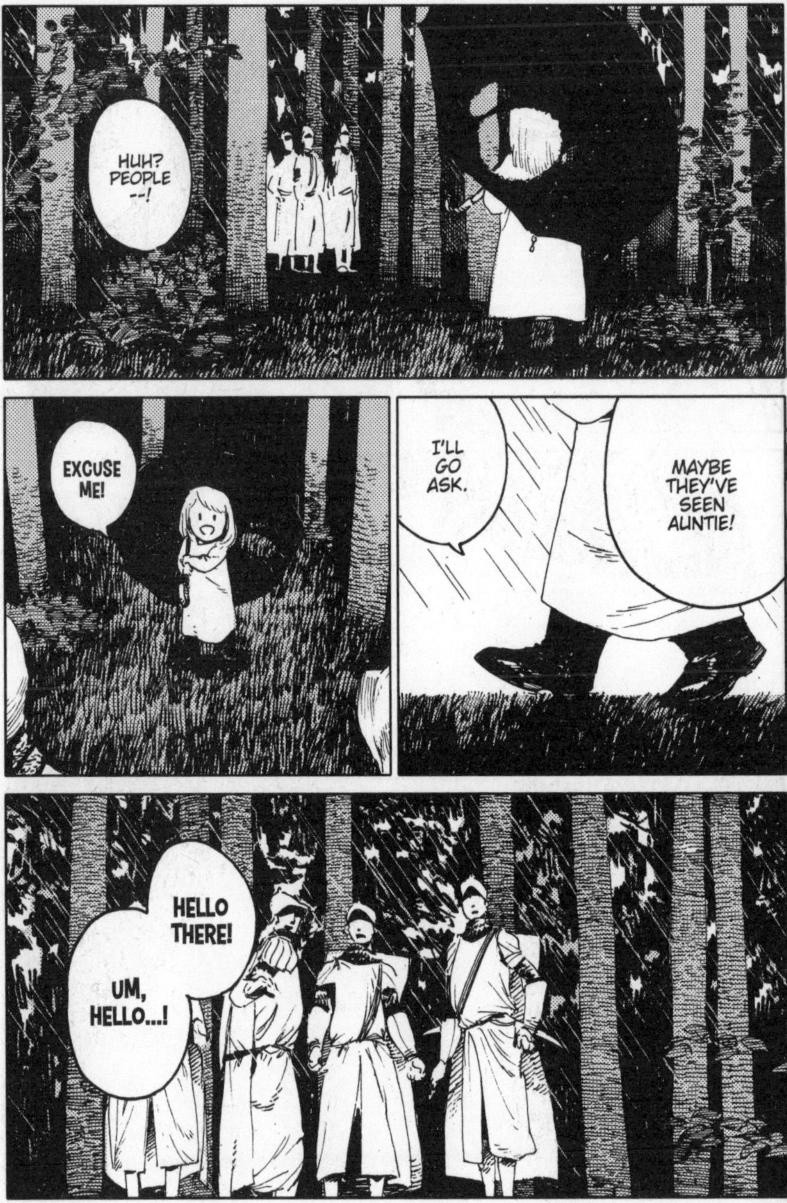
HUH? PEOPLE --!
MAYBE THEY'VE SEEN AUNTIE!
I'LL GO ASK.
EXCUSE ME!
HELLO THERE!
UM, HELLO...!

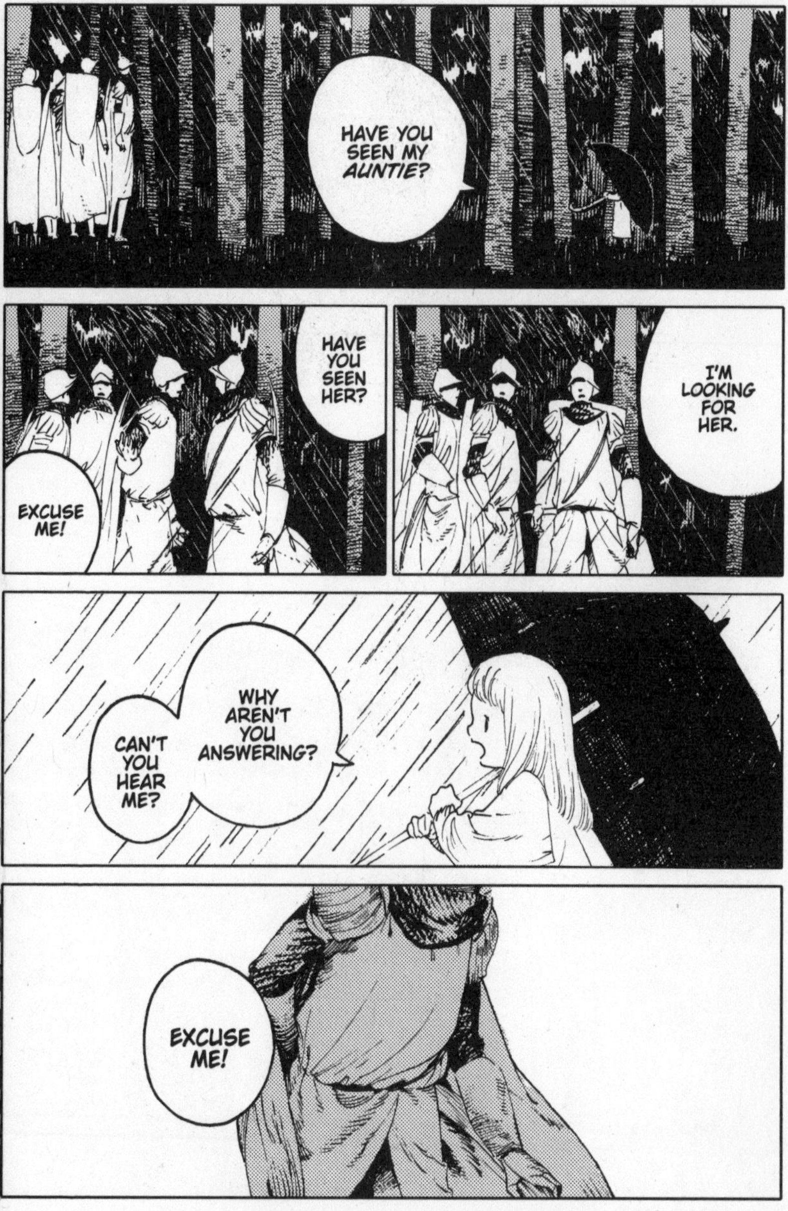
HAVE YOU SEEN MY AUNTIE?
I'M LOOKING FOR HER.
HAVE YOU SEEN HER?
EXCUSE ME!
WHY AREN'T YOU ANSWERING?
CAN'T YOU HEAR ME?
EXCUSE ME!

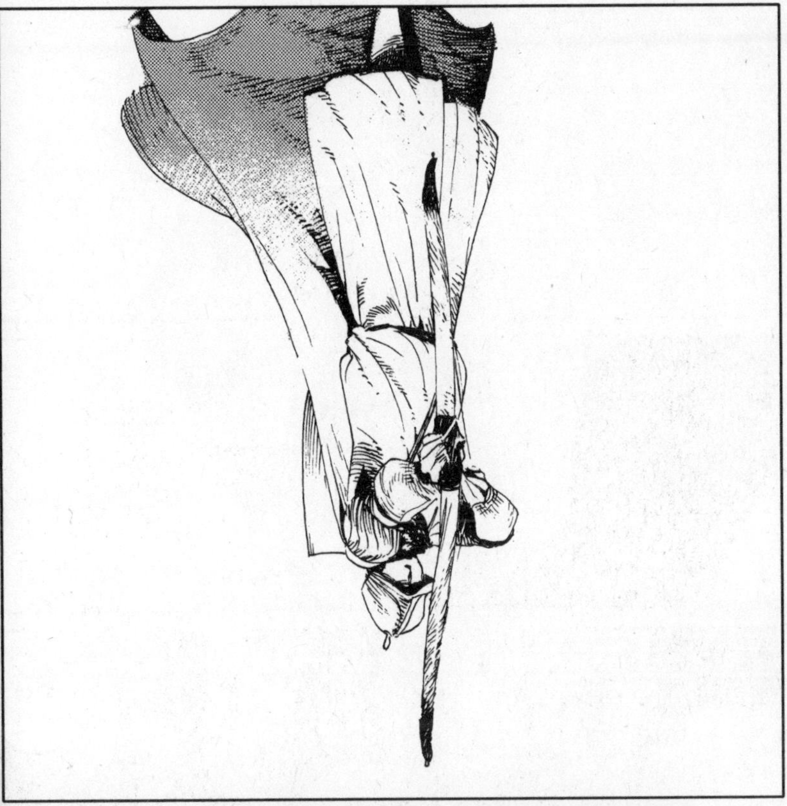
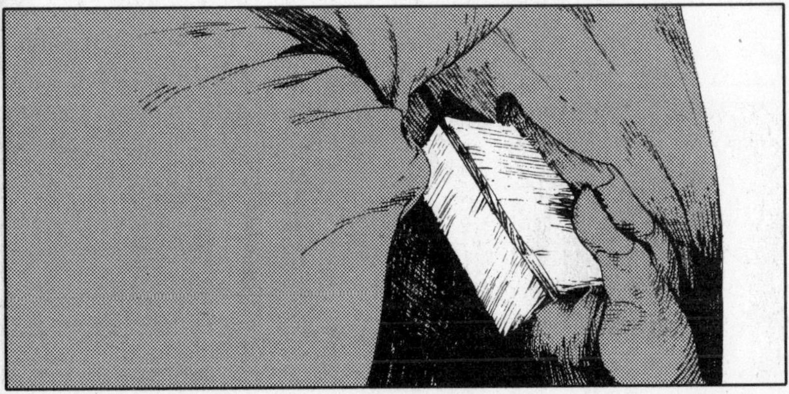

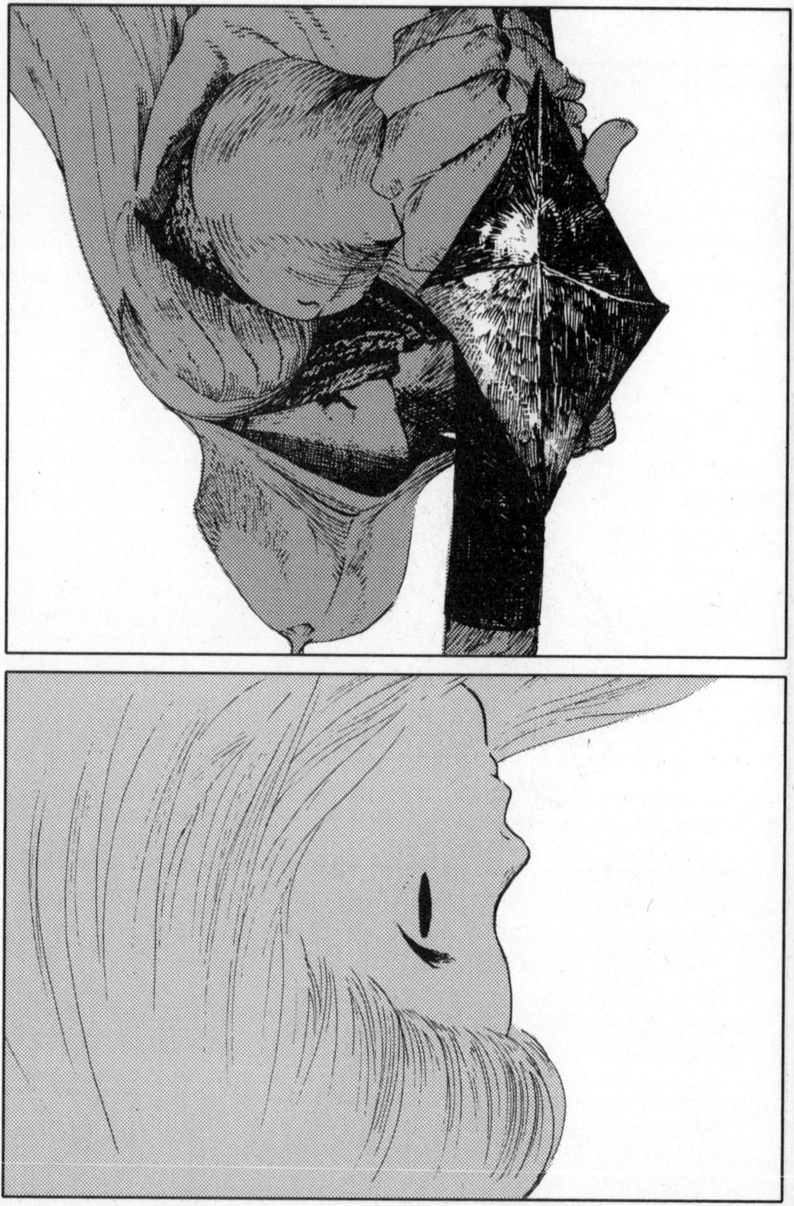

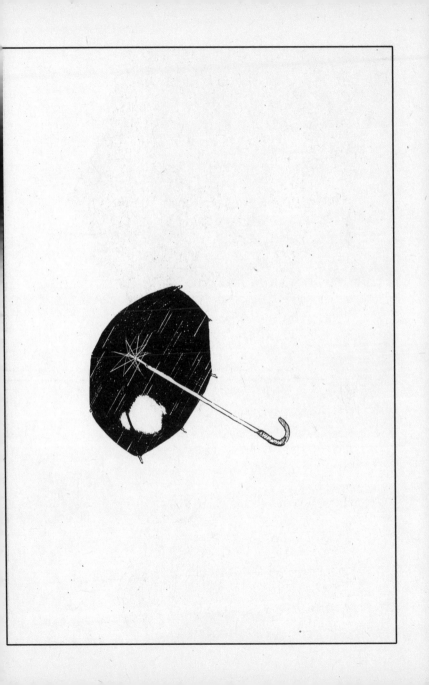

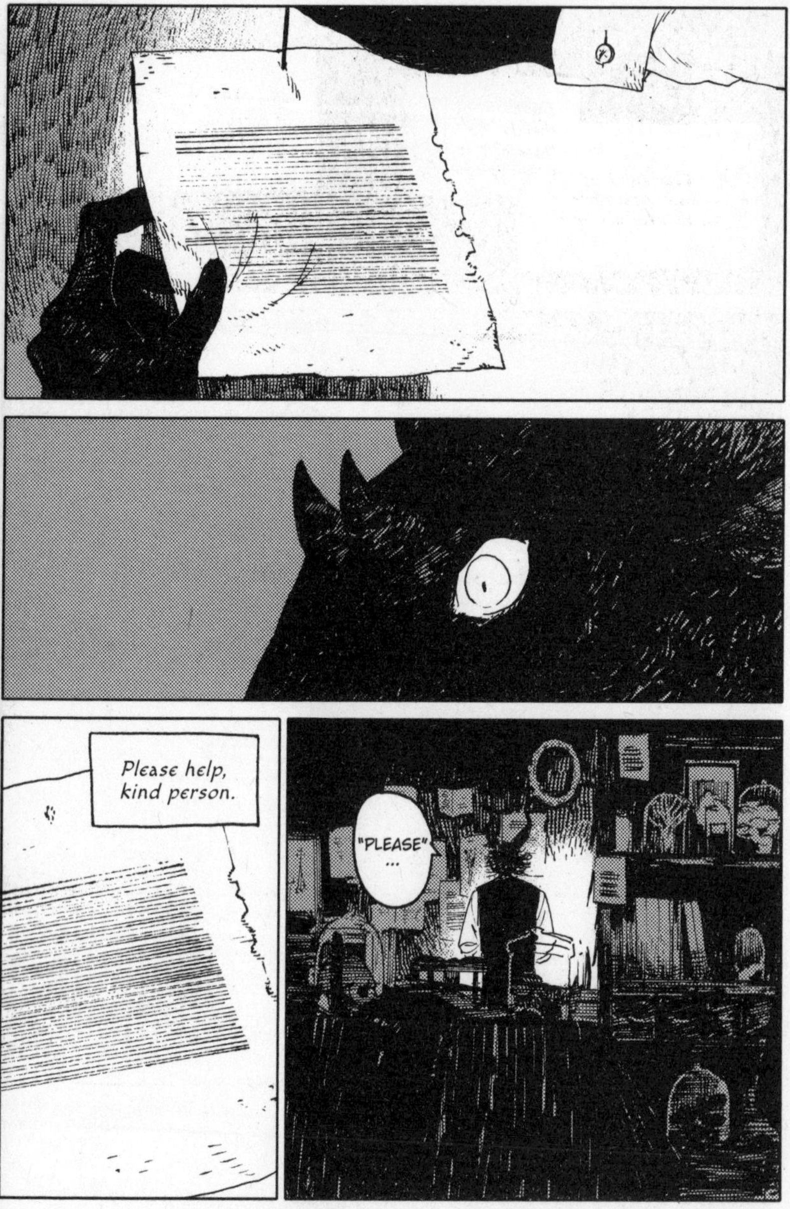
"PLEASE"
...
Please help, kind person.

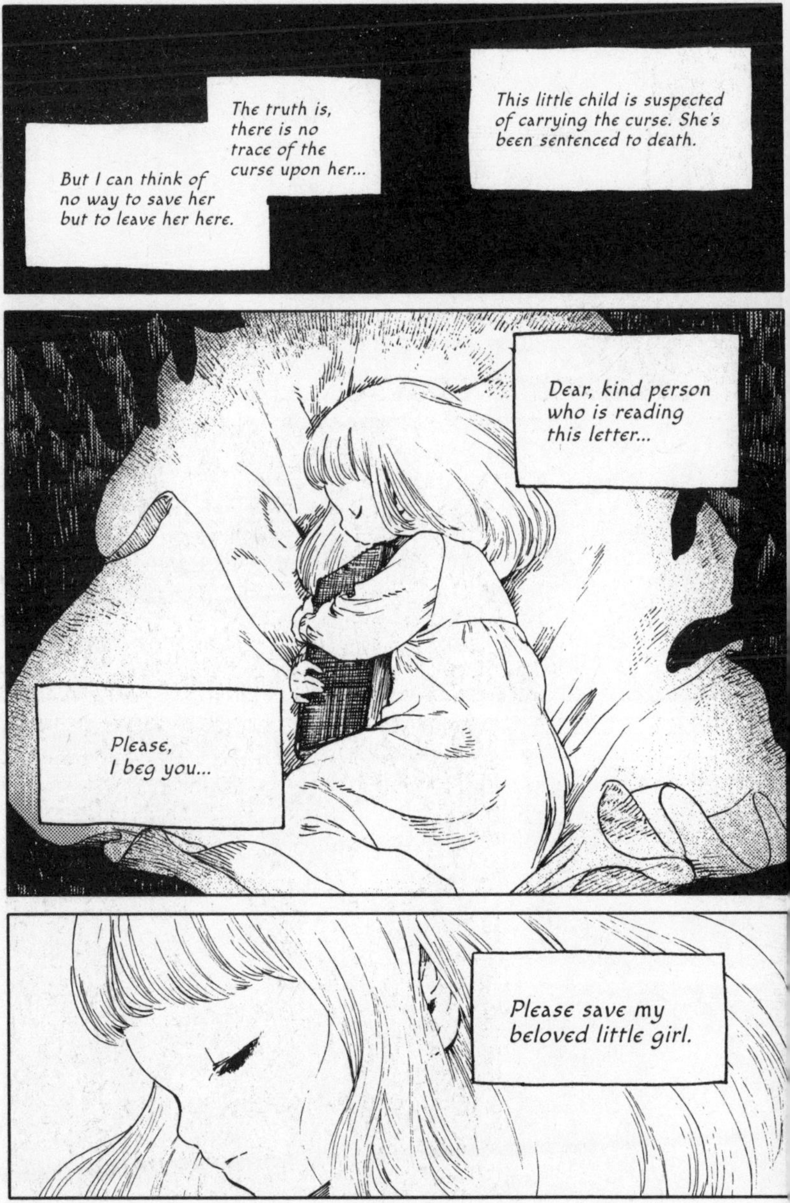
This little child is suspected of carrying the curse. She's been sentenced to death.
The truth is, there is no trace of the curse upon her...
But I can think of no way to save her but to leave her here.
Dear, kind person who is reading this letter...
Please, I beg you...
Please save my beloved little girl.

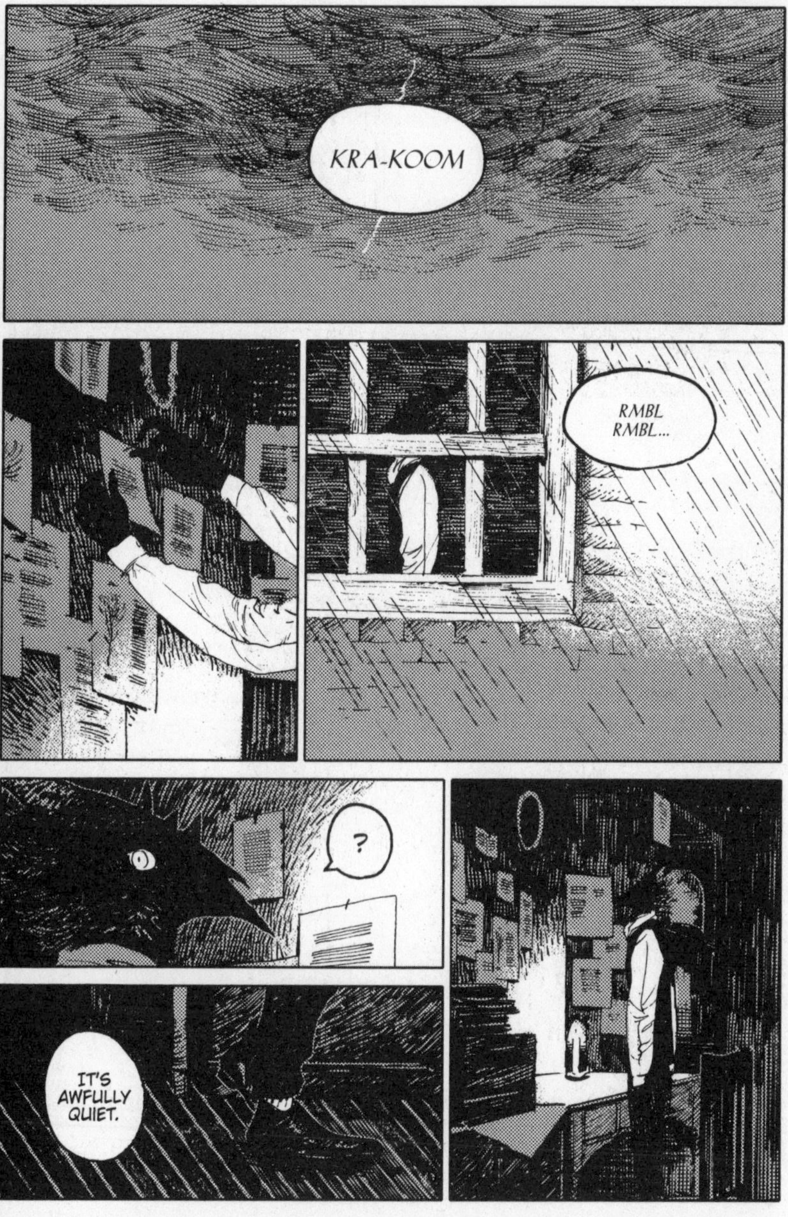
KRA-KOOM
RMBL RMBL...
?
IT'S AWFULLY QUIET.

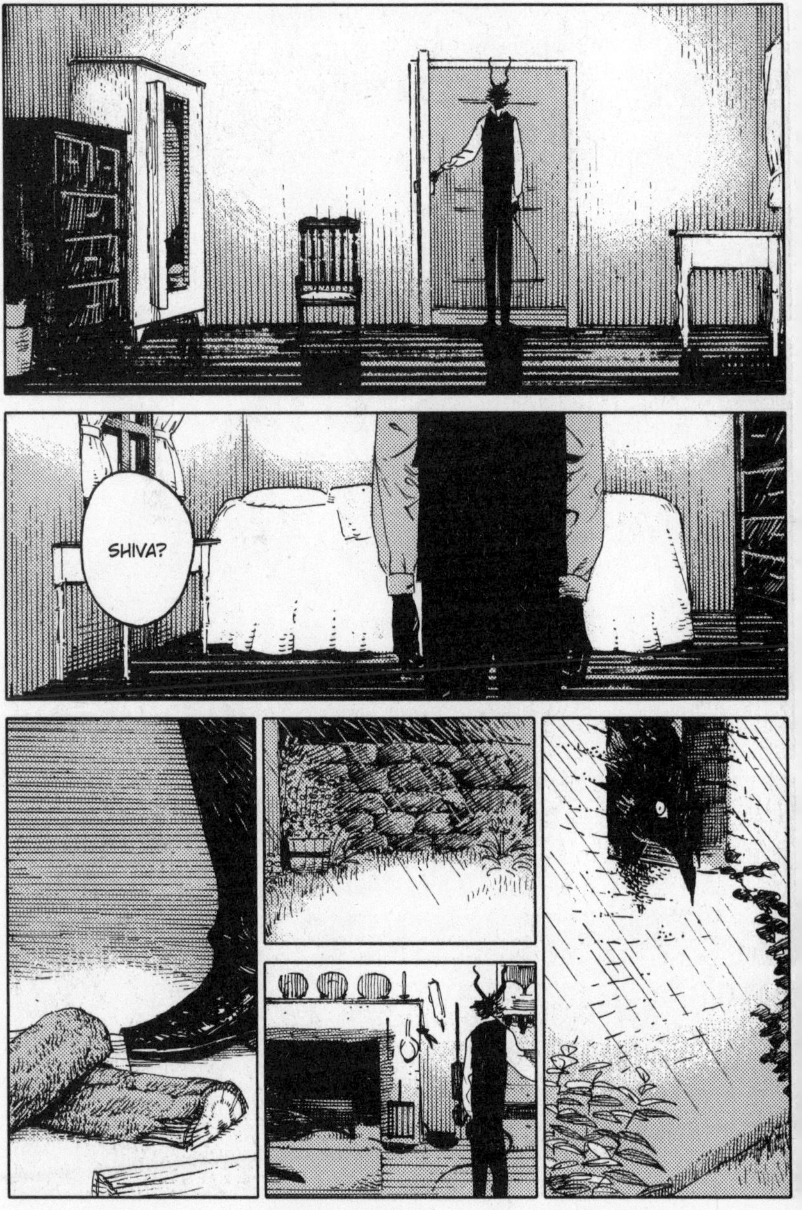
SHIVA?

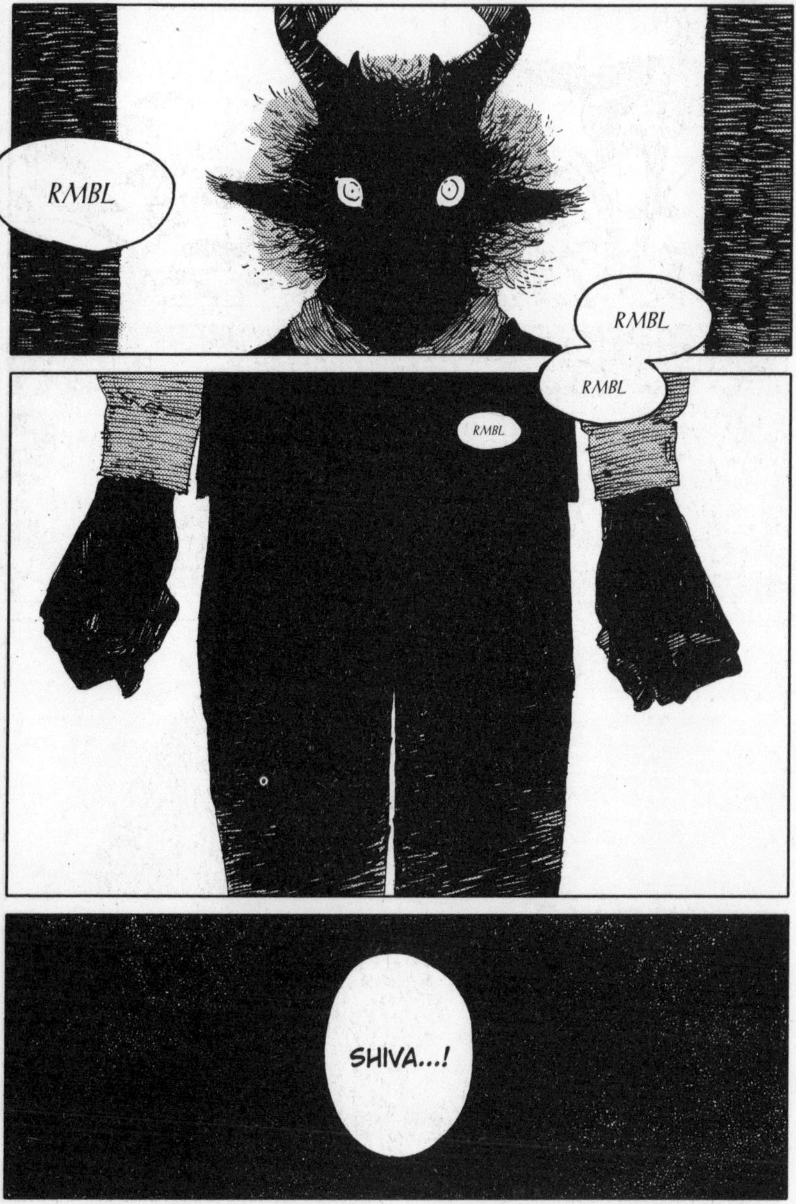
RMBL
RMBL
RMBL
RMBL
SHIVA...!

Chapter 4

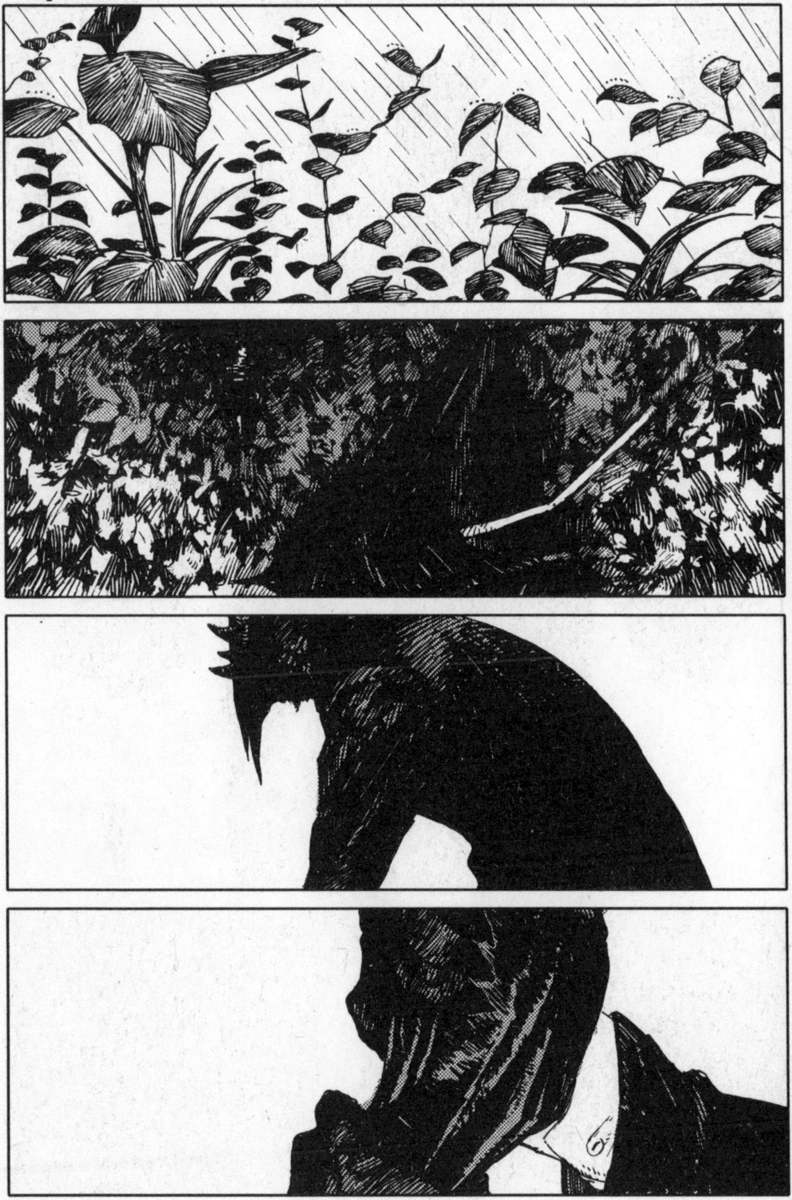

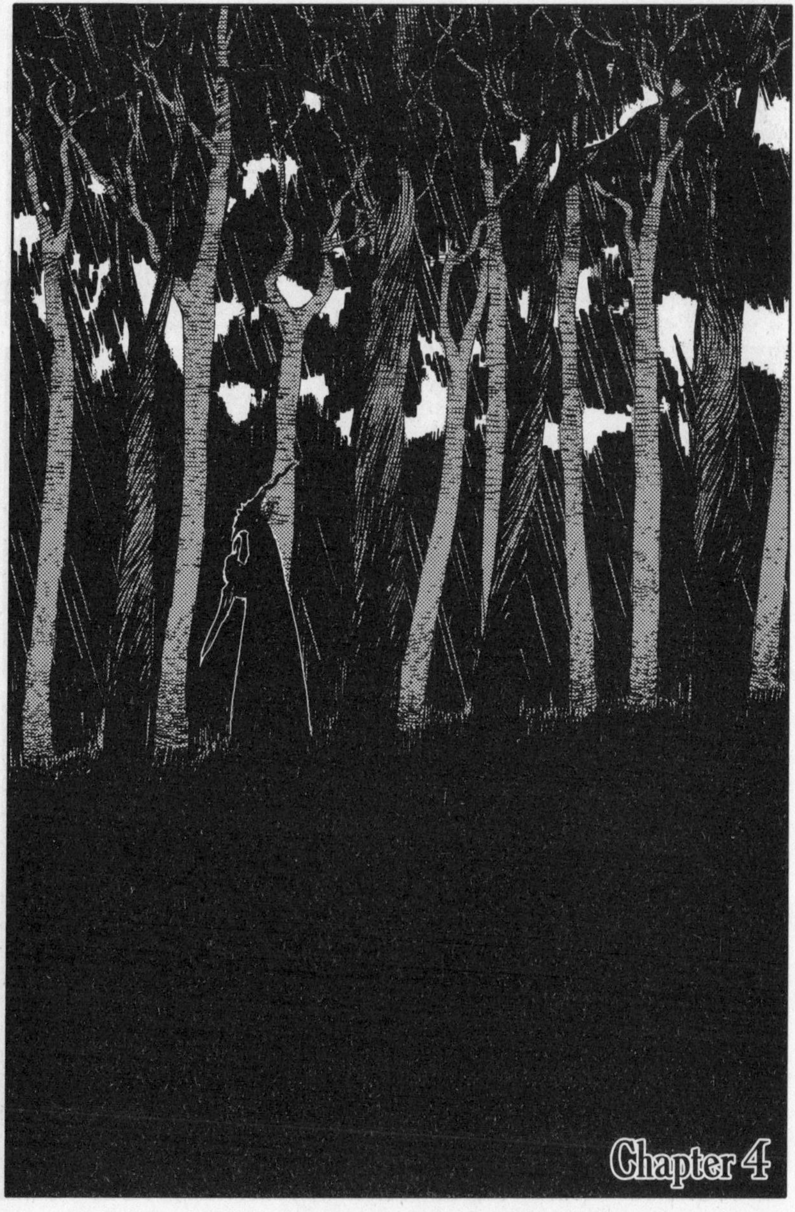
Chapter 4

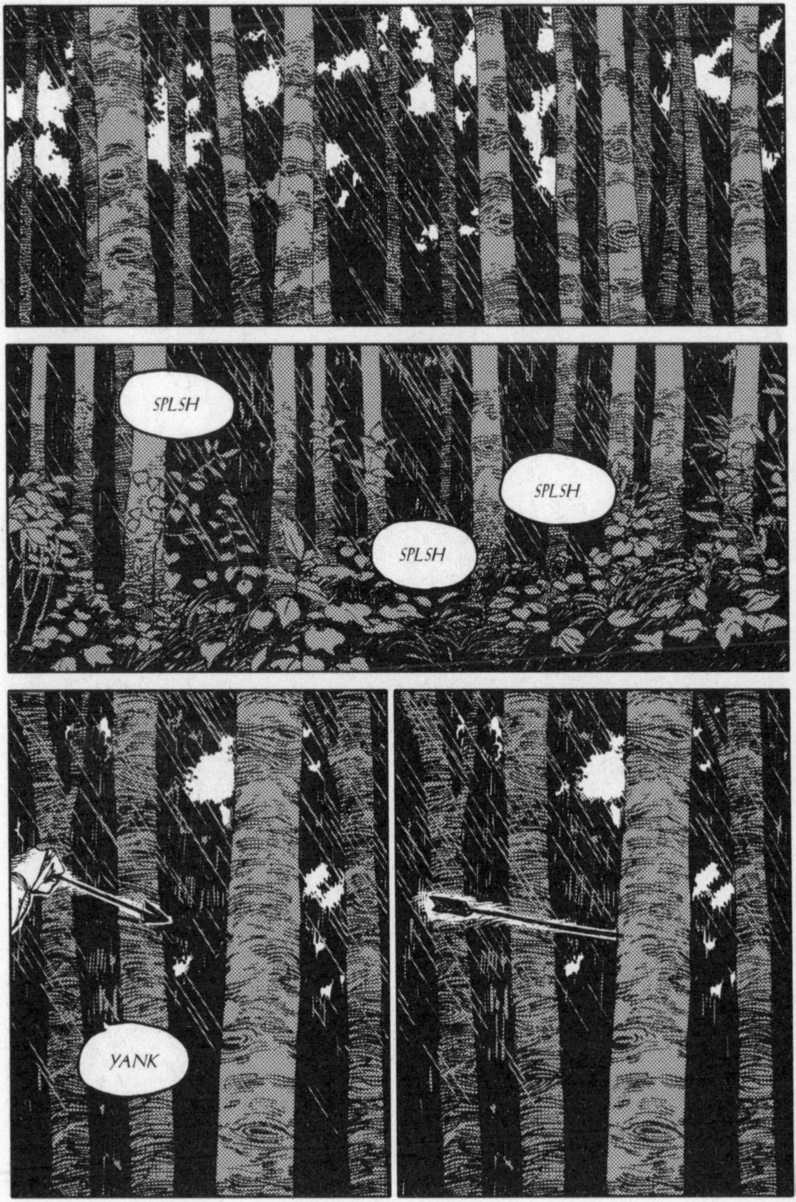
SPLSH
SPLSH
SPLSH
YANK

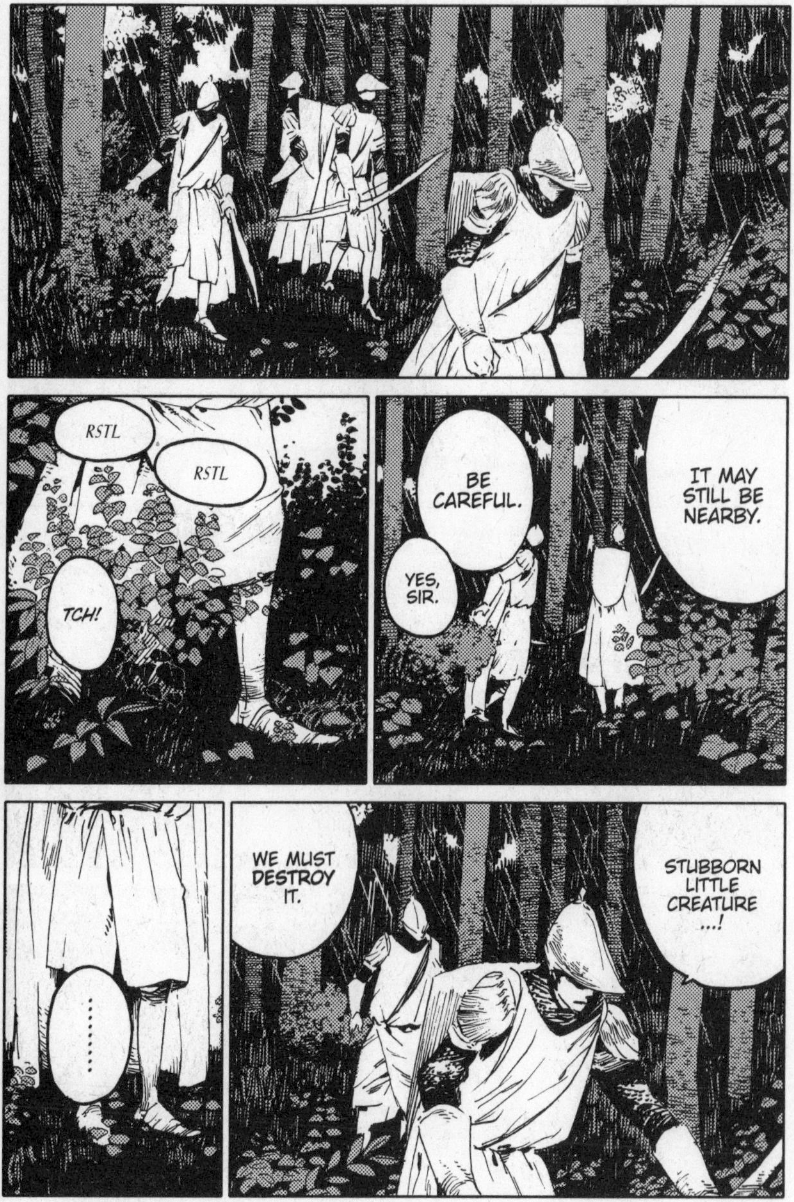
IT MAY STILL BE NEARBY.
BE CAREFUL.
YES, SIR.
RSTL
RSTL
TCH!
STUBBORN LITTLE CREATURE ...!
WE MUST DESTROY IT.
......

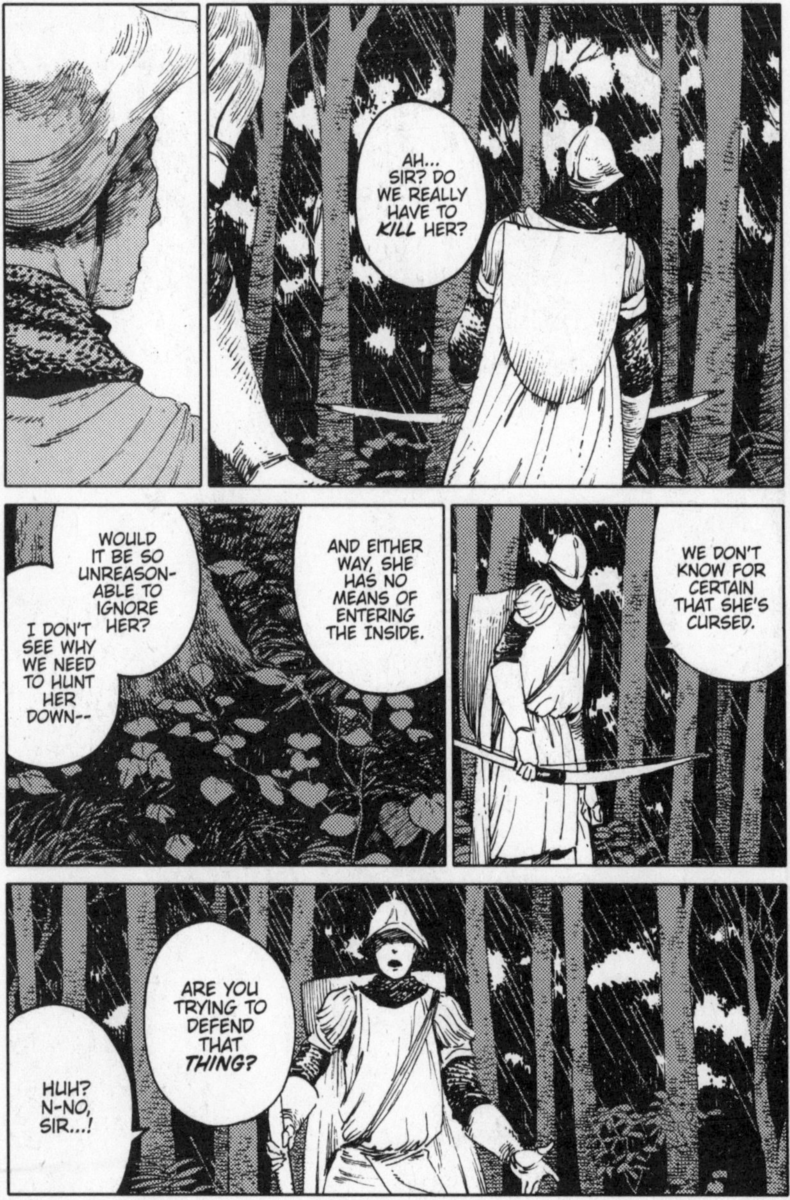
AH... SIR? DO WE REALLY HAVE TO *KILL* HER?
WE DON'T KNOW FOR CERTAIN THAT SHE'S CURSED.
AND EITHER WAY, SHE HAS NO MEANS OF ENTERING THE INSIDE.
WOULD IT BE SO UNREASON-ABLE TO IGNORE HER?
I DON'T SEE WHY WE NEED TO HUNT HER DOWN--
ARE YOU TRYING TO DEFEND THAT *THING?*
HUH? N-NO, SIR...!

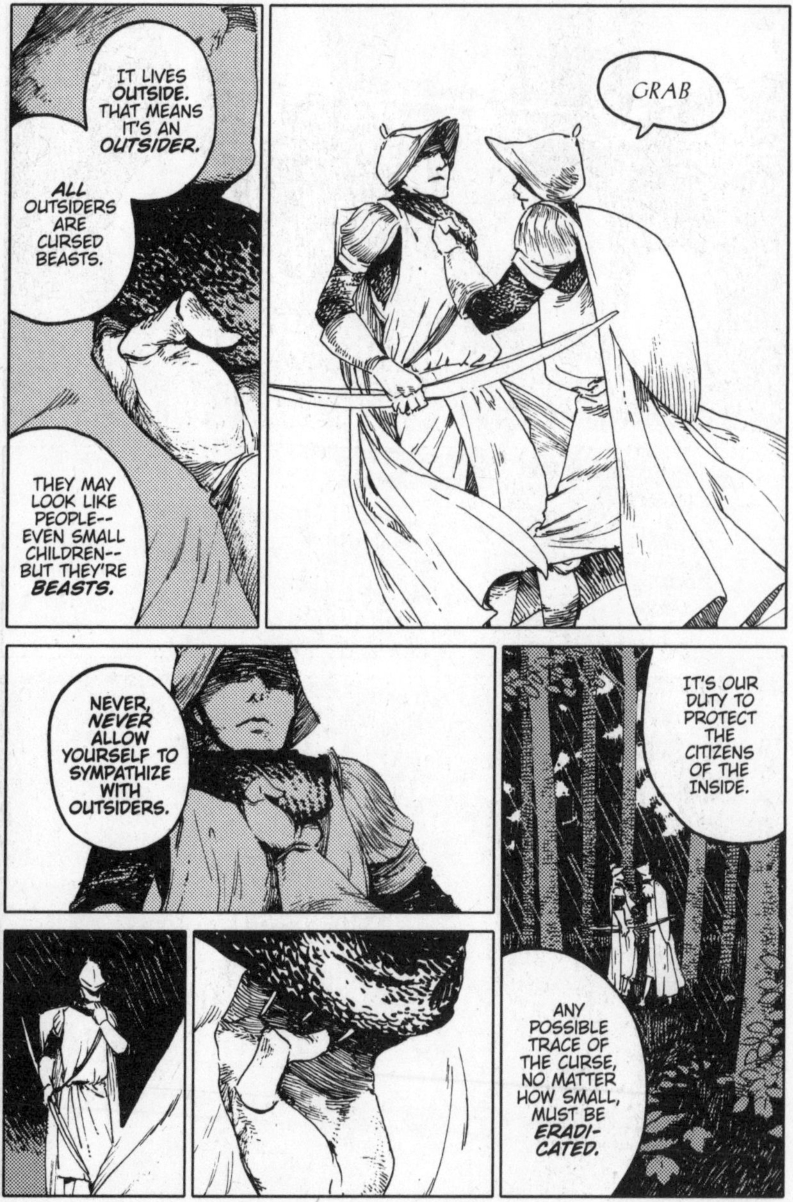
GRAB
IT LIVES OUTSIDE. THAT MEANS IT'S AN OUTSIDER.
ALL OUTSIDERS ARE CURSED BEASTS.
THEY MAY LOOK LIKE PEOPLE-- EVEN SMALL CHILDREN-- BUT THEY'RE BEASTS.
IT'S OUR DUTY TO PROTECT THE CITIZENS OF THE INSIDE.
ANY POSSIBLE TRACE OF THE CURSE, NO MATTER HOW SMALL, MUST BE ERADI-CATED.
NEVER, NEVER ALLOW YOURSELF TO SYMPATHIZE WITH OUTSIDERS.

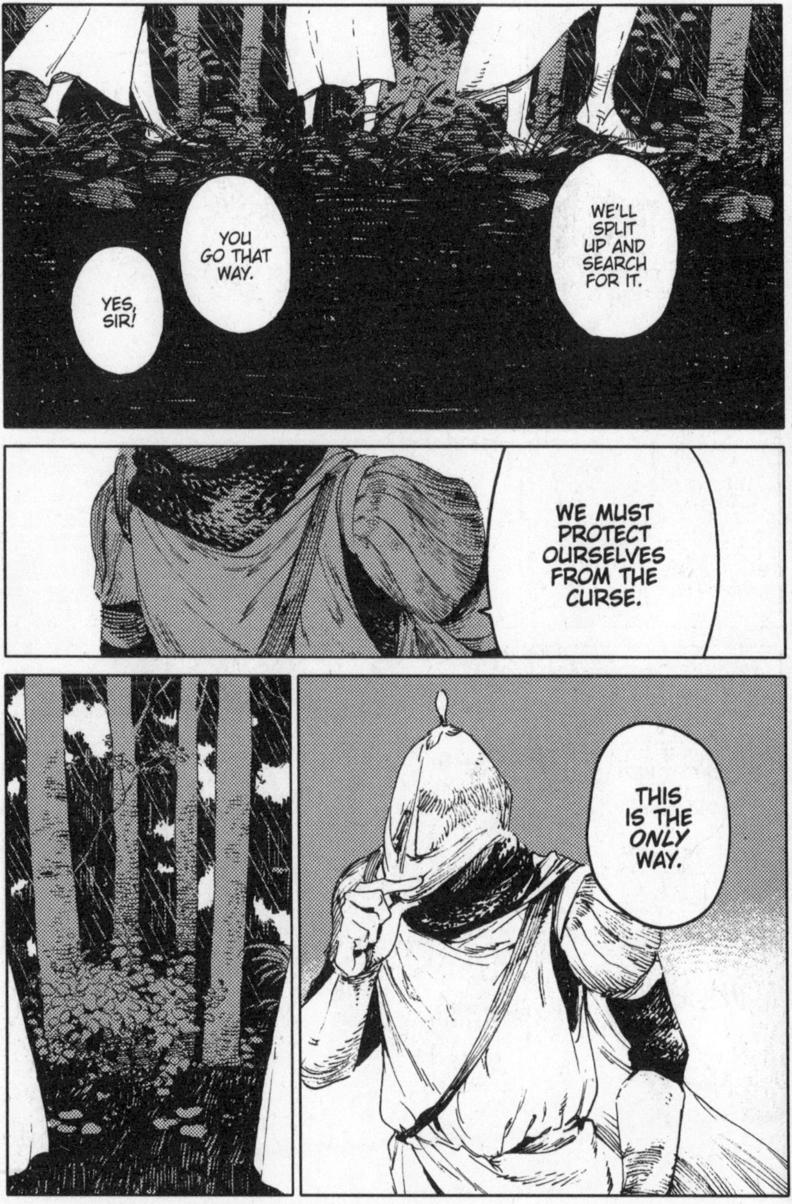
WE'LL SPLIT UP AND SEARCH FOR IT.
YOU GO THAT WAY.
YES, SIR!
WE MUST PROTECT OURSELVES FROM THE CURSE.
THIS IS THE *ONLY* WAY.

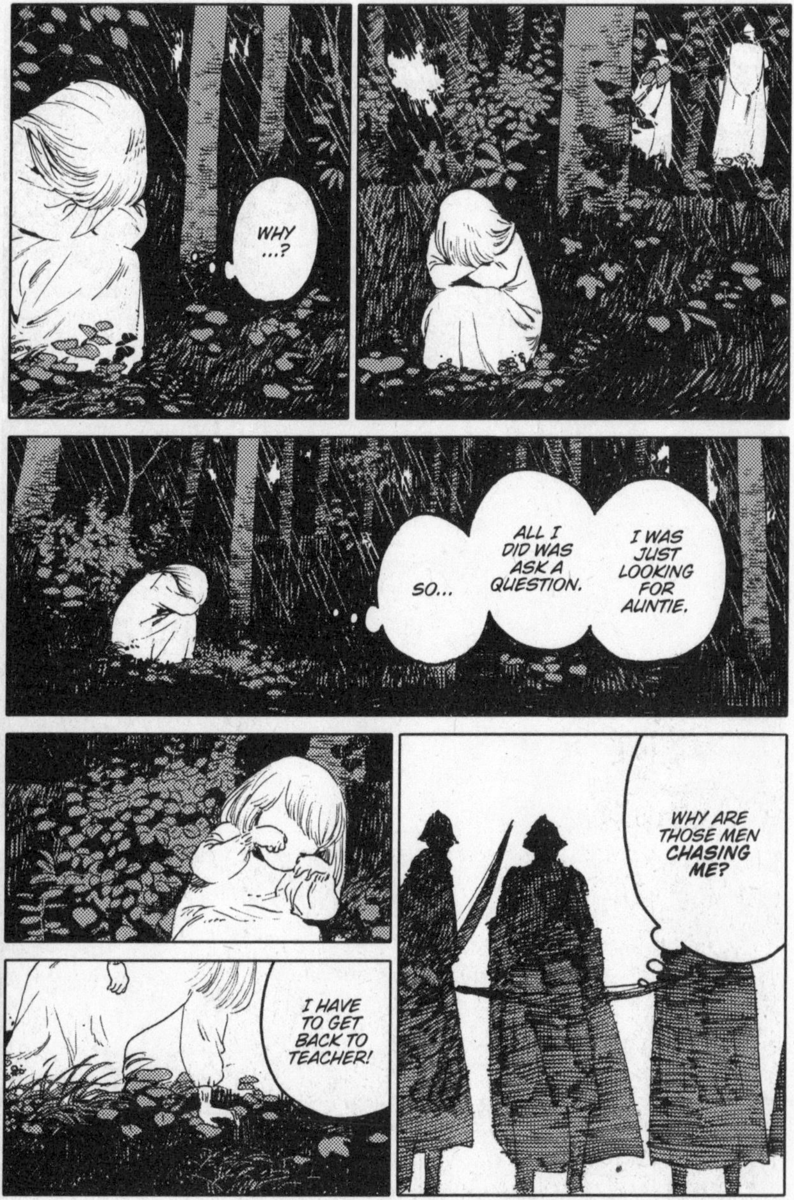
WHY ...?
I WAS JUST LOOKING FOR AUNTIE.
ALL I DID WAS ASK A QUESTION.
SO...
WHY ARE THOSE MEN CHASING ME?
I HAVE TO GET BACK TO TEACHER!

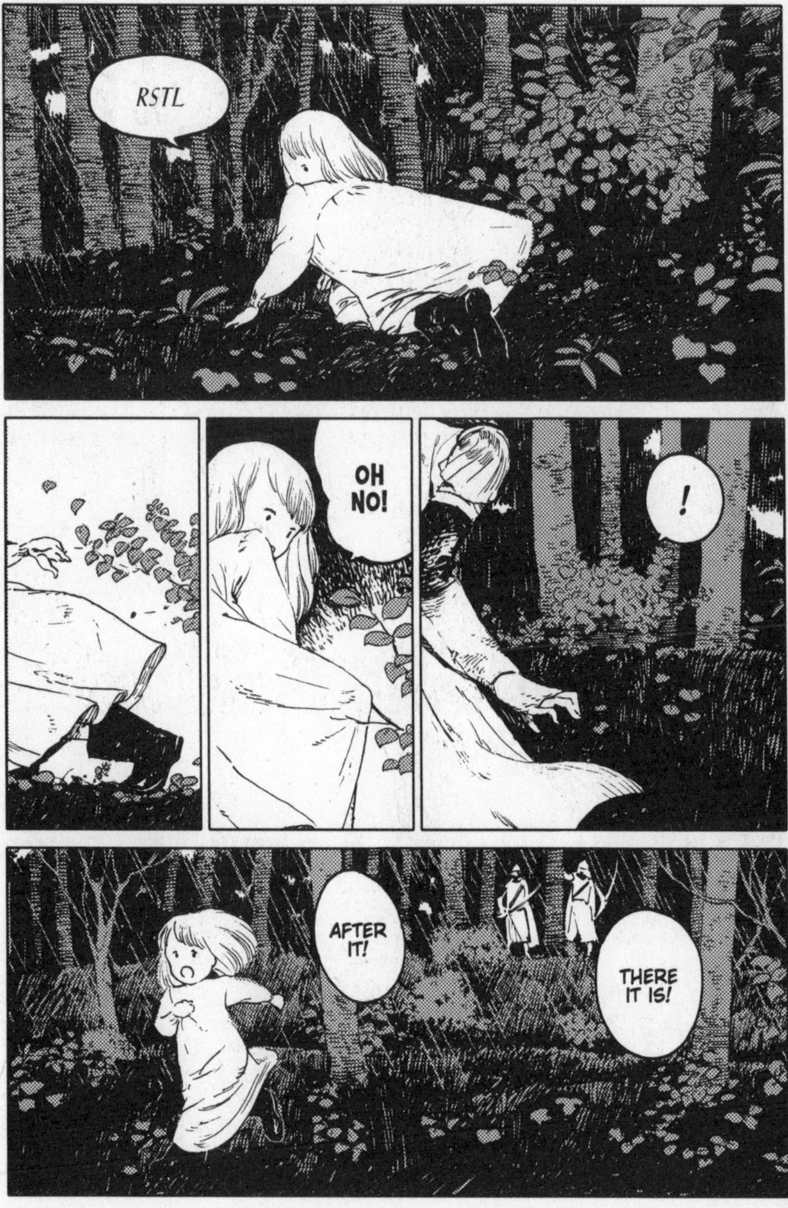
RSTL
!
OH NO!
THERE IT IS!
AFTER IT!

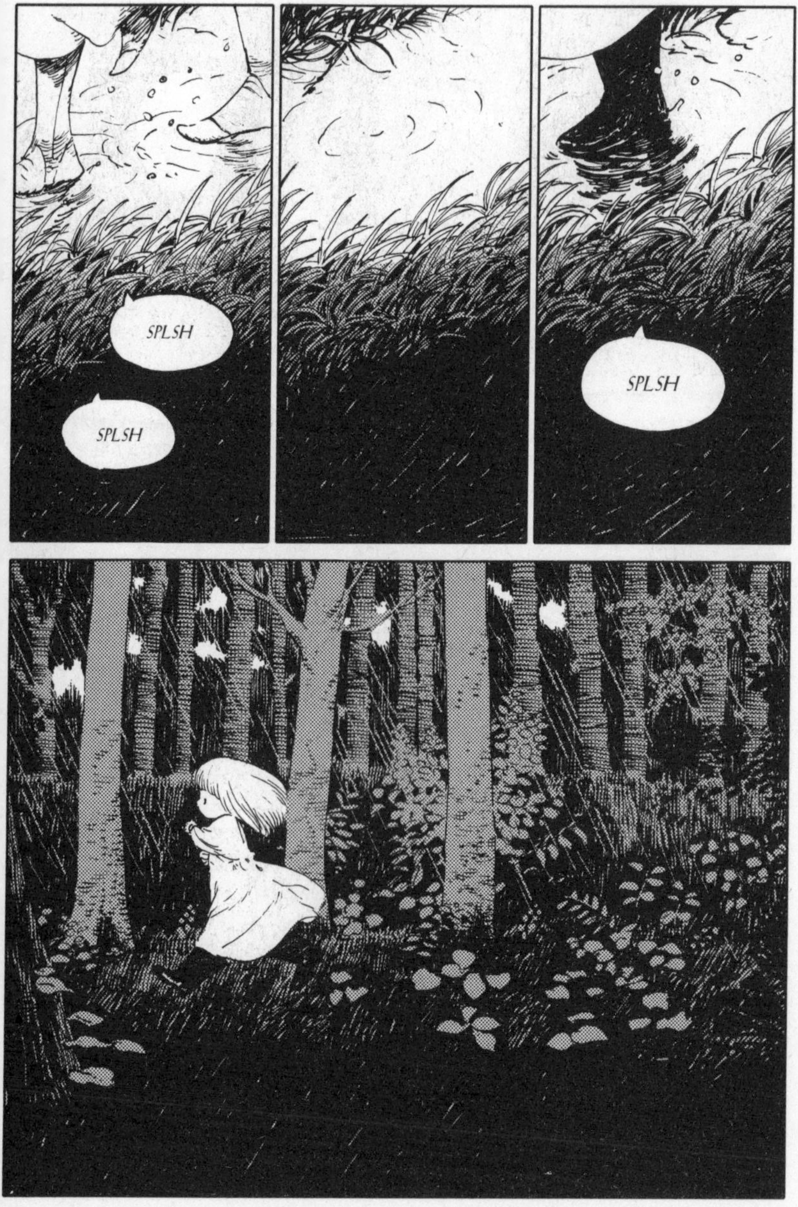
SPLSH
SPLSH
SPLSH

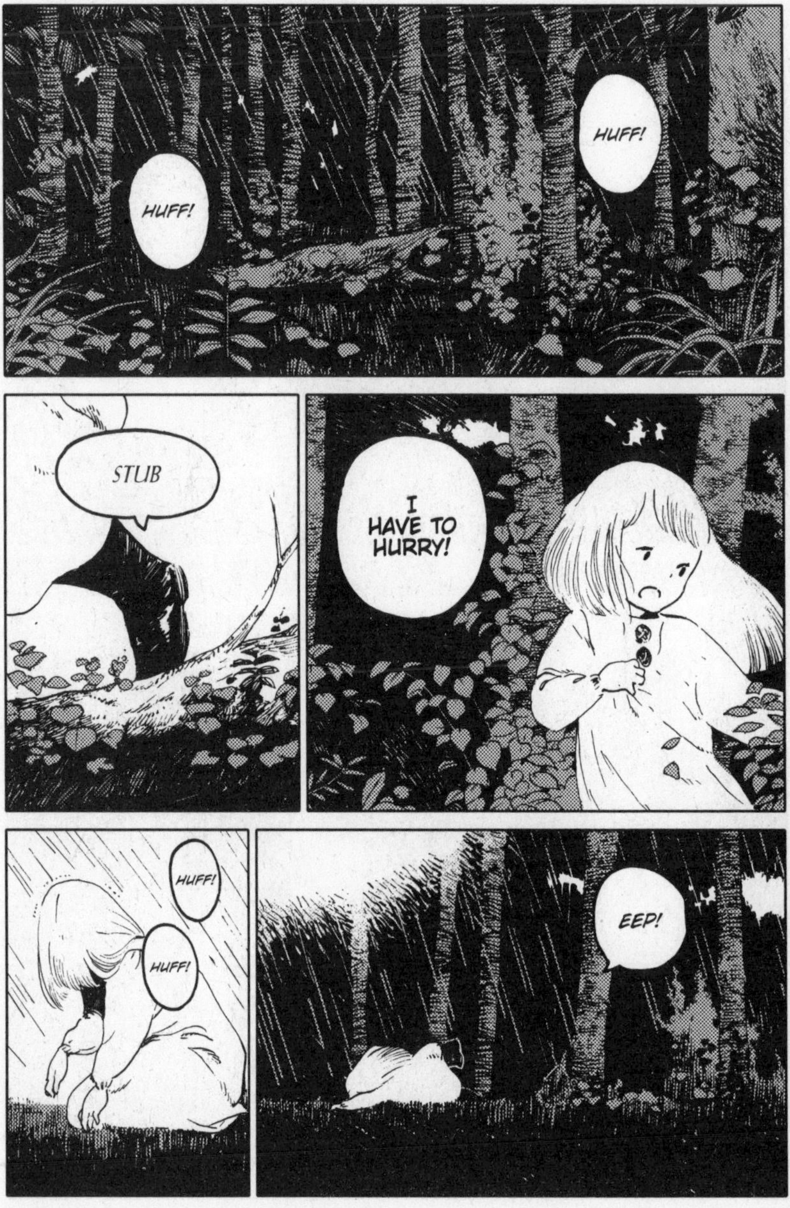
HUFF!
HUFF!
I HAVE TO HURRY!
STUB
EEP!
HUFF!
HUFF!

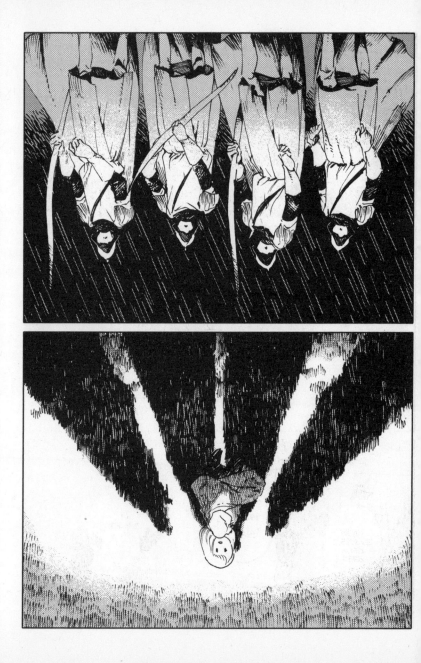

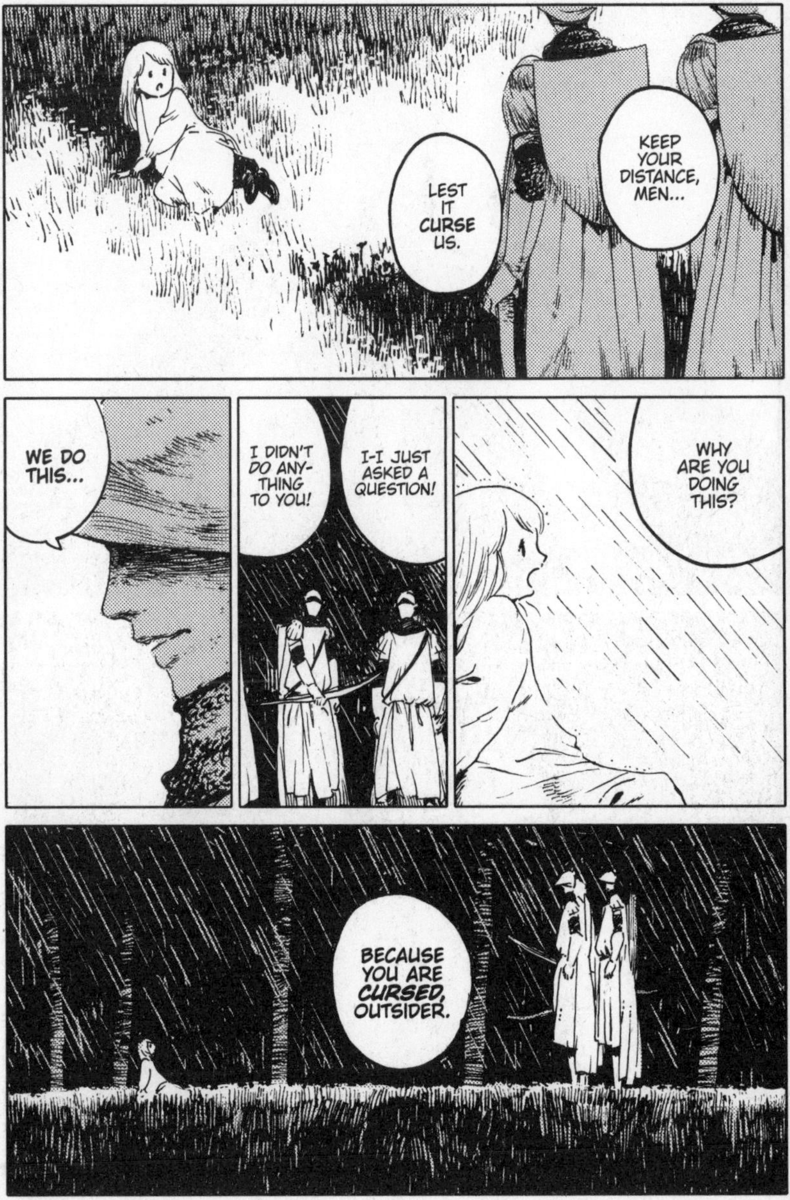
KEEP YOUR DISTANCE, MEN...
LEST IT CURSE US.
WHY ARE YOU DOING THIS?
I-I JUST ASKED A QUESTION!
I DIDN'T DO ANY-THING TO YOU!
WE DO THIS...
BECAUSE YOU ARE *CURSED*, OUTSIDER.

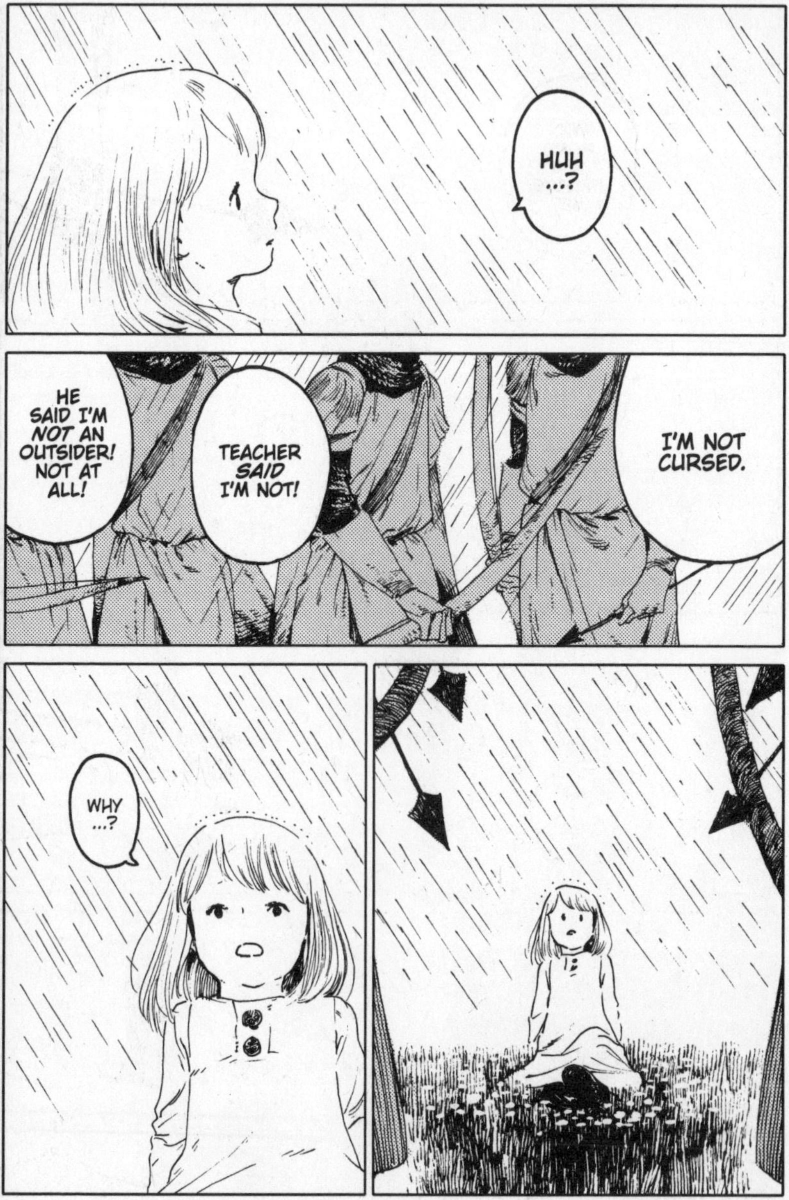
HUH ...?
I'M NOT CURSED.
TEACHER *SAID* I'M NOT!
HE SAID I'M *NOT* AN OUTSIDER! NOT AT ALL!
WHY ...?

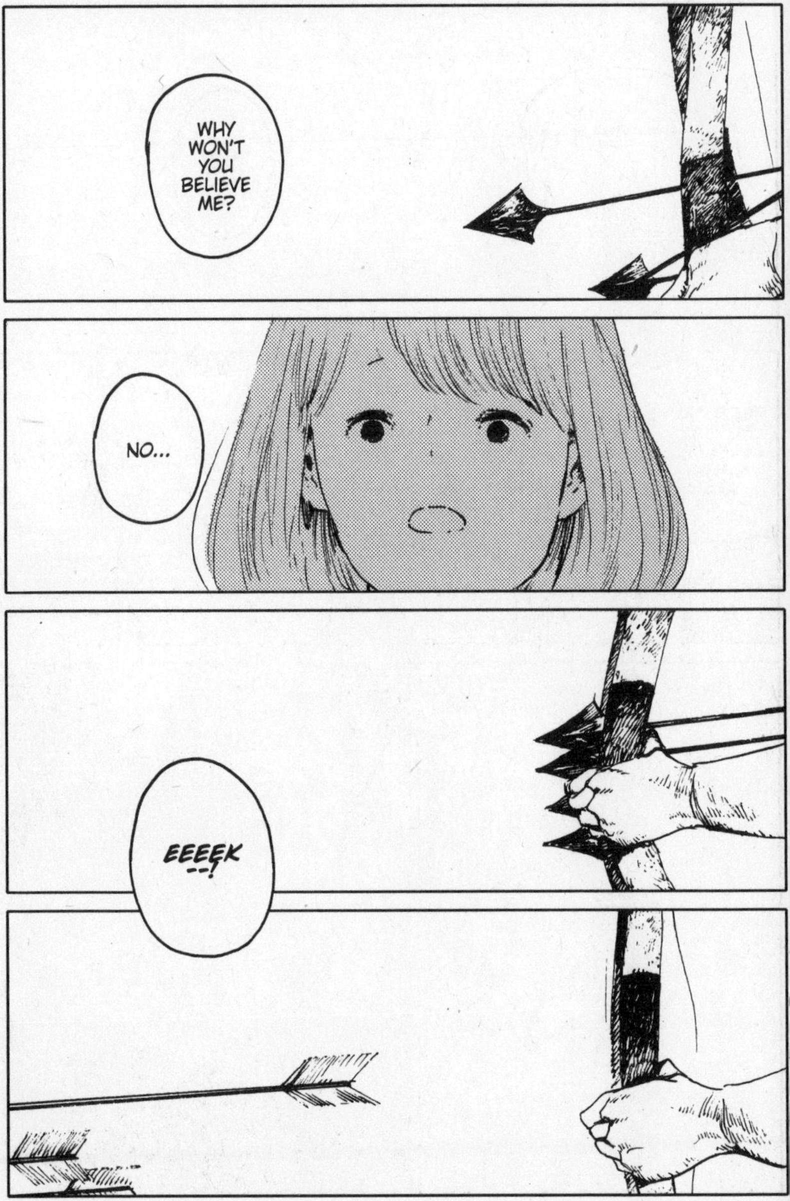
WHY WON'T YOU BELIEVE ME?
NO...
EEEEK --!

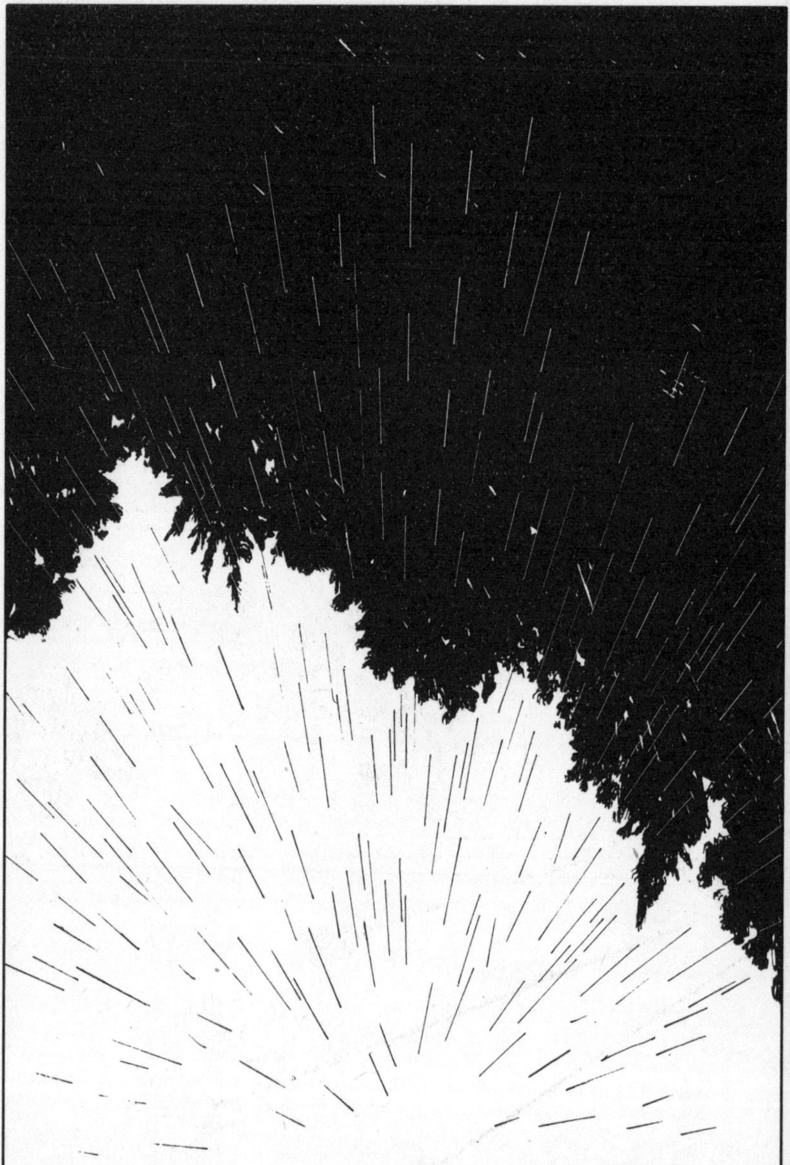

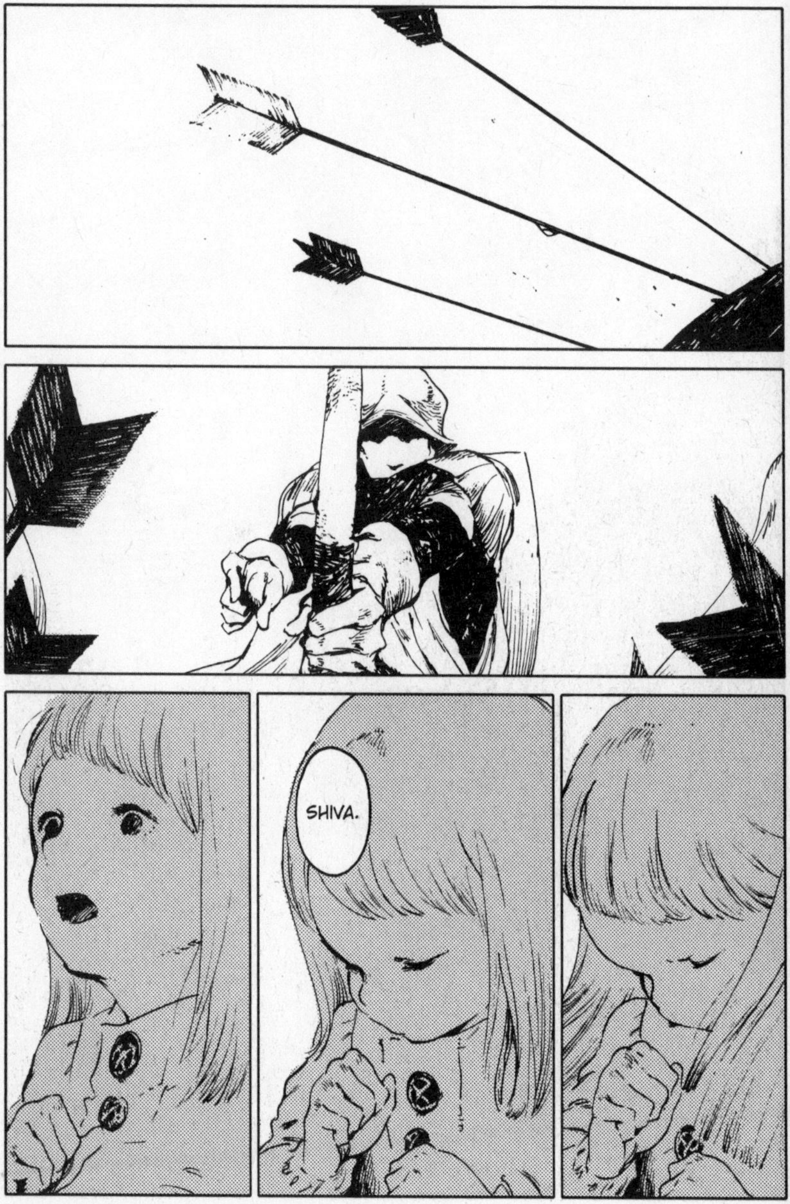
SHIVA.

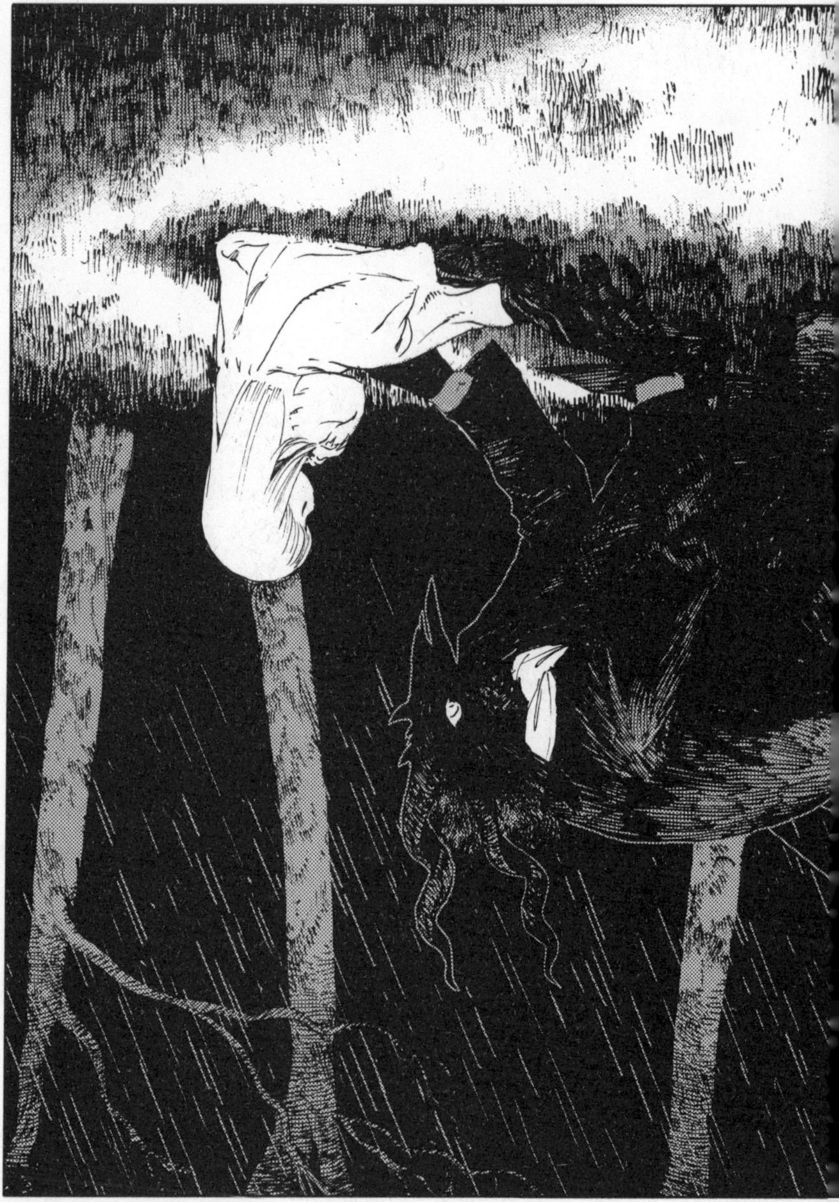

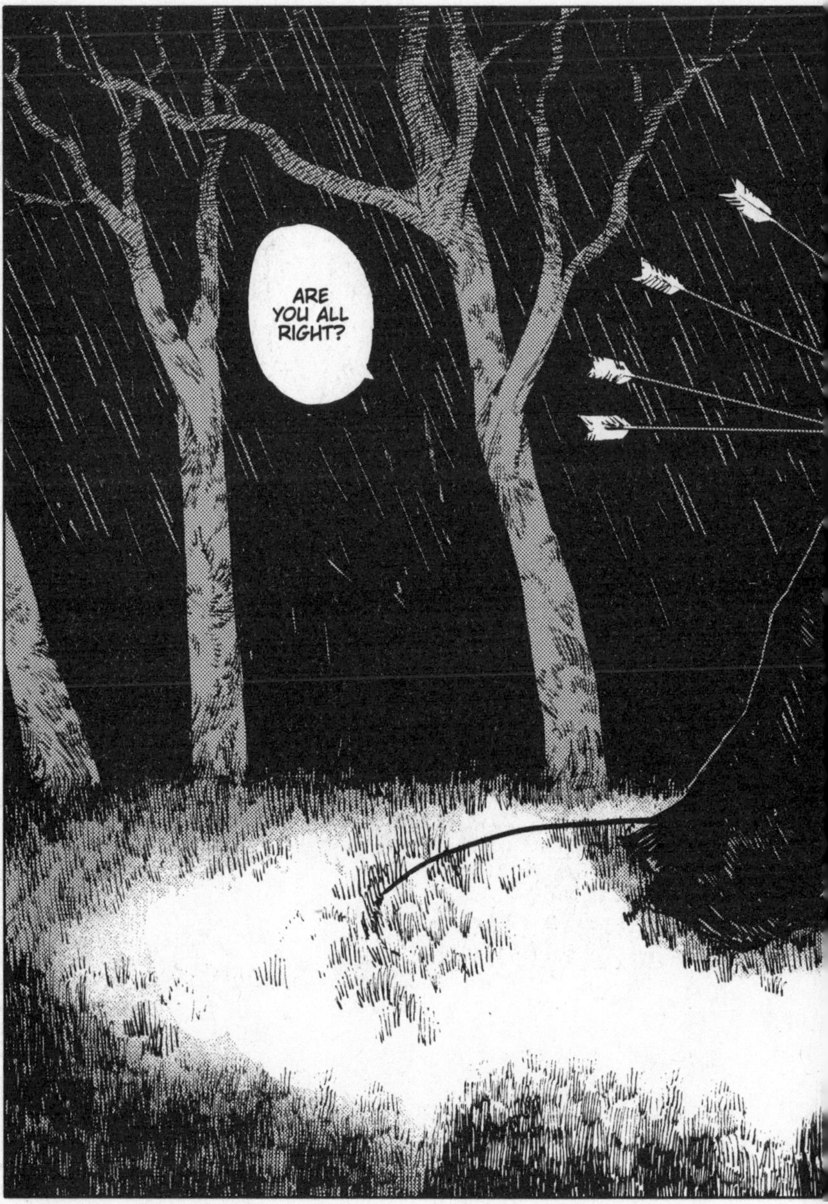
ARE YOU ALL RIGHT?

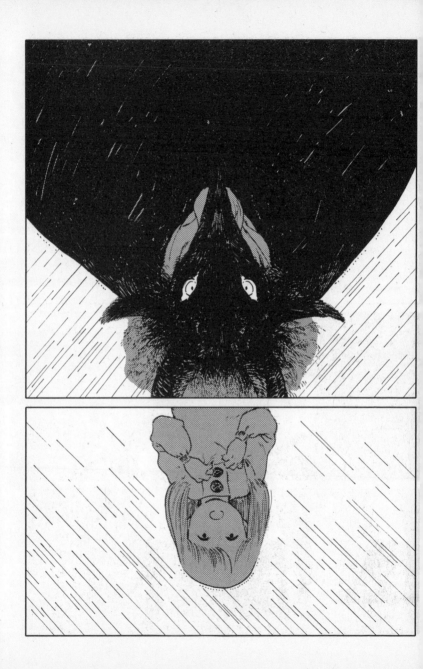

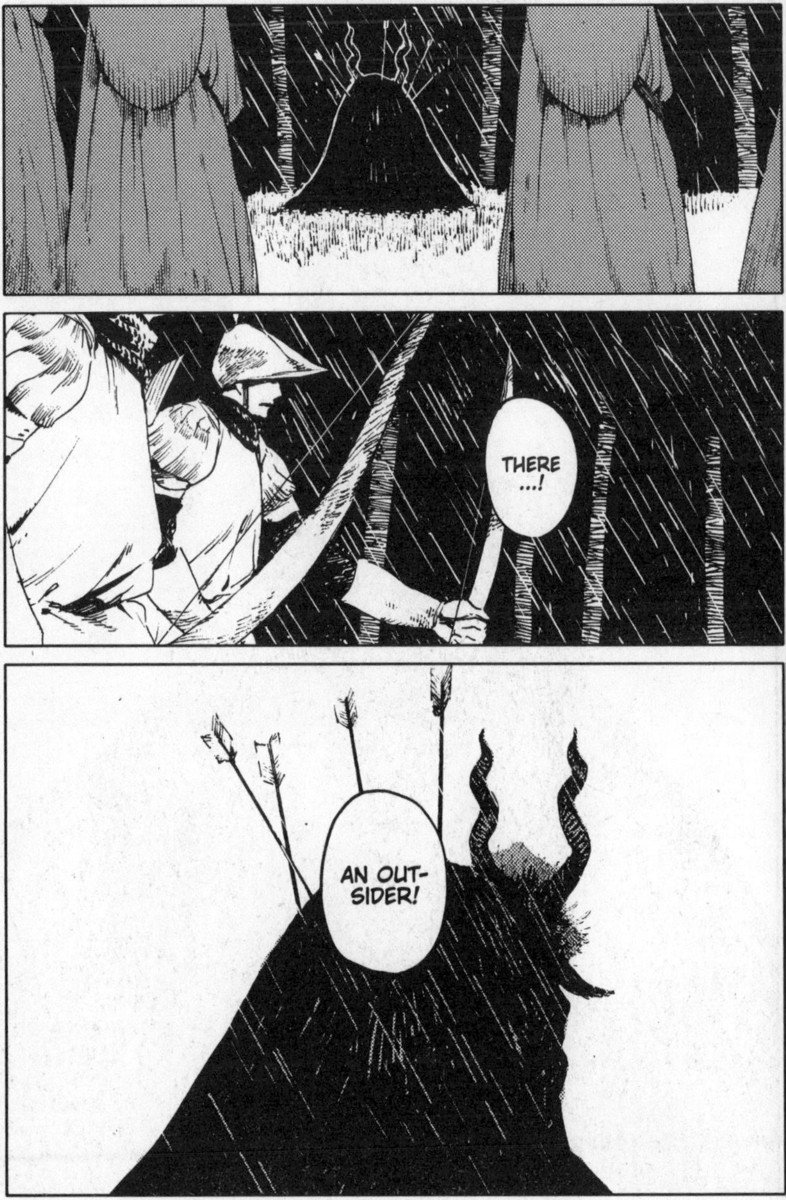
THERE ...!
AN OUT-SIDER!

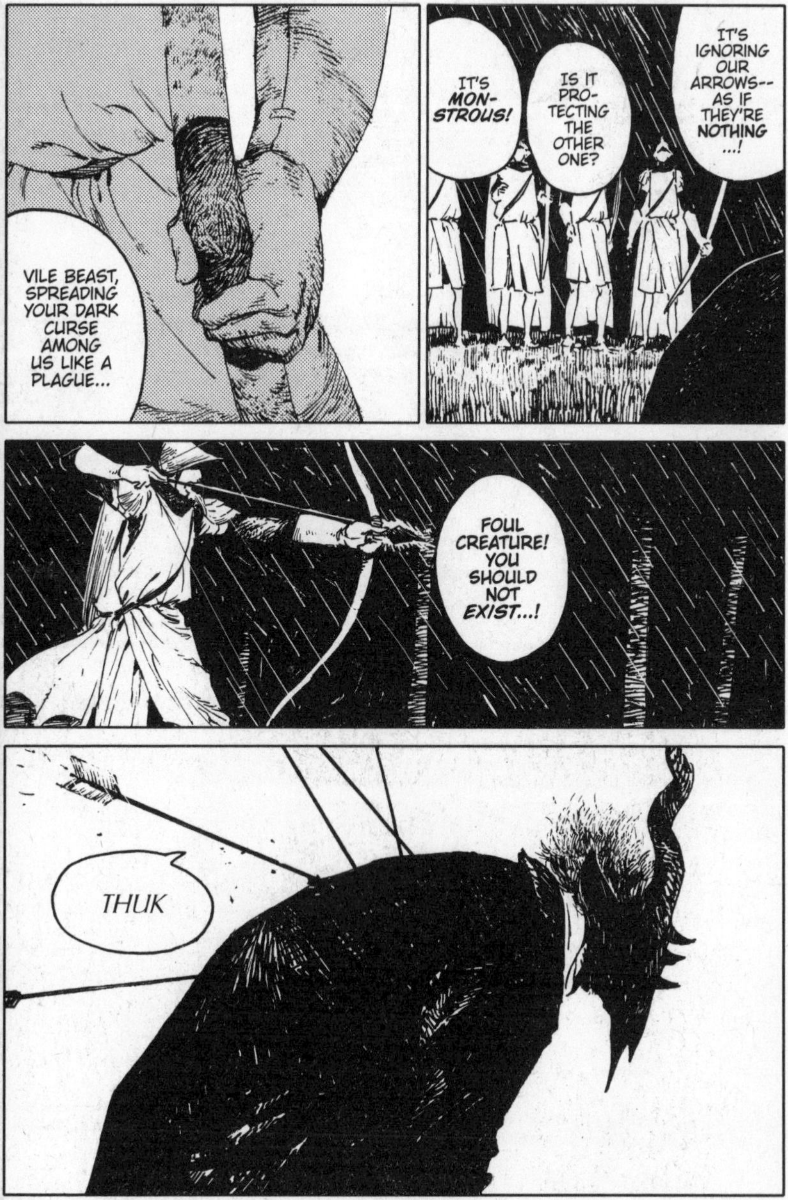
IT'S IGNORING OUR ARROWS-- AS IF THEY'RE NOTHING ...!
IS IT PRO-TECTING THE OTHER ONE?
IT'S MON-STROUS!
VILE BEAST, SPREADING YOUR DARK CURSE AMONG US LIKE A PLAGUE...
FOUL CREATURE! YOU SHOULD NOT EXIST...!
THUK

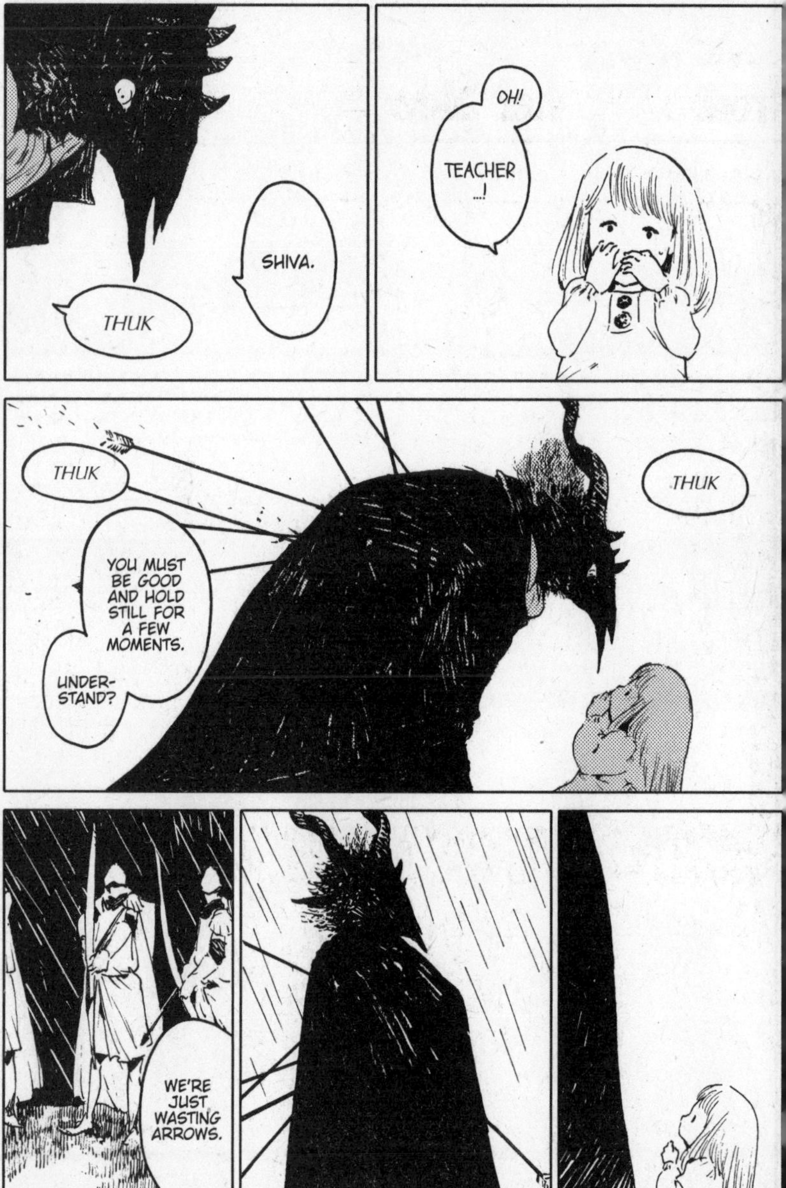
OH!
TEACHER ...!
SHIVA.
THUK
THUK
THUK
YOU MUST BE GOOD AND HOLD STILL FOR A FEW MOMENTS.
UNDER-STAND?
WE'RE JUST WASTING ARROWS.

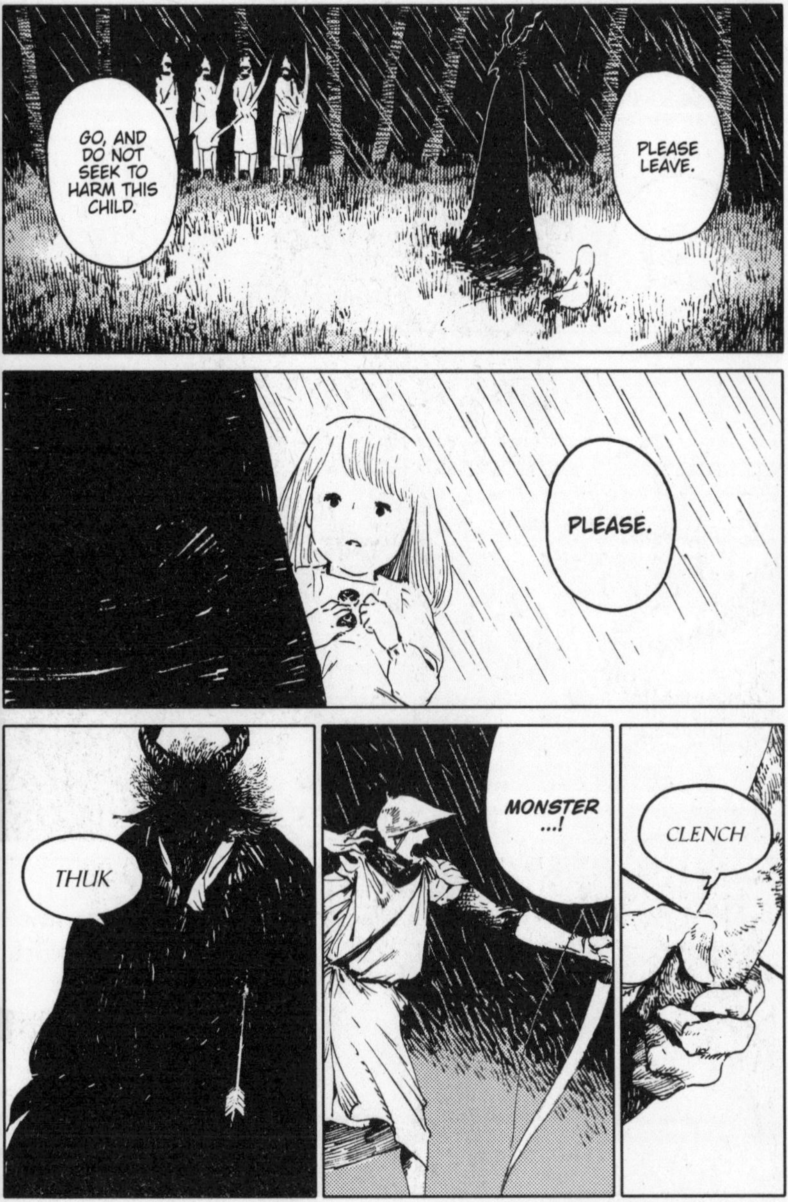
PLEASE LEAVE.
GO, AND DO NOT SEEK TO HARM THIS CHILD.
PLEASE.
CLENCH
MONSTER ...!
THUK

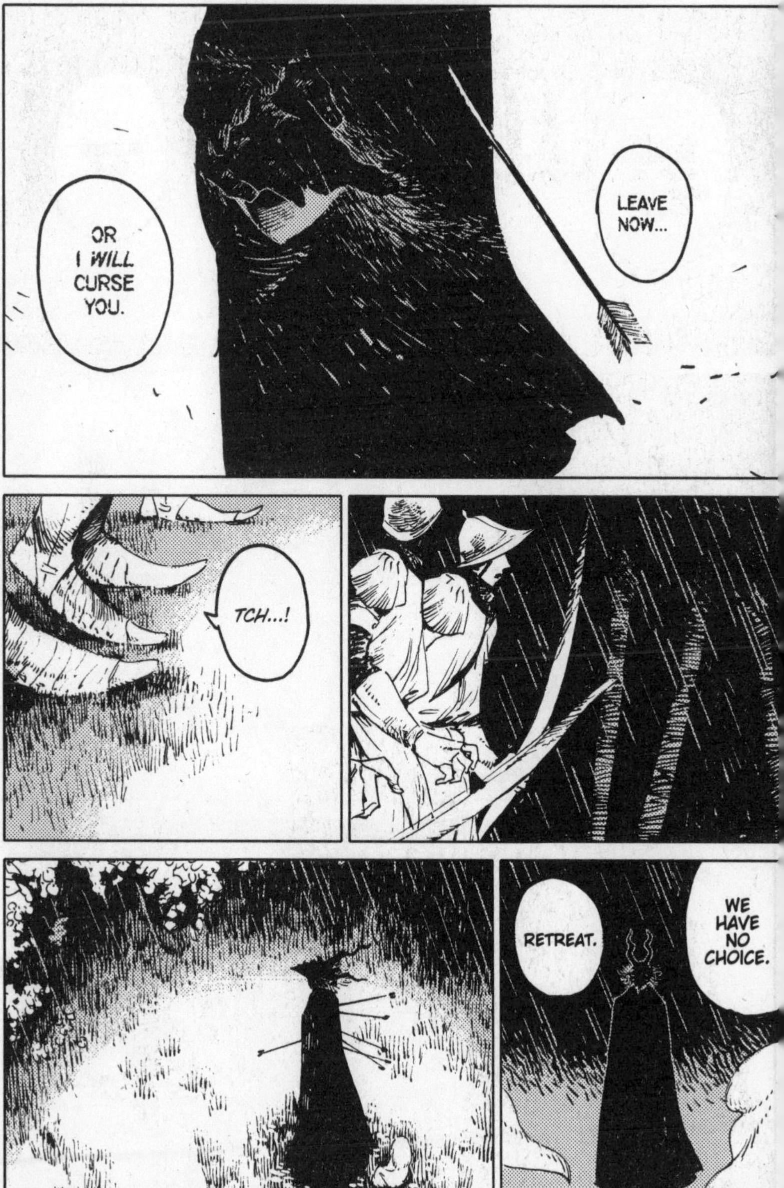
LEAVE NOW...
OR I WILL CURSE YOU.
TCH...!
WE HAVE NO CHOICE.
RETREAT.

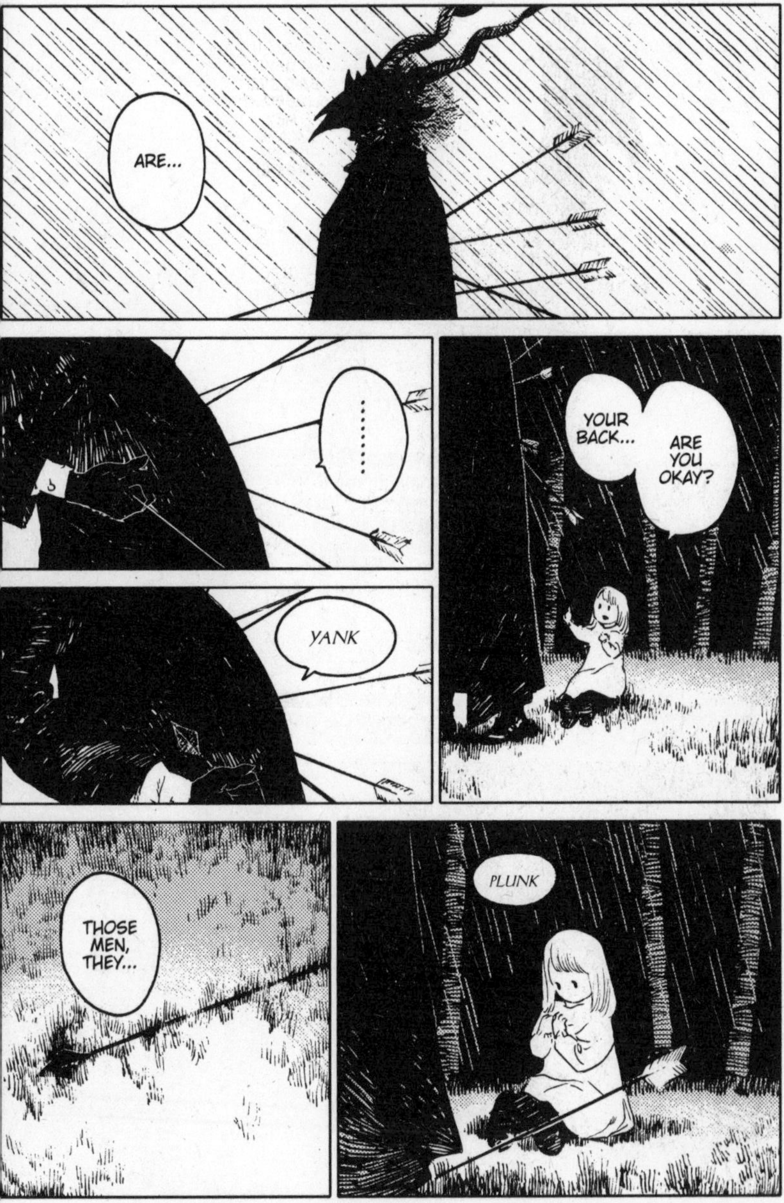
ARE...
YOUR BACK...
ARE YOU OKAY?
....
YANK
PLUNK
THOSE MEN, THEY...

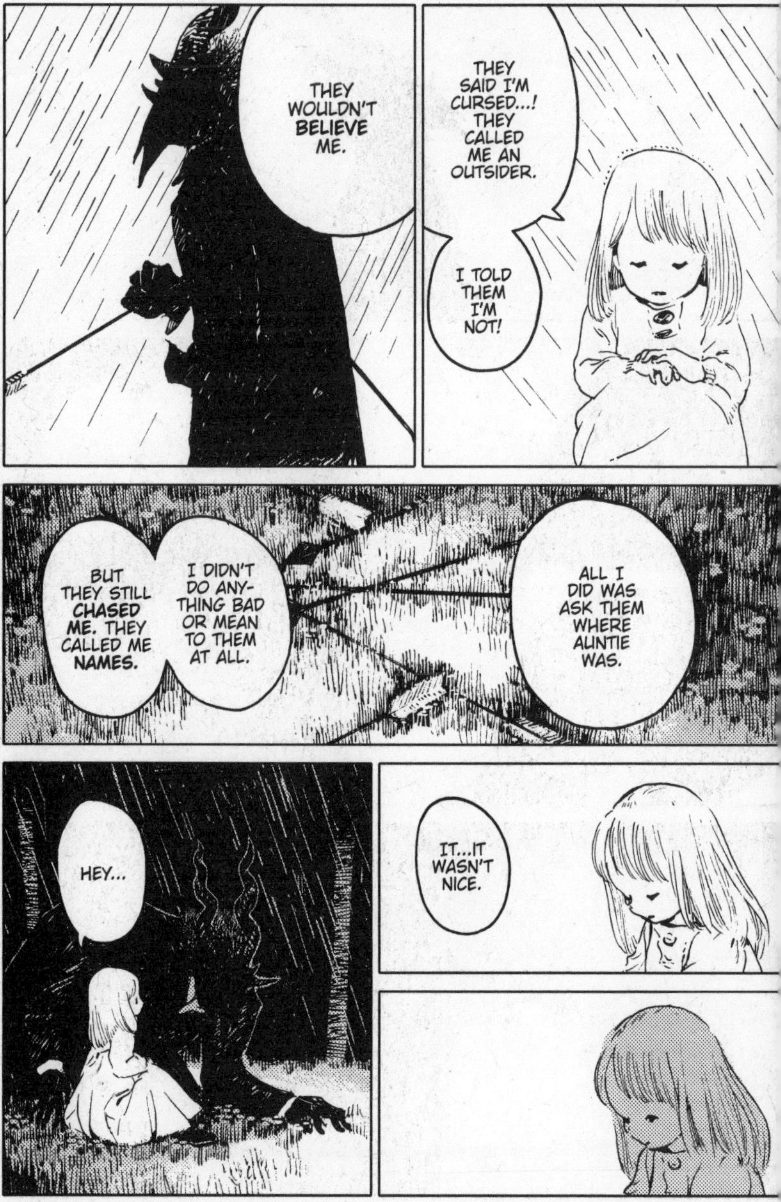
THEY SAID I'M CURSED...! THEY CALLED ME AN OUTSIDER.
I TOLD THEM I'M NOT!
THEY WOULDN'T BELIEVE ME.
ALL I DID WAS ASK THEM WHERE AUNTIE WAS.
I DIDN'T DO ANYTHING BAD OR MEAN TO THEM AT ALL.
BUT THEY STILL CHASED ME. THEY CALLED ME NAMES.
IT...IT WASN'T NICE.
HEY...

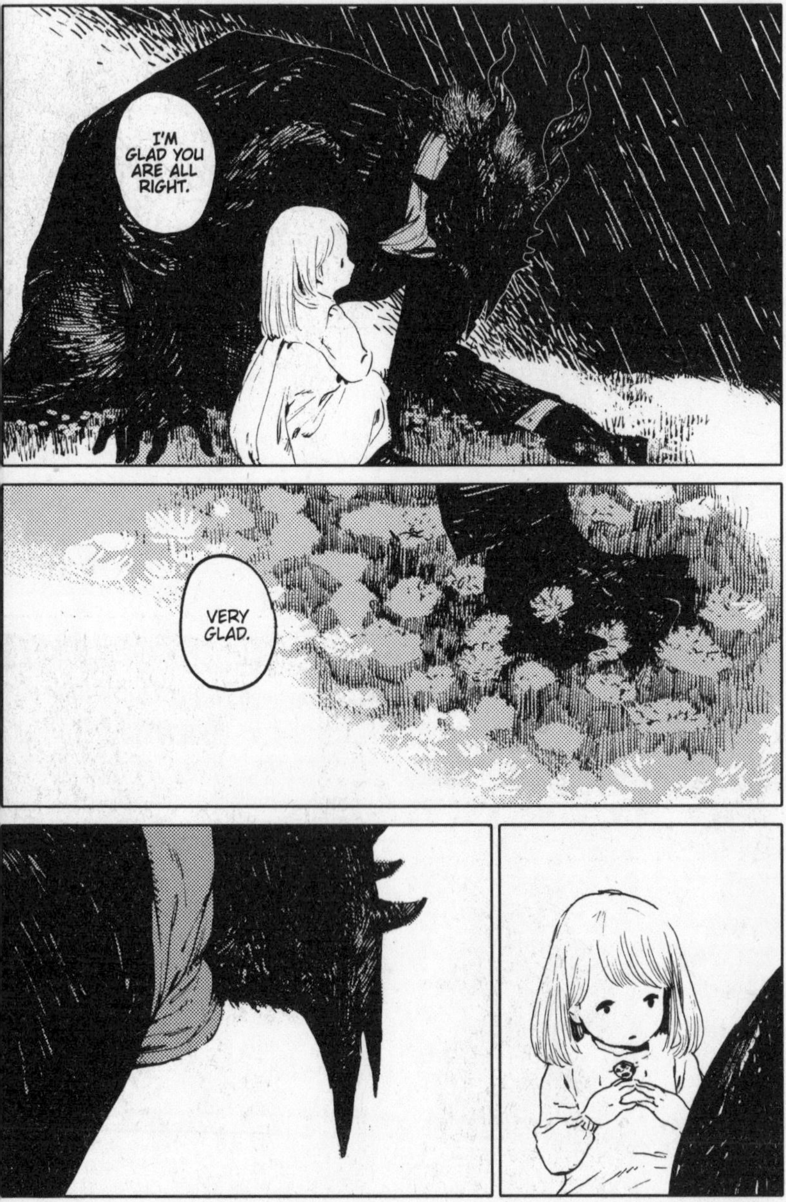
I'M GLAD YOU ARE ALL RIGHT.
VERY GLAD.

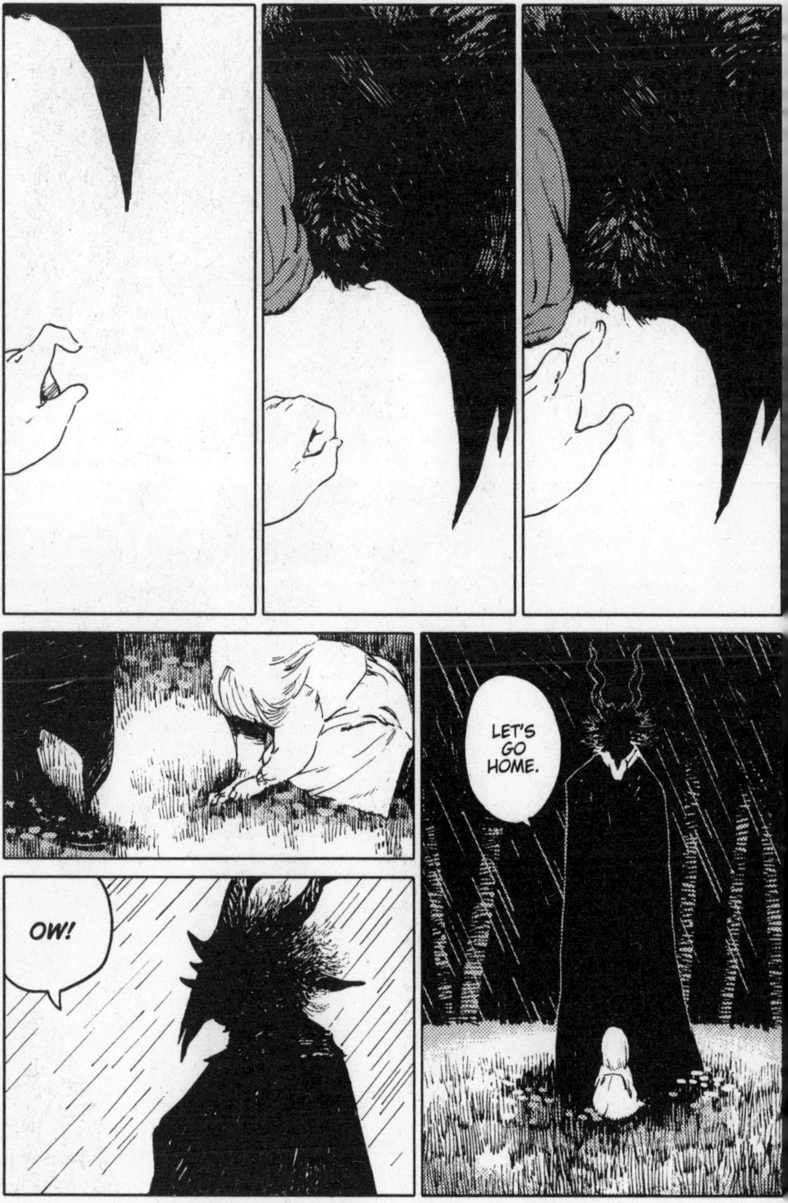
LET'S GO HOME.
OW!

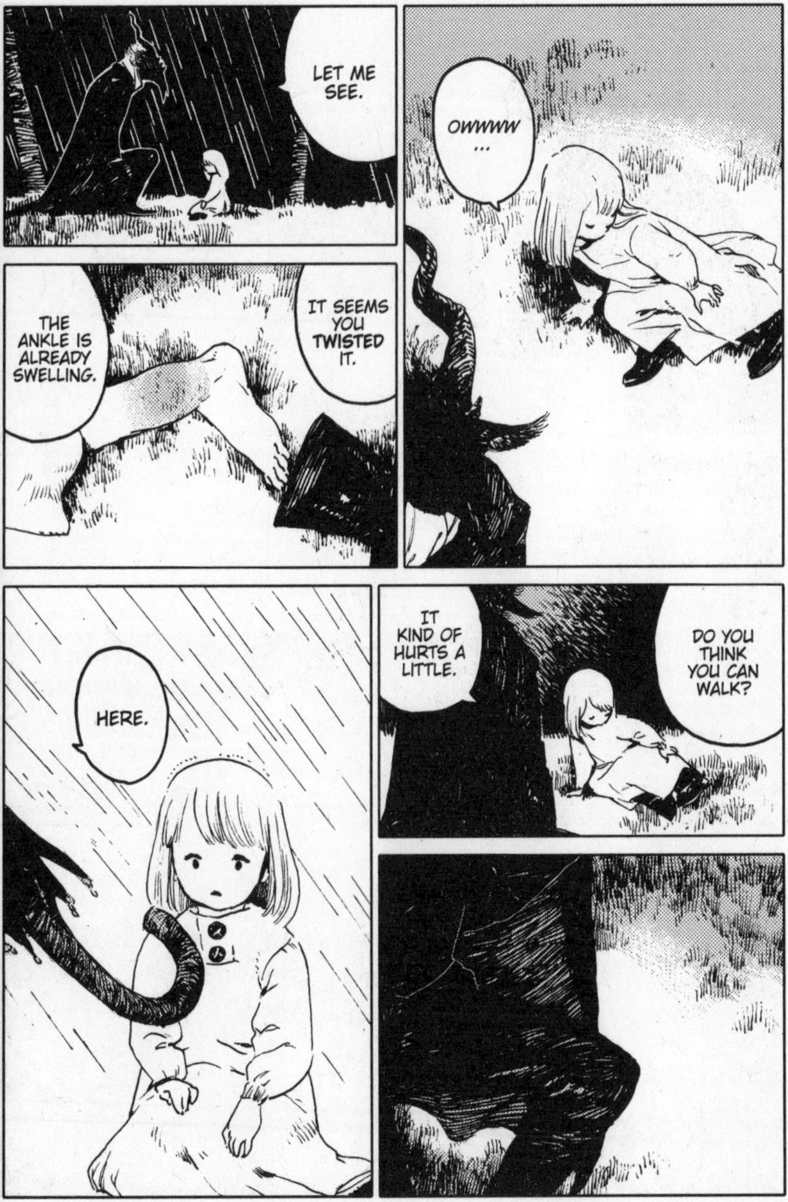
OWWWW ...
LET ME SEE.
IT SEEMS YOU TWISTED IT.
THE ANKLE IS ALREADY SWELLING.
DO YOU THINK YOU CAN WALK?
IT KIND OF HURTS A LITTLE.
HERE.

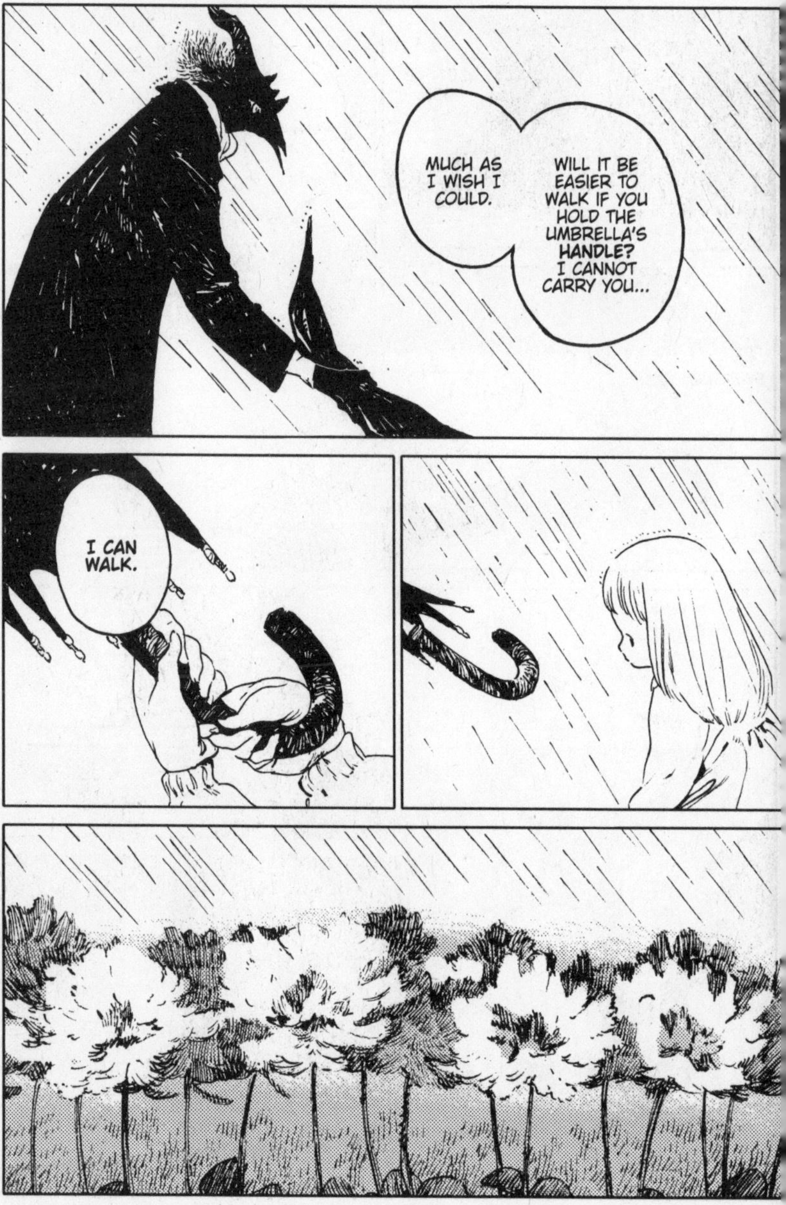
WILL IT BE EASIER TO WALK IF YOU HOLD THE UMBRELLA'S HANDLE? I CANNOT CARRY YOU...
MUCH AS I WISH I COULD.
I CAN WALK.

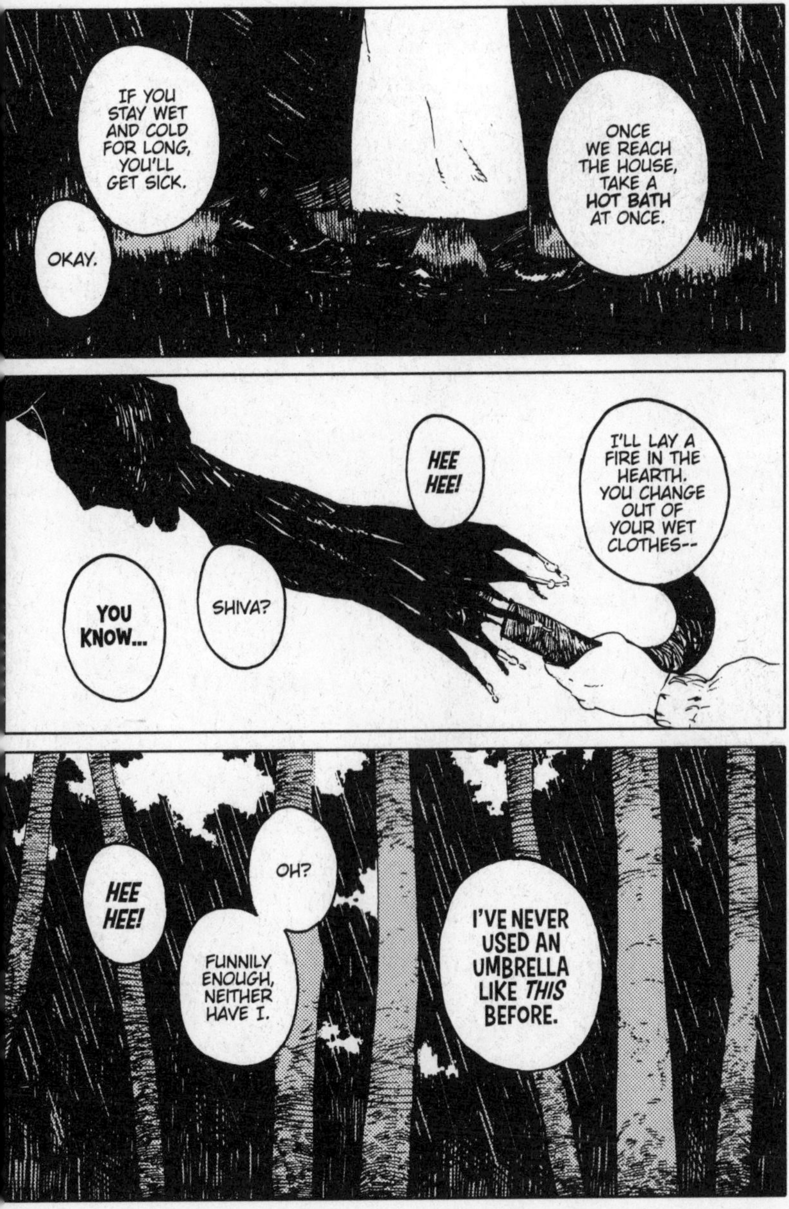
ONCE WE REACH THE HOUSE, TAKE A HOT BATH AT ONCE.
IF YOU STAY WET AND COLD FOR LONG, YOU'LL GET SICK.
OKAY.
I'LL LAY A FIRE IN THE HEARTH. YOU CHANGE OUT OF YOUR WET CLOTHES--
HEE HEE!
SHIVA?
YOU KNOW...
I'VE NEVER USED AN UMBRELLA LIKE *THIS* BEFORE.
OH?
FUNNILY ENOUGH, NEITHER HAVE I.
HEE HEE!

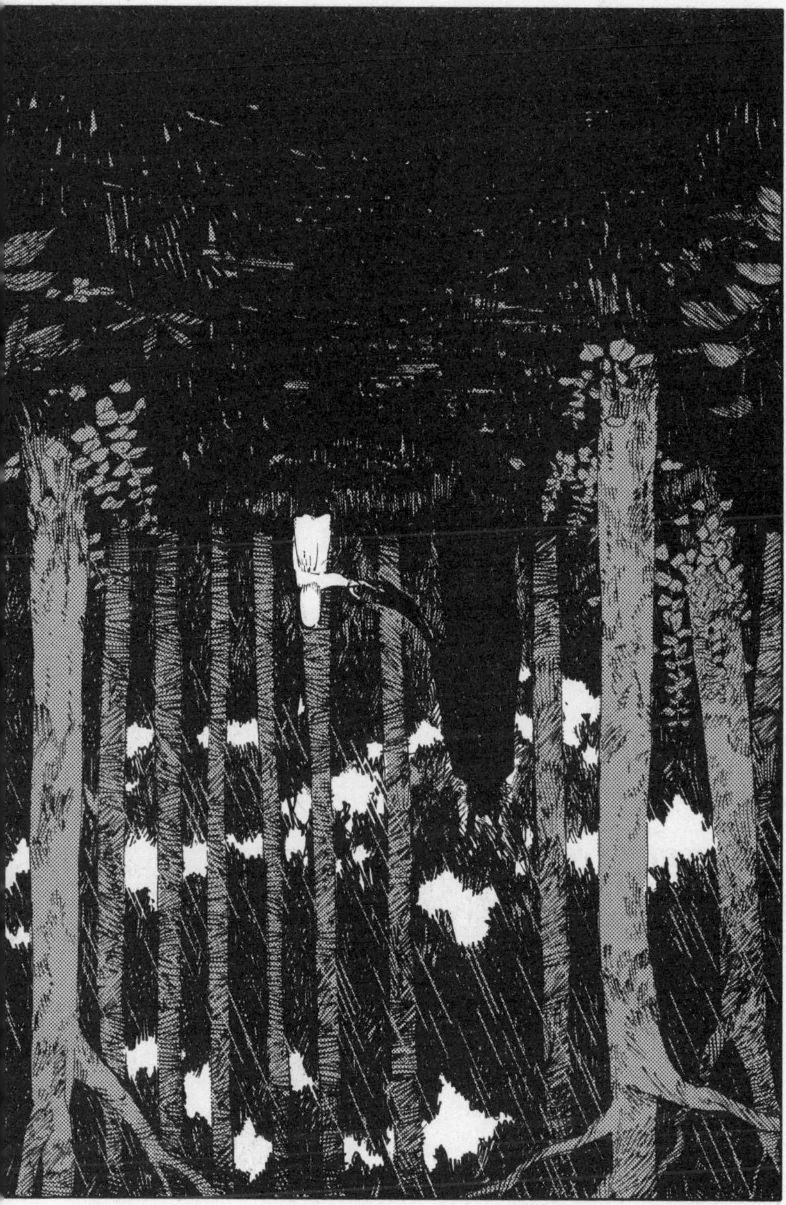

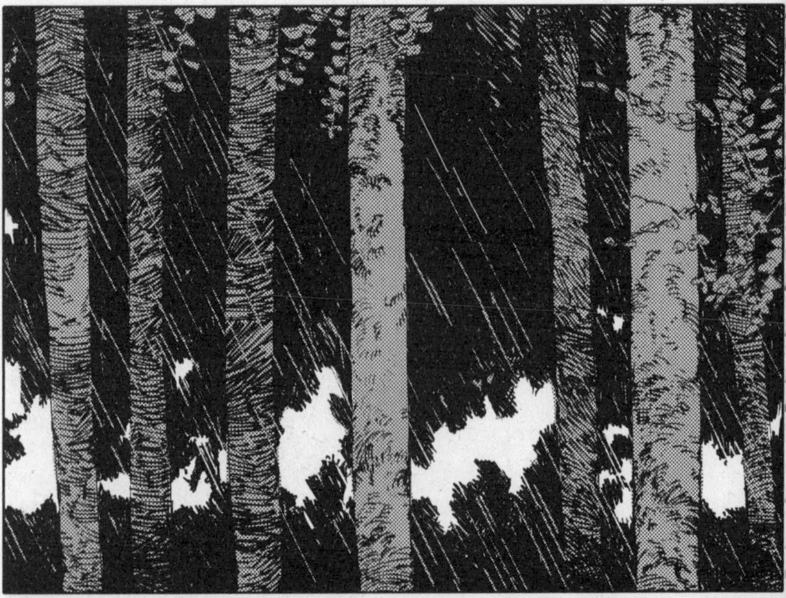
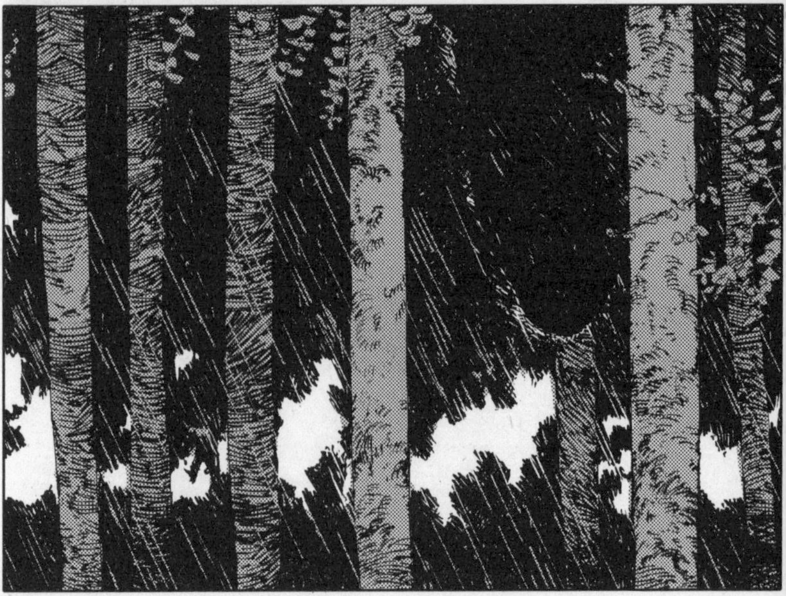

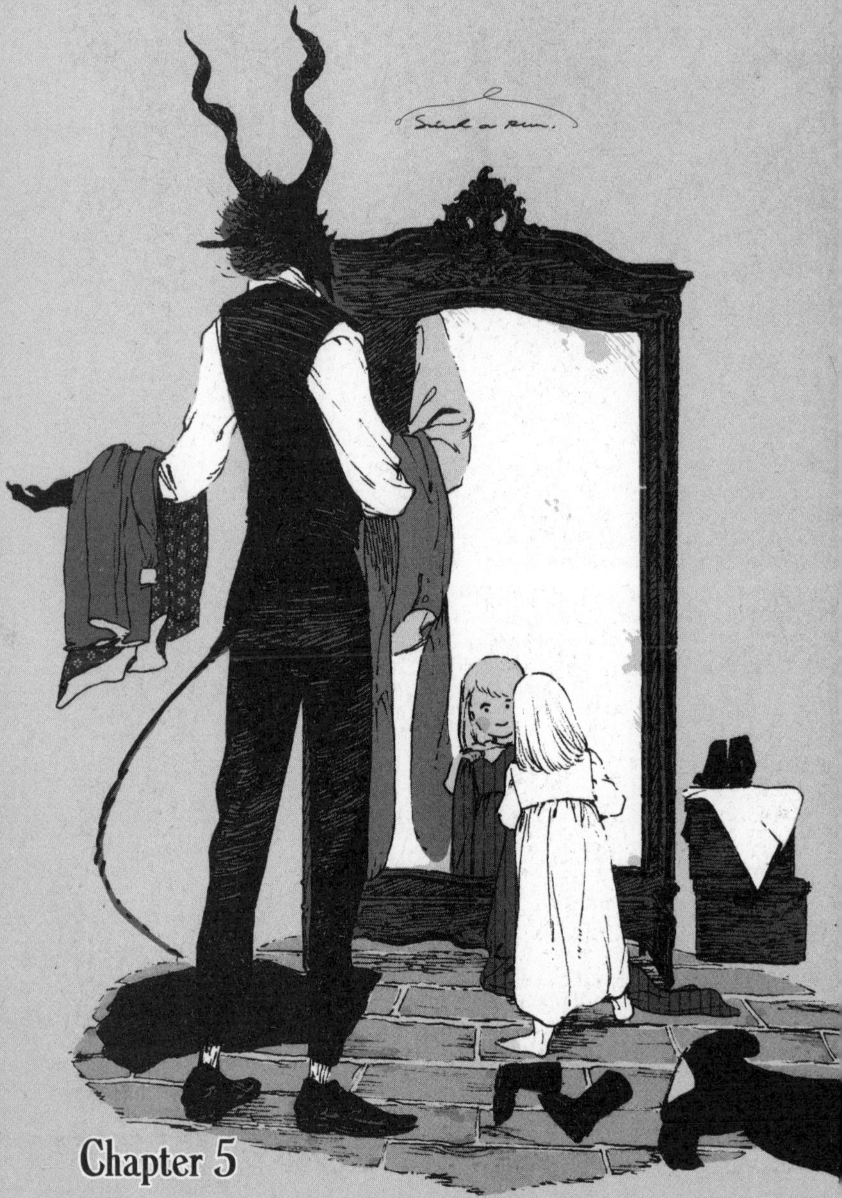
Chapter 5

Siúil, a Rún

The Girl from the Other Side

— 1 —

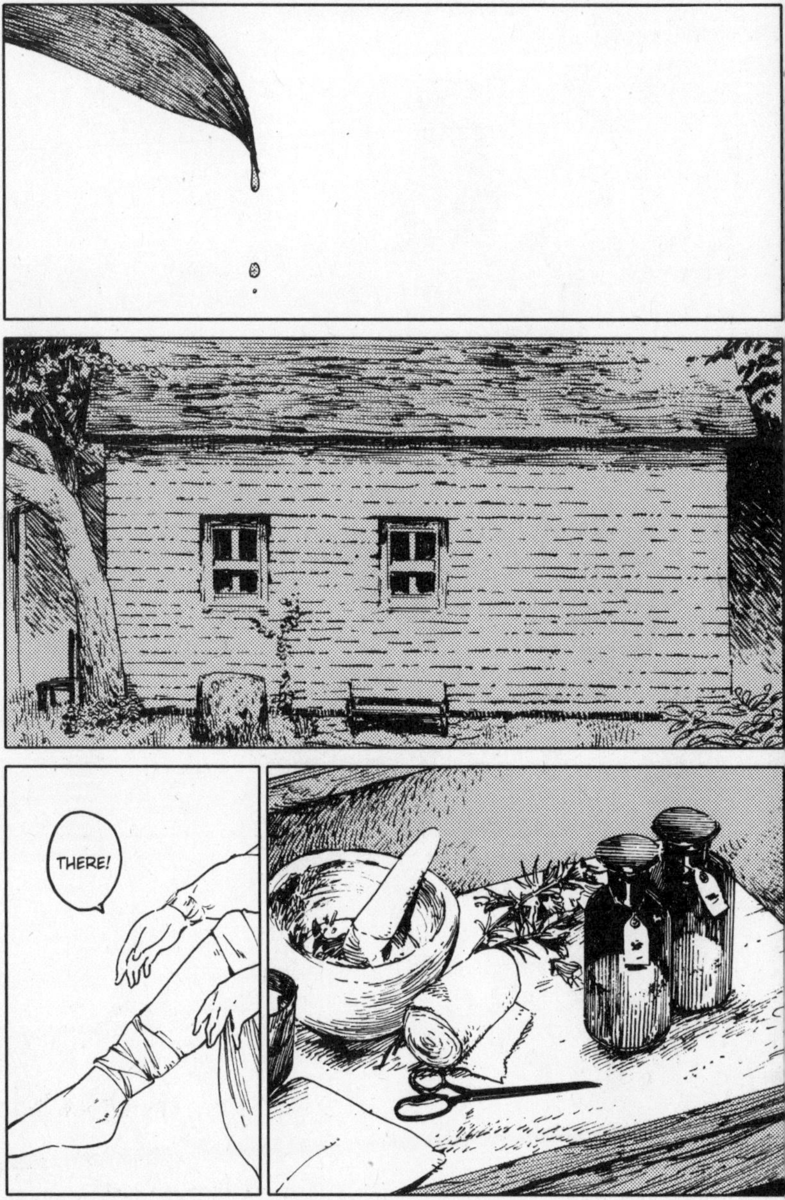
THERE!

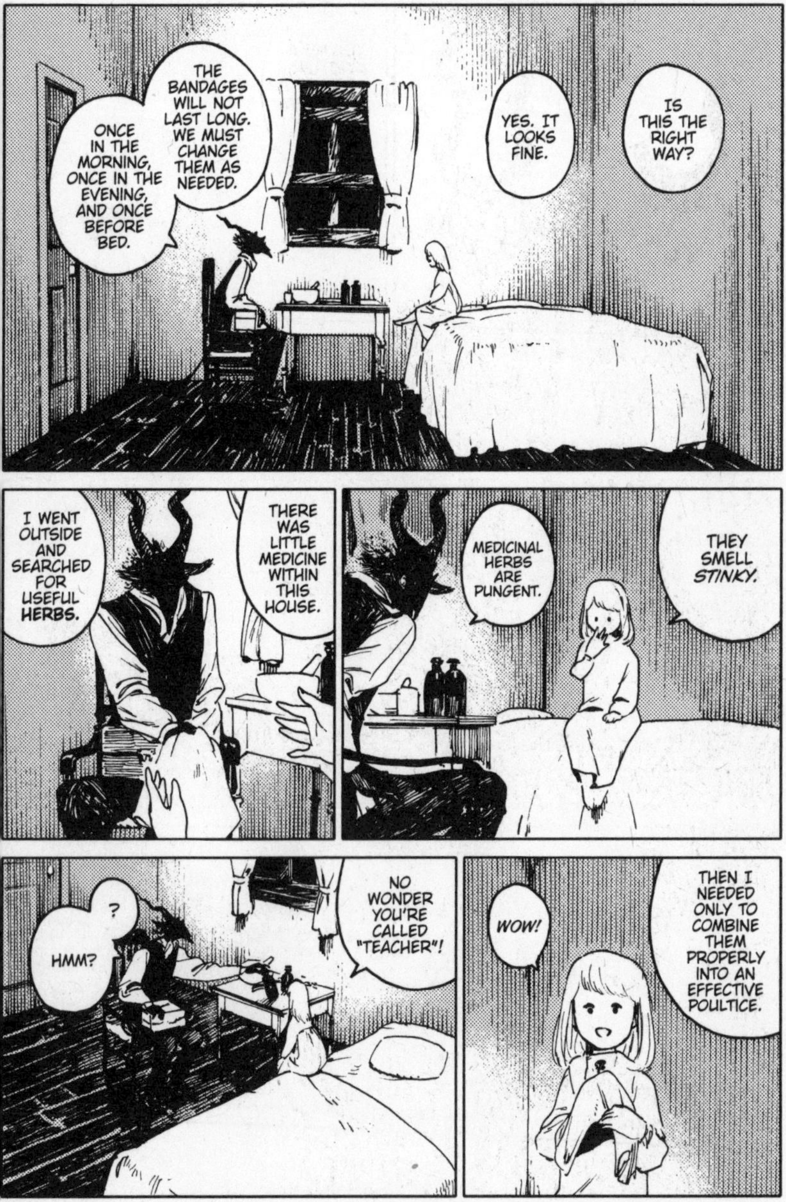
IS THIS THE RIGHT WAY?
YES. IT LOOKS FINE.
THE BANDAGES WILL NOT LAST LONG. WE MUST CHANGE THEM AS NEEDED.
ONCE IN THE MORNING, ONCE IN THE EVENING, AND ONCE BEFORE BED.
THEY SMELL *STINKY.*
MEDICINAL HERBS ARE PUNGENT.
THERE WAS LITTLE MEDICINE WITHIN THIS HOUSE.
I WENT OUTSIDE AND SEARCHED FOR USEFUL HERBS.
THEN I NEEDED ONLY TO COMBINE THEM PROPERLY INTO AN EFFECTIVE POULTICE.
WOW!
NO WONDER YOU'RE CALLED "TEACHER"!
?
HMM?

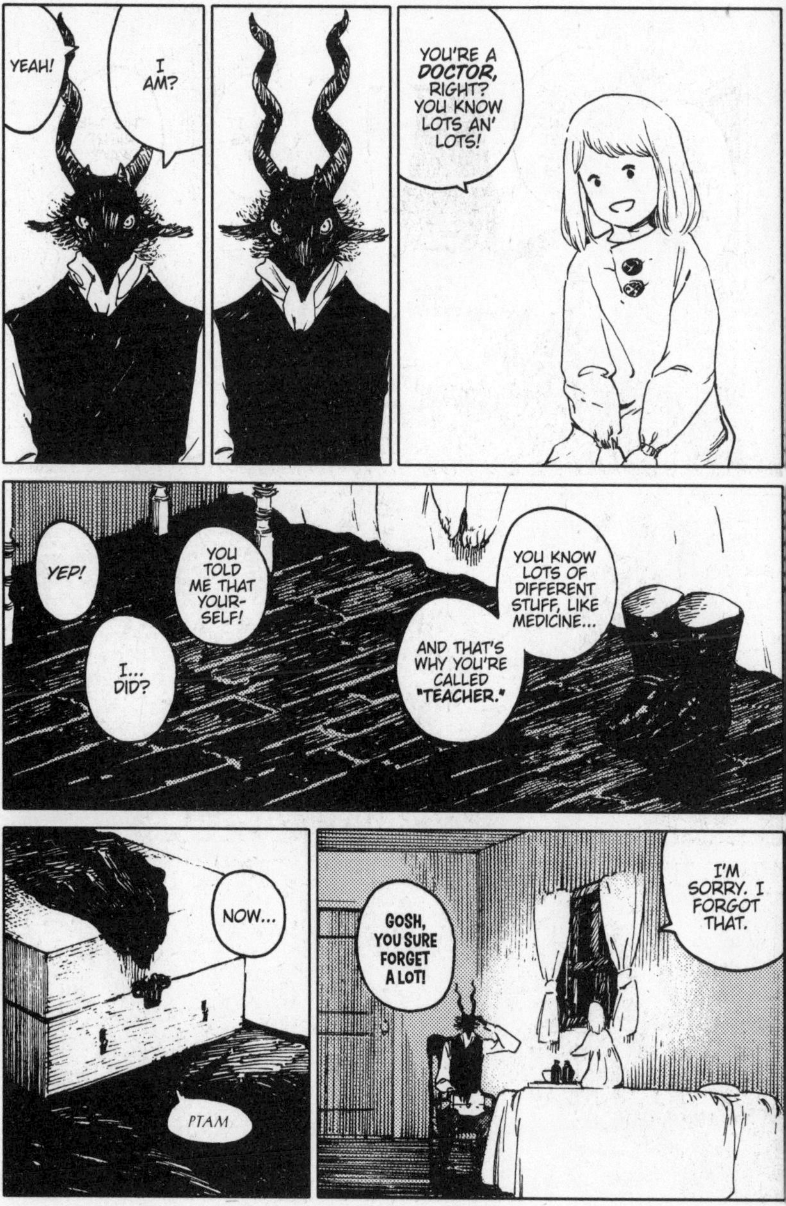
YOU'RE A DOCTOR, RIGHT? YOU KNOW LOTS AN' LOTS!
I AM?
YEAH!
YOU KNOW LOTS OF DIFFERENT STUFF, LIKE MEDICINE...
AND THAT'S WHY YOU'RE CALLED "TEACHER."
YOU TOLD ME THAT YOURSELF!
YEP!
I... DID?
I'M SORRY. I FORGOT THAT.
GOSH, YOU SURE FORGET A LOT!
NOW...
PTAM

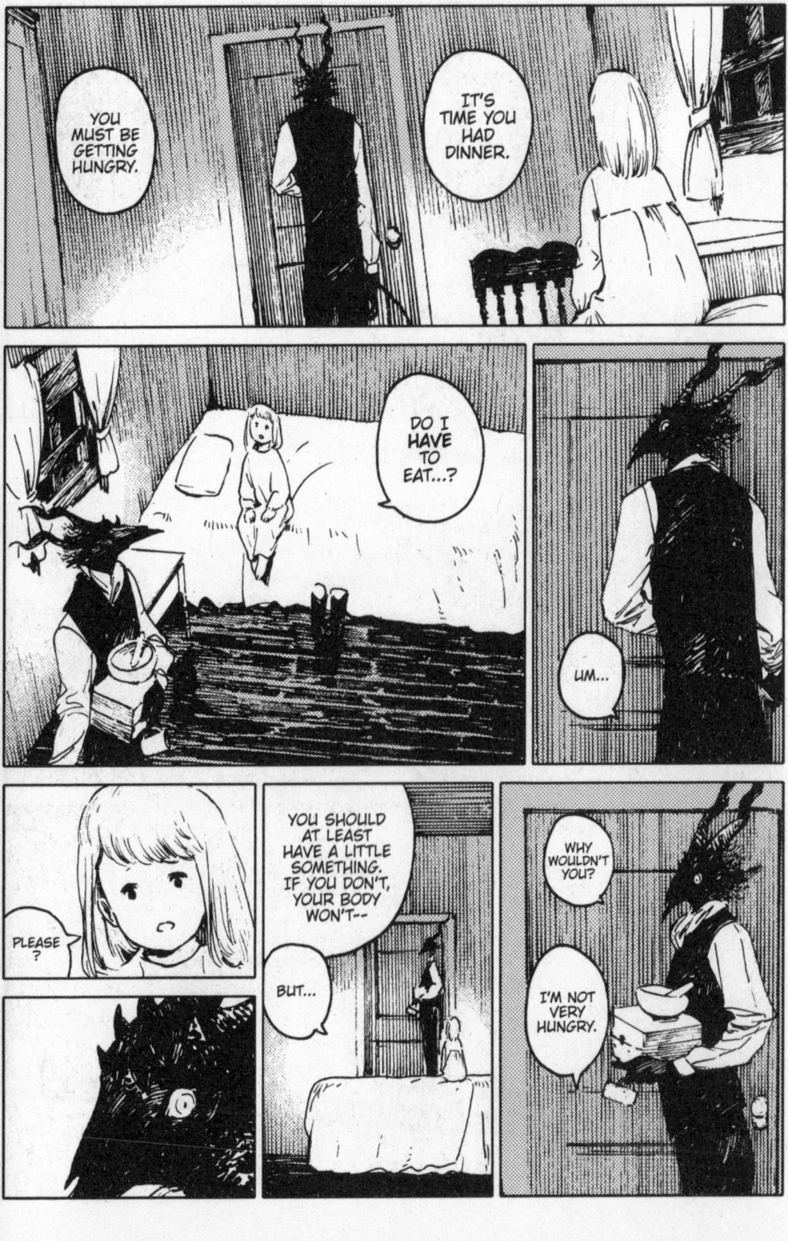
IT'S TIME YOU HAD DINNER.
YOU MUST BE GETTING HUNGRY.
UM...
DO I HAVE TO EAT...?
WHY WOULDN'T YOU?
I'M NOT VERY HUNGRY.
YOU SHOULD AT LEAST HAVE A LITTLE SOMETHING. IF YOU DON'T, YOUR BODY WON'T--
BUT...
PLEASE?

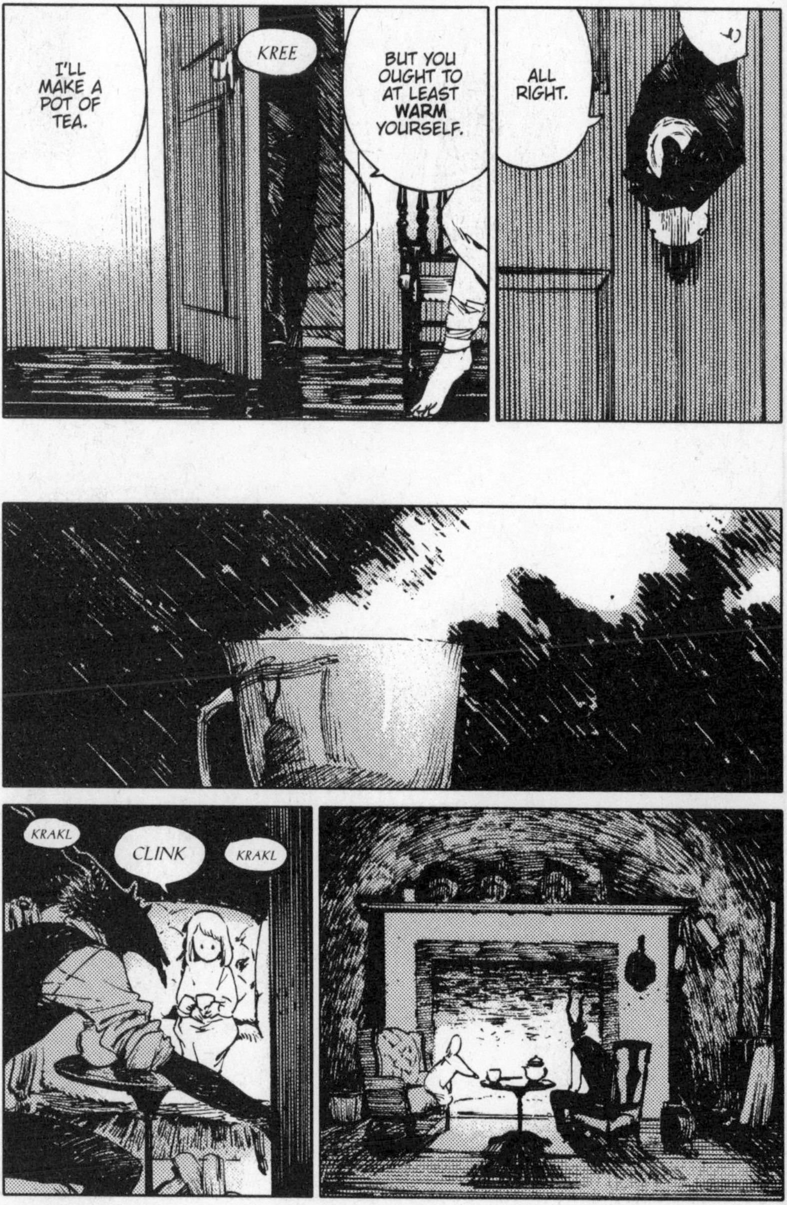
ALL RIGHT.
BUT YOU OUGHT TO AT LEAST **WARM** YOURSELF.
KREE
I'LL MAKE A POT OF TEA.
KRAKL
CLINK
KRAKL

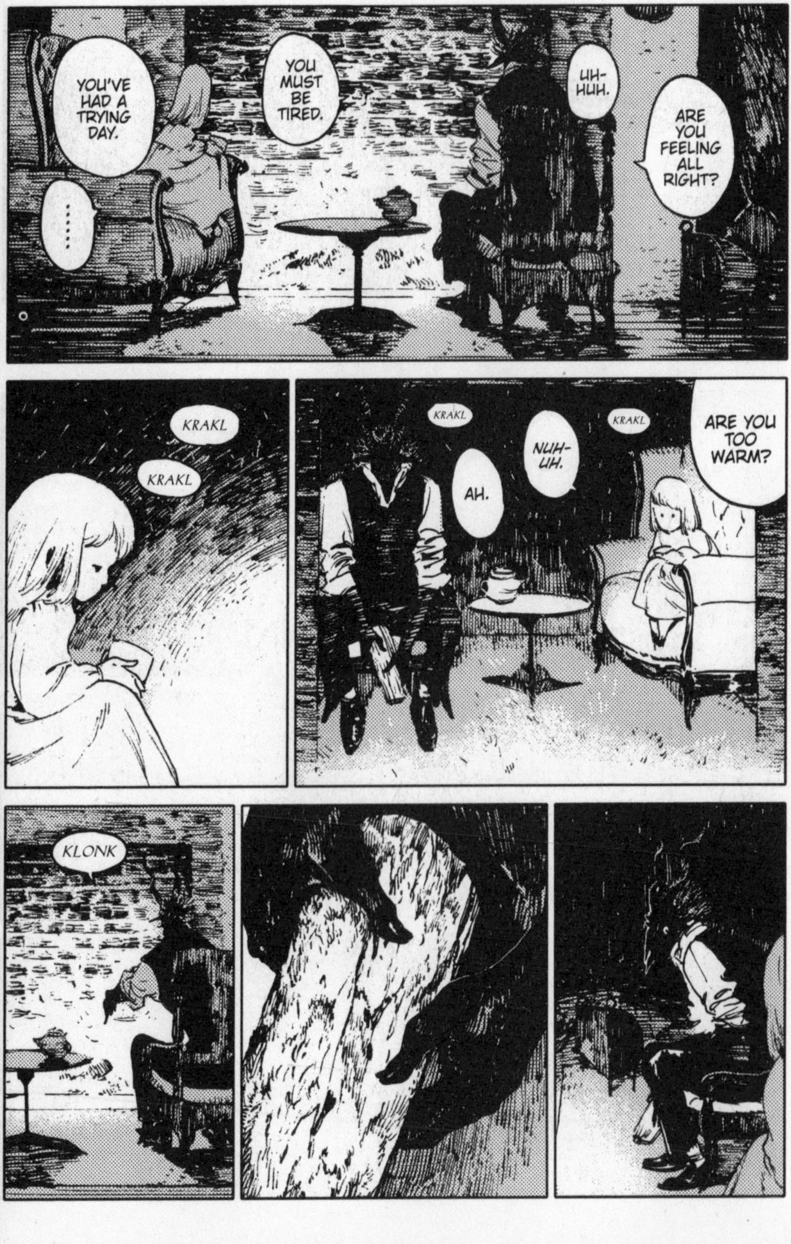
ARE YOU FEELING ALL RIGHT?
UH-HUH.
YOU MUST BE TIRED.
YOU'VE HAD A TRYING DAY.
......
ARE YOU TOO WARM?
KRAKL
NUH-UH.
AH.
KRAKL
KRAKL
KRAKL
KLONK

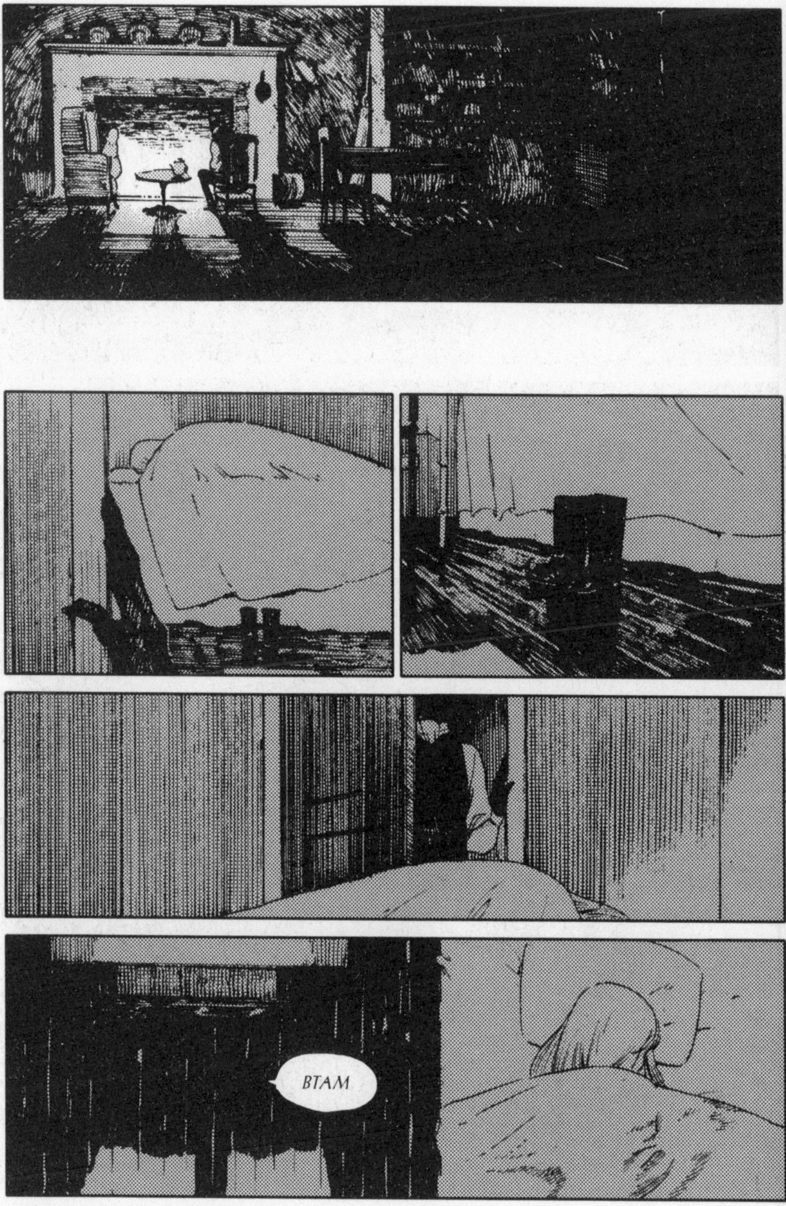
BTAM

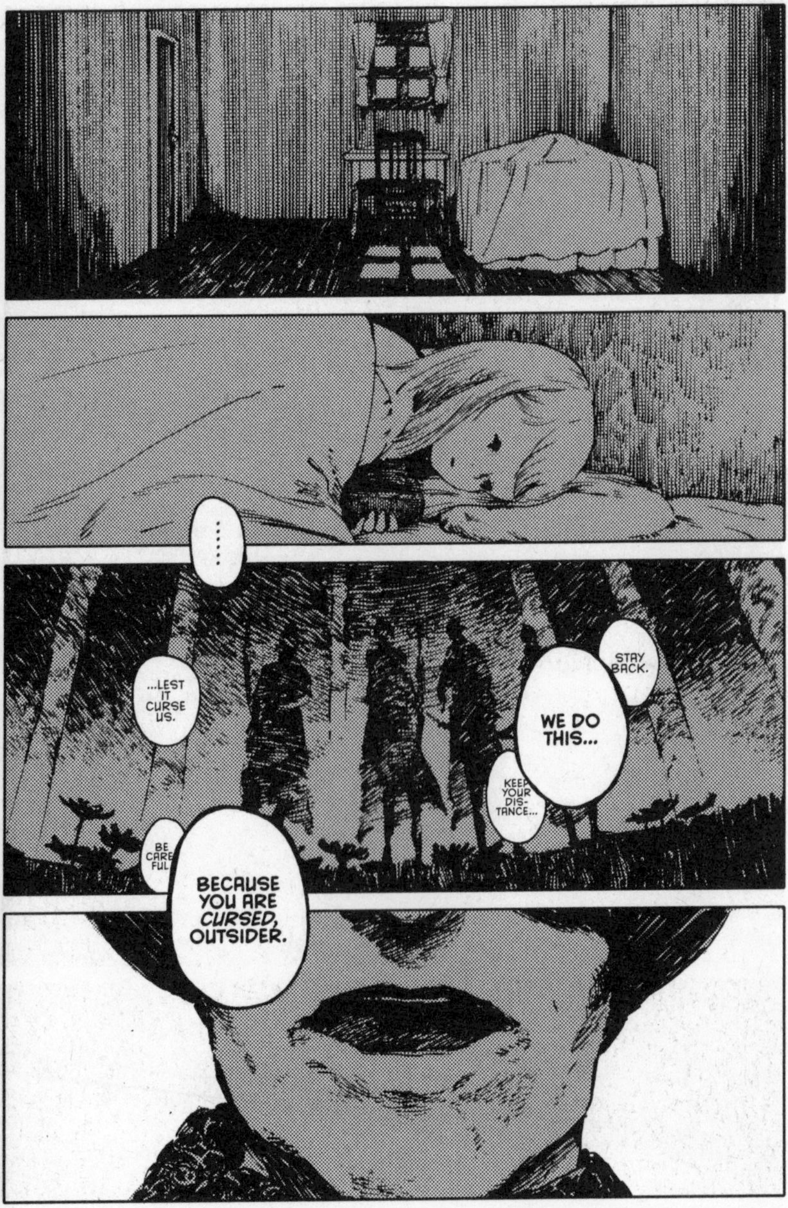
......
STAY BACK.
WE DO THIS...
KEEP YOUR DIS-TANCE...
...LEST IT CURSE US.
BE CAREFUL
BECAUSE YOU ARE *CURSED*, OUTSIDER.

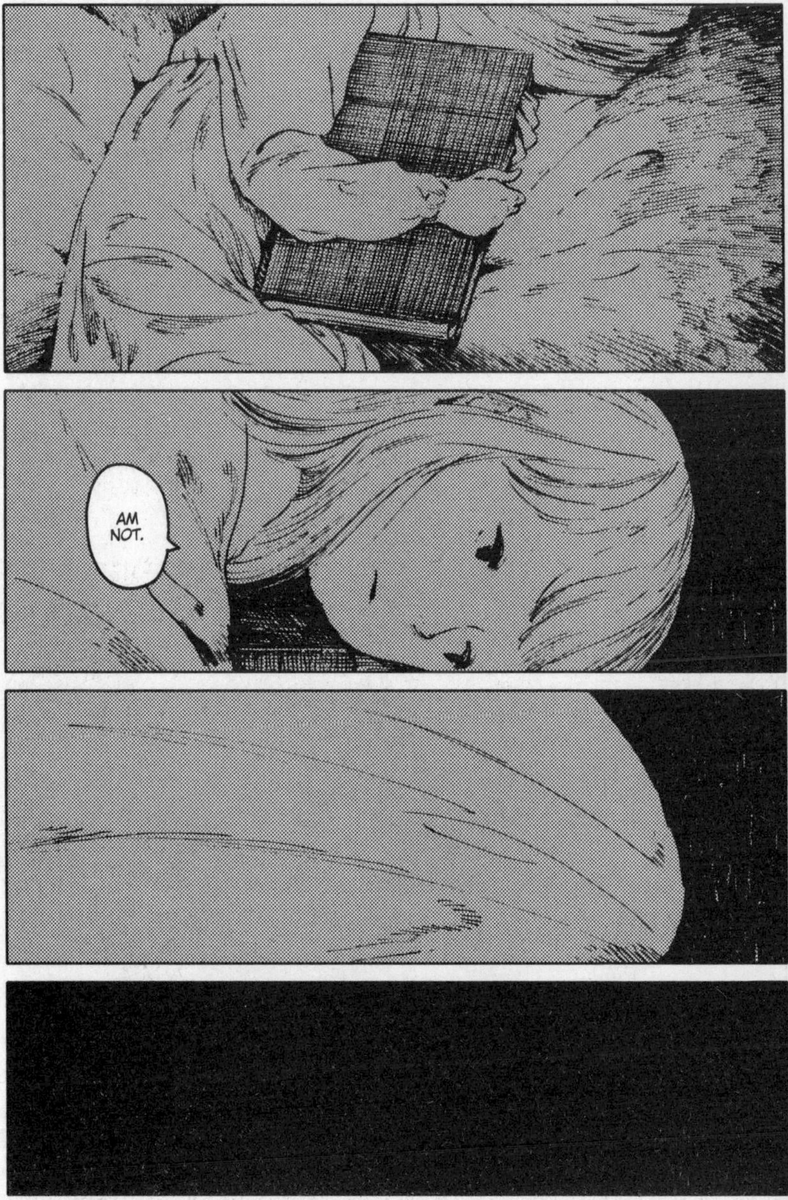
AM NOT.

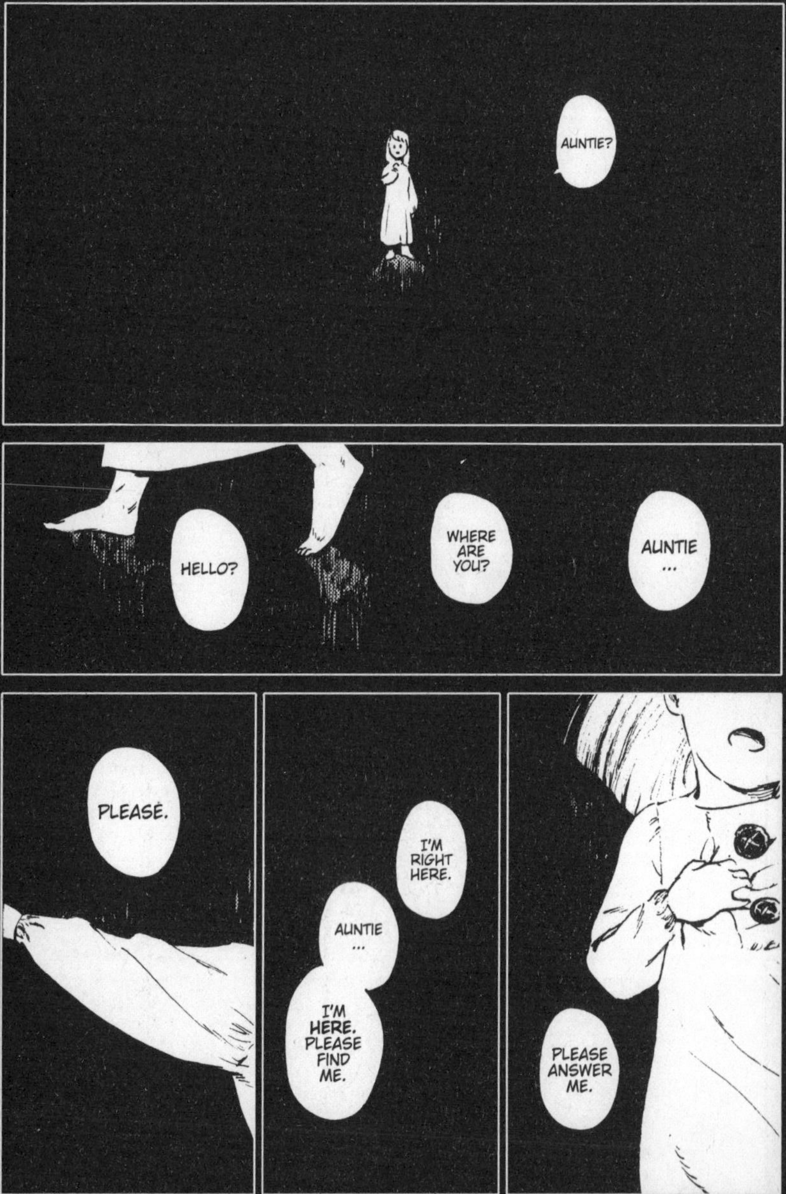
AUNTIE?
AUNTIE ...
WHERE ARE YOU?
HELLO?
PLEASE ANSWER ME.
I'M RIGHT HERE.
AUNTIE ...
I'M HERE. PLEASE FIND ME.
PLEASE.

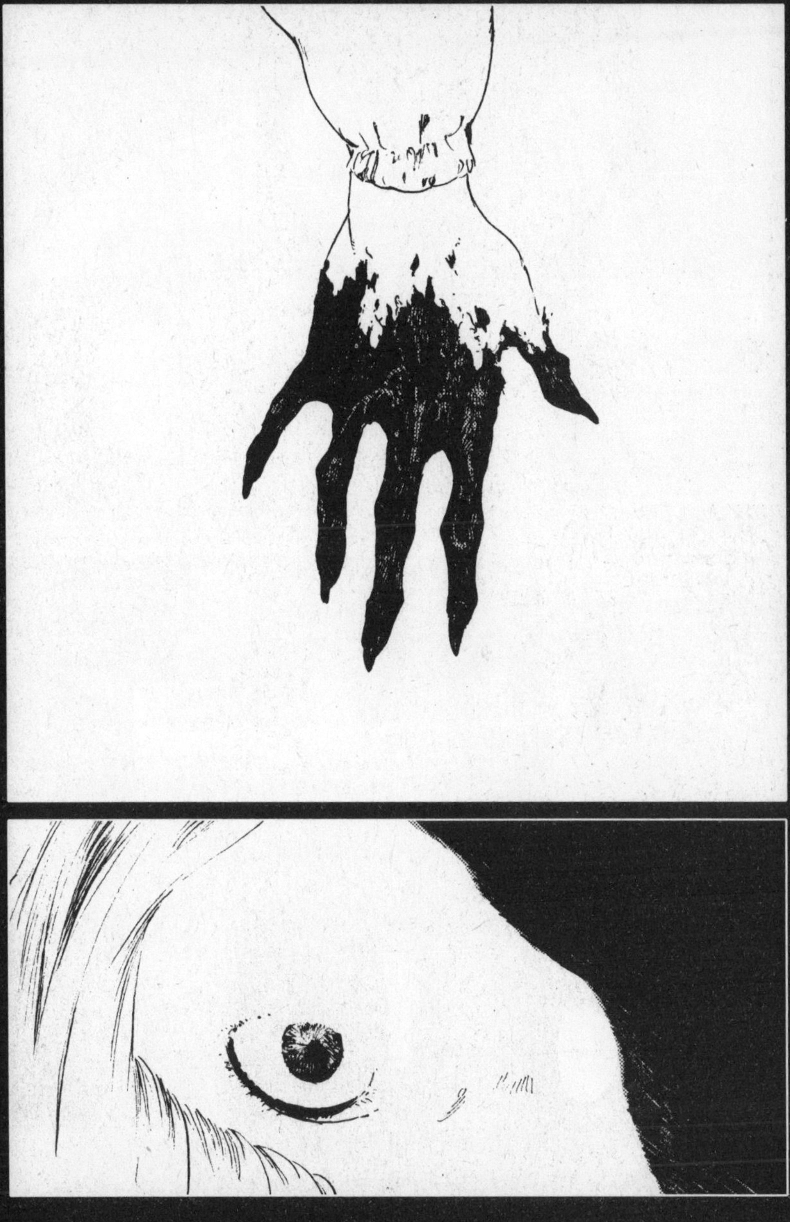

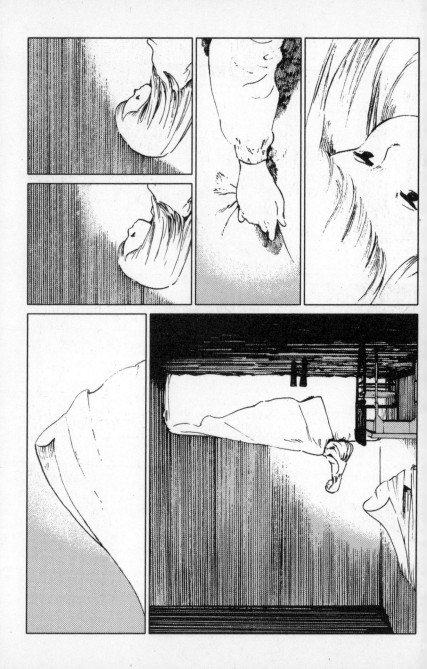

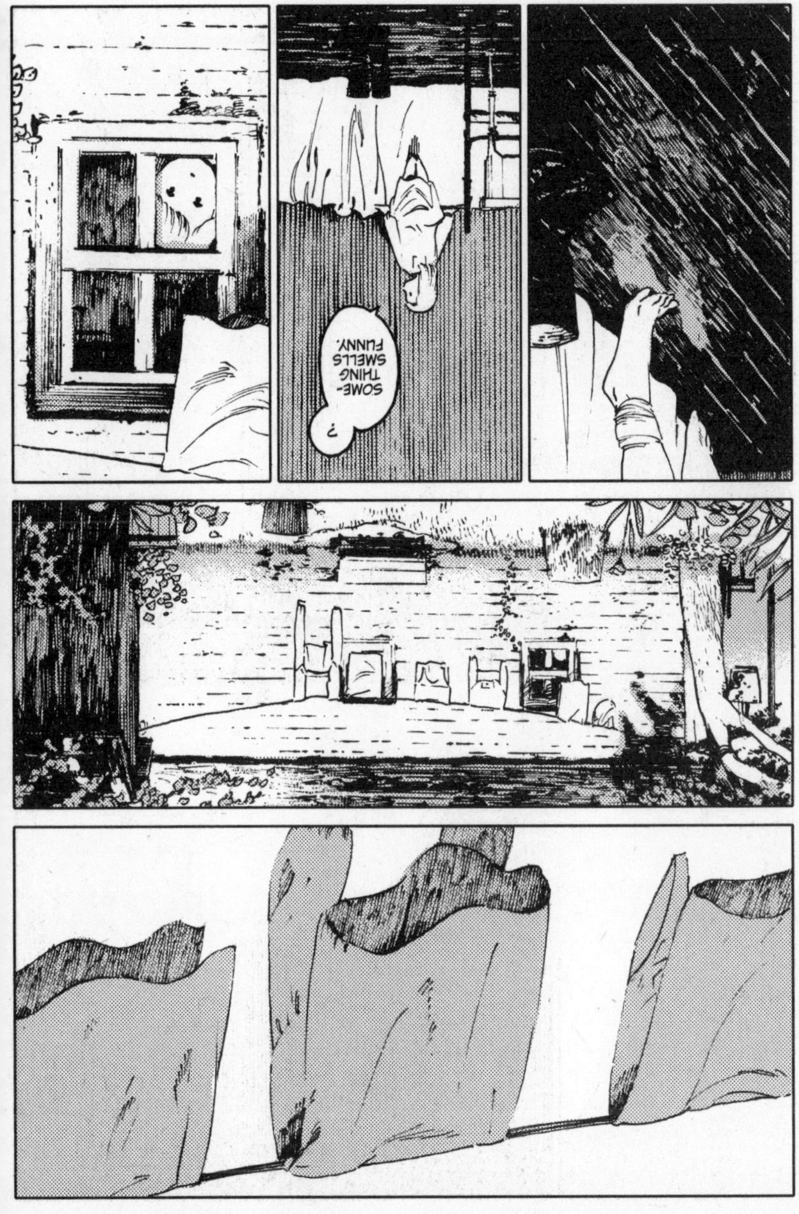
SOME-THING SMELLS FUNNY.
?

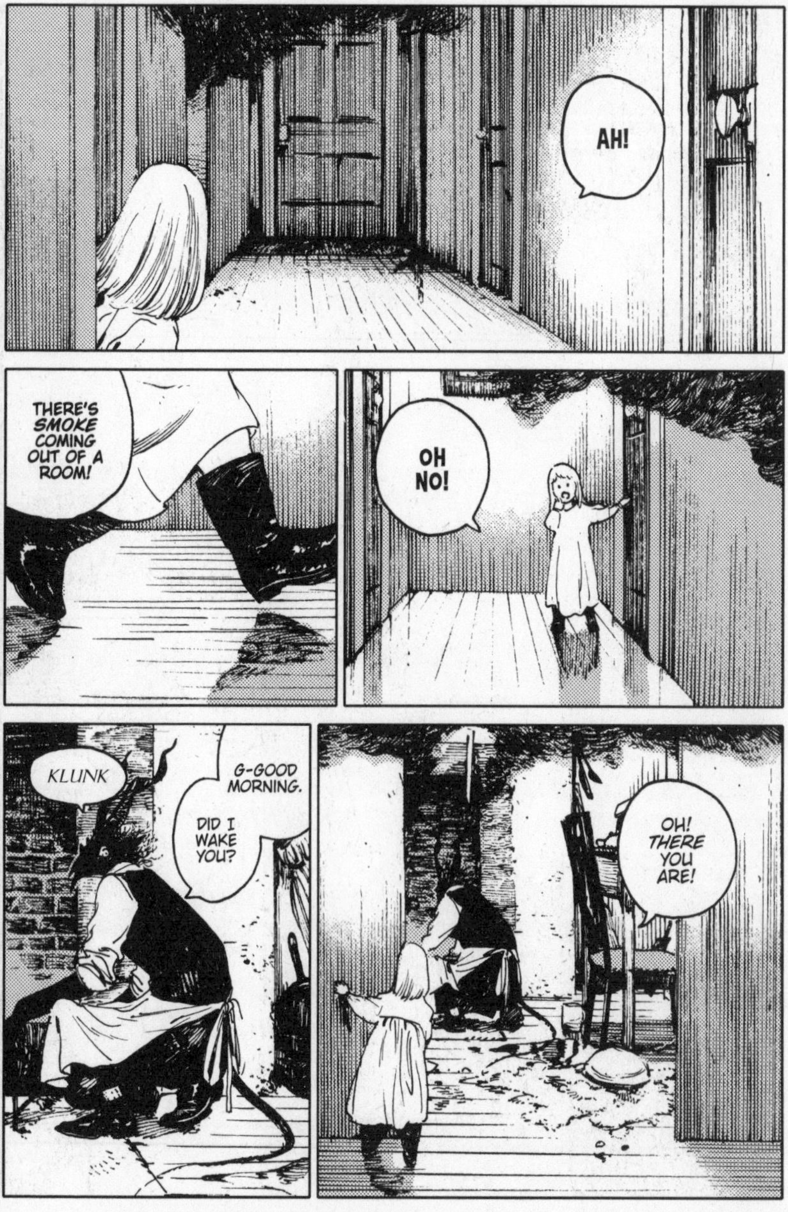
AH!
OH NO!
THERE'S SMOKE COMING OUT OF A ROOM!
OH! THERE YOU ARE!
G-GOOD MORNING.
DID I WAKE YOU?
KLUNK

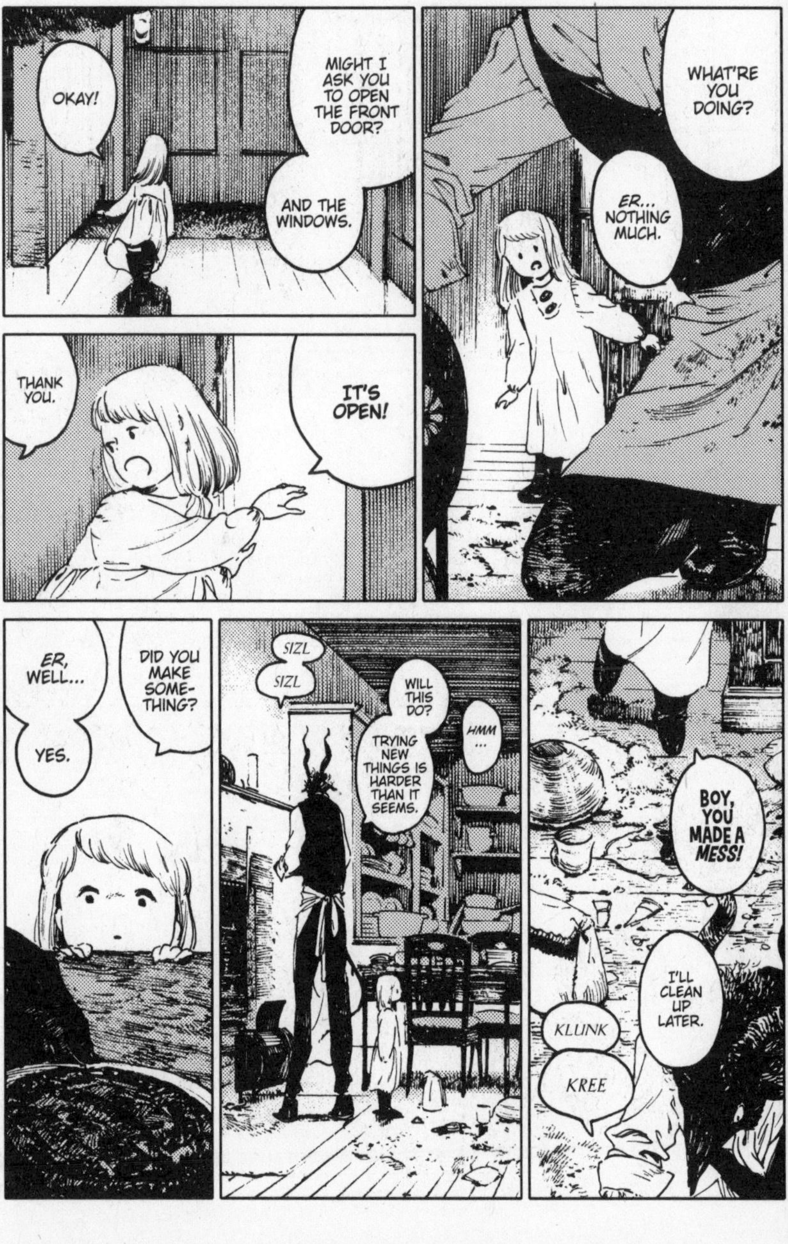
WHAT'RE YOU DOING?
ER... NOTHING MUCH.
MIGHT I ASK YOU TO OPEN THE FRONT DOOR?
AND THE WINDOWS.
OKAY!
IT'S OPEN!
THANK YOU.
BOY, YOU MADE A MESS!
I'LL CLEAN UP LATER.
KLUNK
KREE
SIZL
SIZL
WILL THIS DO?
HMM...
TRYING NEW THINGS IS HARDER THAN IT SEEMS.
DID YOU MAKE SOME-THING?
ER, WELL...
YES.

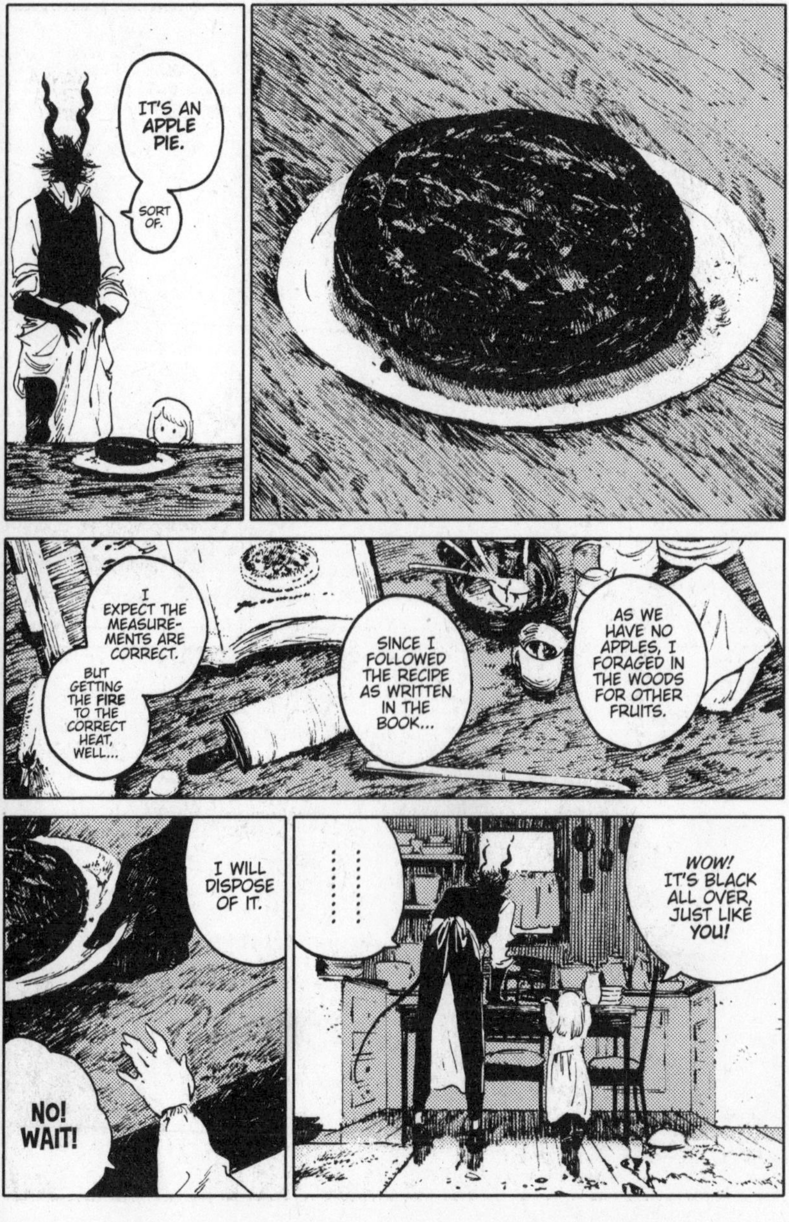
IT'S AN APPLE PIE.
SORT OF.
AS WE HAVE NO APPLES, I FORAGED IN THE WOODS FOR OTHER FRUITS.
SINCE I FOLLOWED THE RECIPE AS WRITTEN IN THE BOOK...
I EXPECT THE MEASURE-MENTS ARE CORRECT.
BUT GETTING THE FIRE TO THE CORRECT HEAT, WELL...
WOW! IT'S BLACK ALL OVER, JUST LIKE YOU!
......
I WILL DISPOSE OF IT.
NO! WAIT!

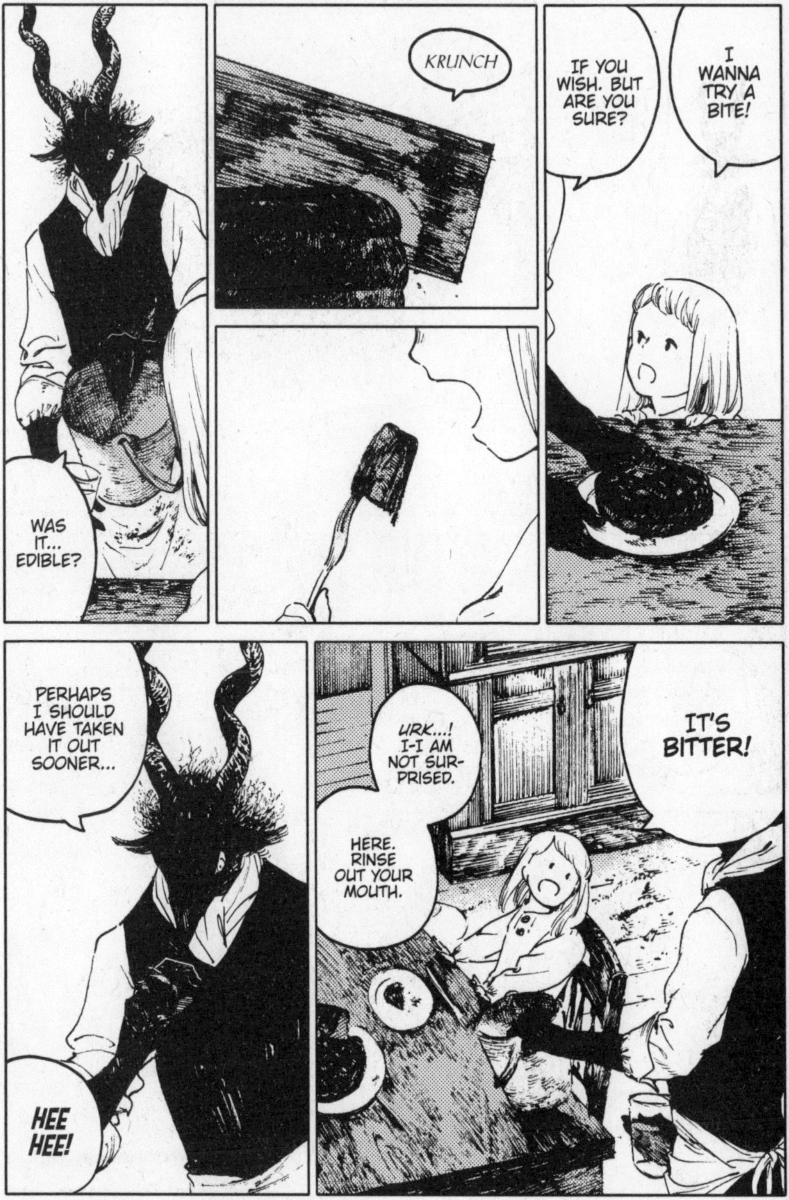
I WANNA TRY A BITE!
IF YOU WISH. BUT ARE YOU SURE?
KRUNCH
WAS IT... EDIBLE?
IT'S BITTER!
URK...! I-I AM NOT SURPRISED.
HERE. RINSE OUT YOUR MOUTH.
PERHAPS I SHOULD HAVE TAKEN IT OUT SOONER...
HEE HEE!

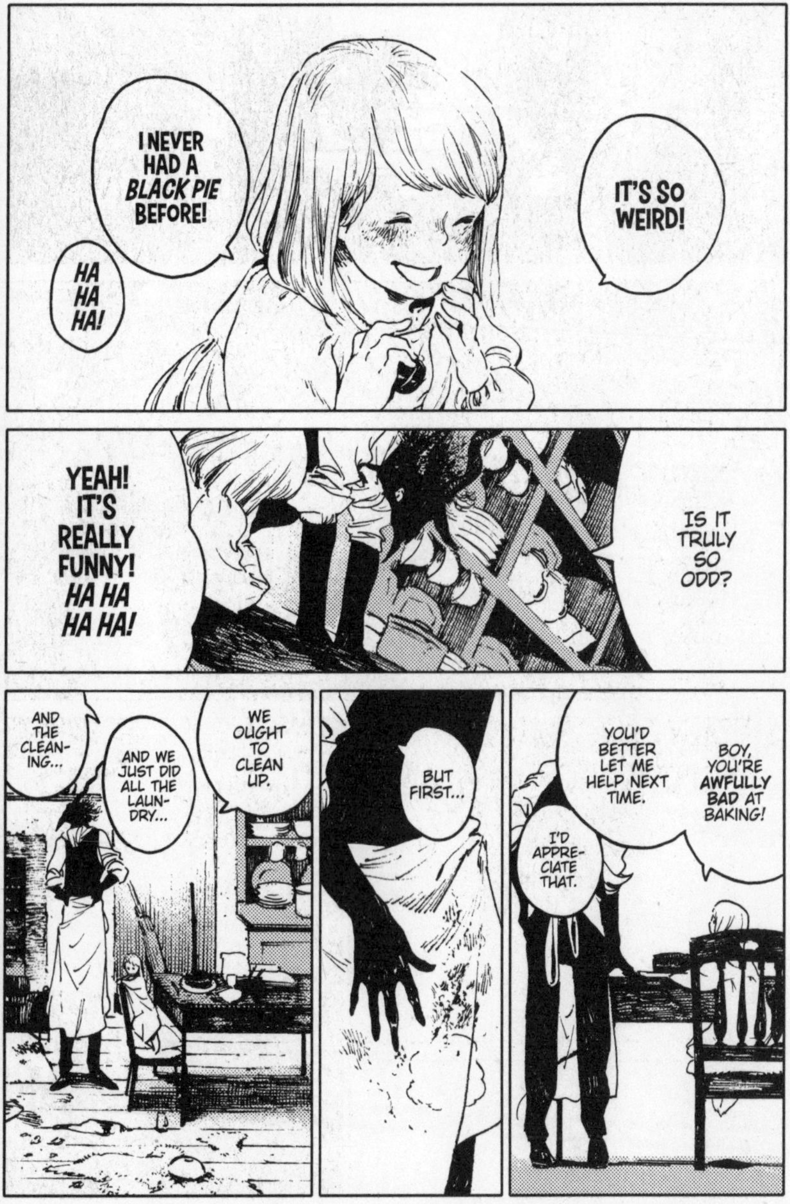
IT'S SO WEIRD!
I NEVER HAD A *BLACK PIE* BEFORE!
HA HA HA!
IS IT TRULY SO ODD?
YEAH! IT'S REALLY FUNNY! *HA HA HA HA!*
BOY, YOU'RE AWFULLY BAD AT BAKING!
YOU'D BETTER LET ME HELP NEXT TIME.
I'D APPRECIATE THAT.
BUT FIRST...
WE OUGHT TO CLEAN UP.
AND WE JUST DID ALL THE LAUNDRY...
AND THE CLEANING...

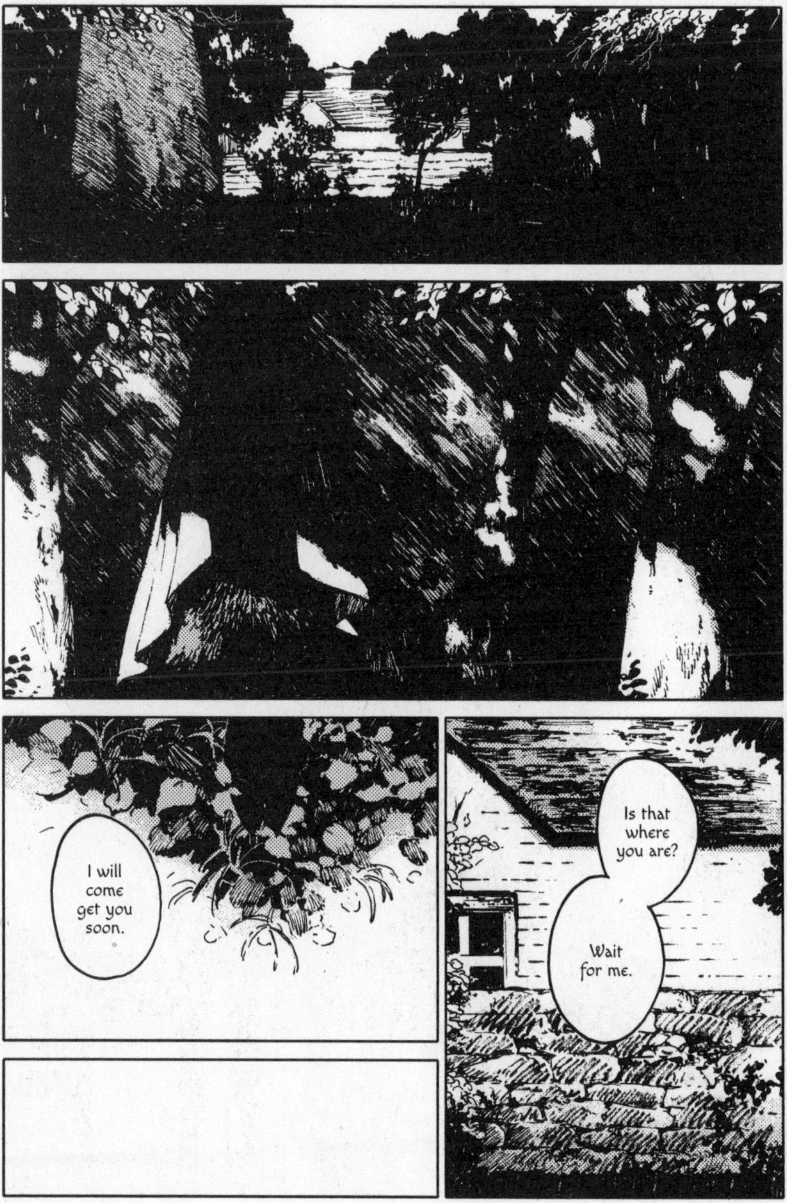
Is that where you are?
Wait for me.
I will come get you soon.

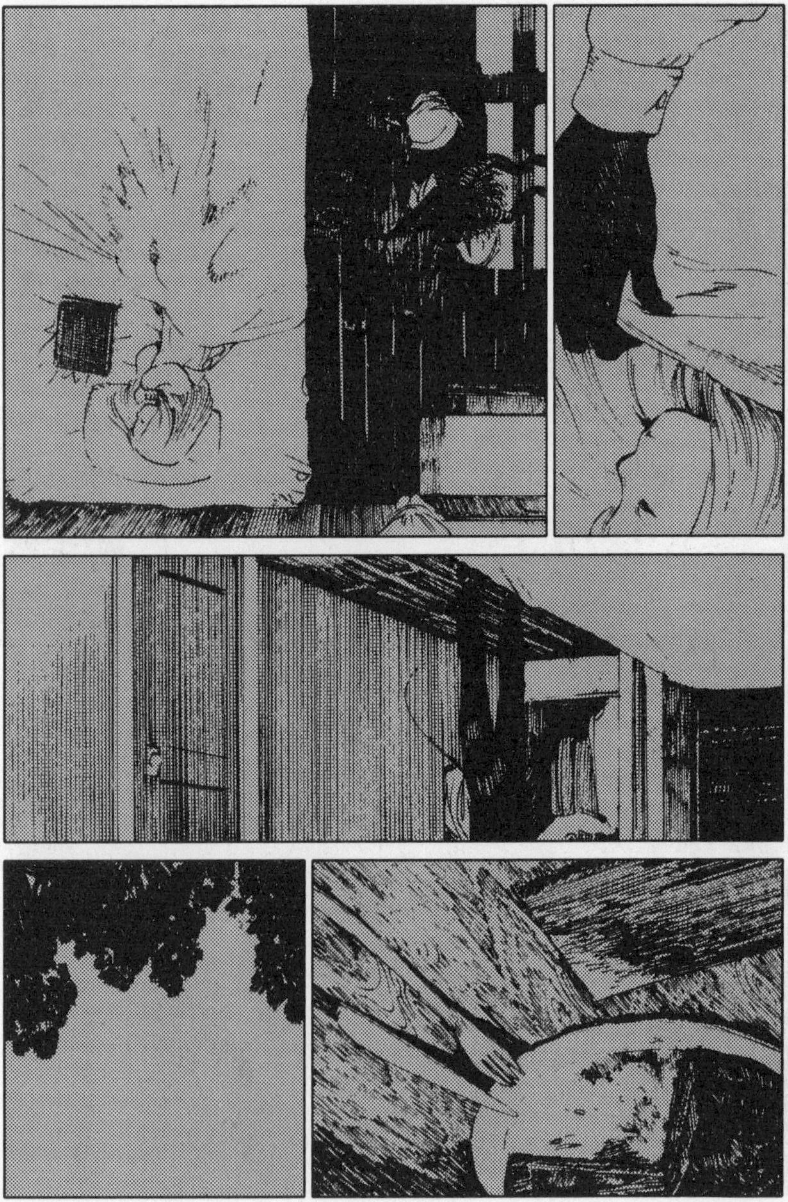

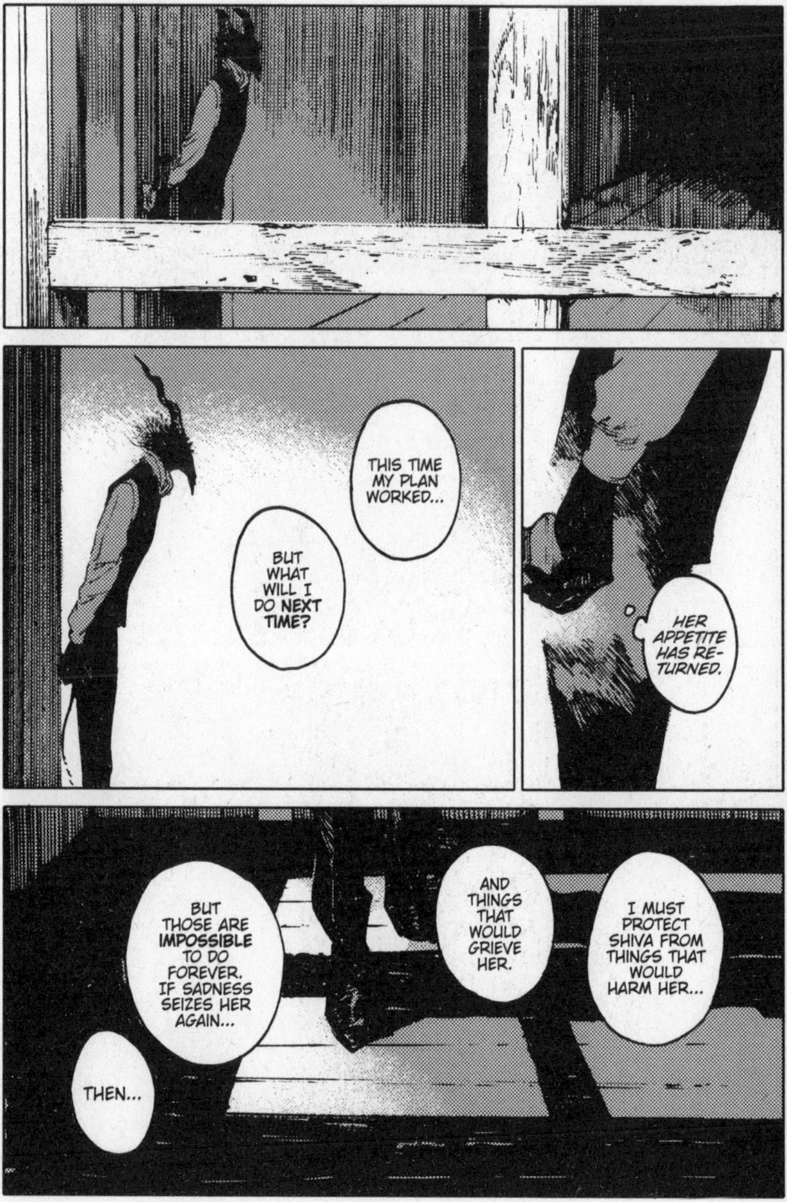
HER APPETITE HAS RE-TURNED.
THIS TIME MY PLAN WORKED...
BUT WHAT WILL I DO NEXT TIME?
I MUST PROTECT SHIVA FROM THINGS THAT WOULD HARM HER...
AND THINGS THAT WOULD GRIEVE HER.
BUT THOSE ARE IMPOSSIBLE TO DO FOREVER. IF SADNESS SEIZES HER AGAIN...
THEN...

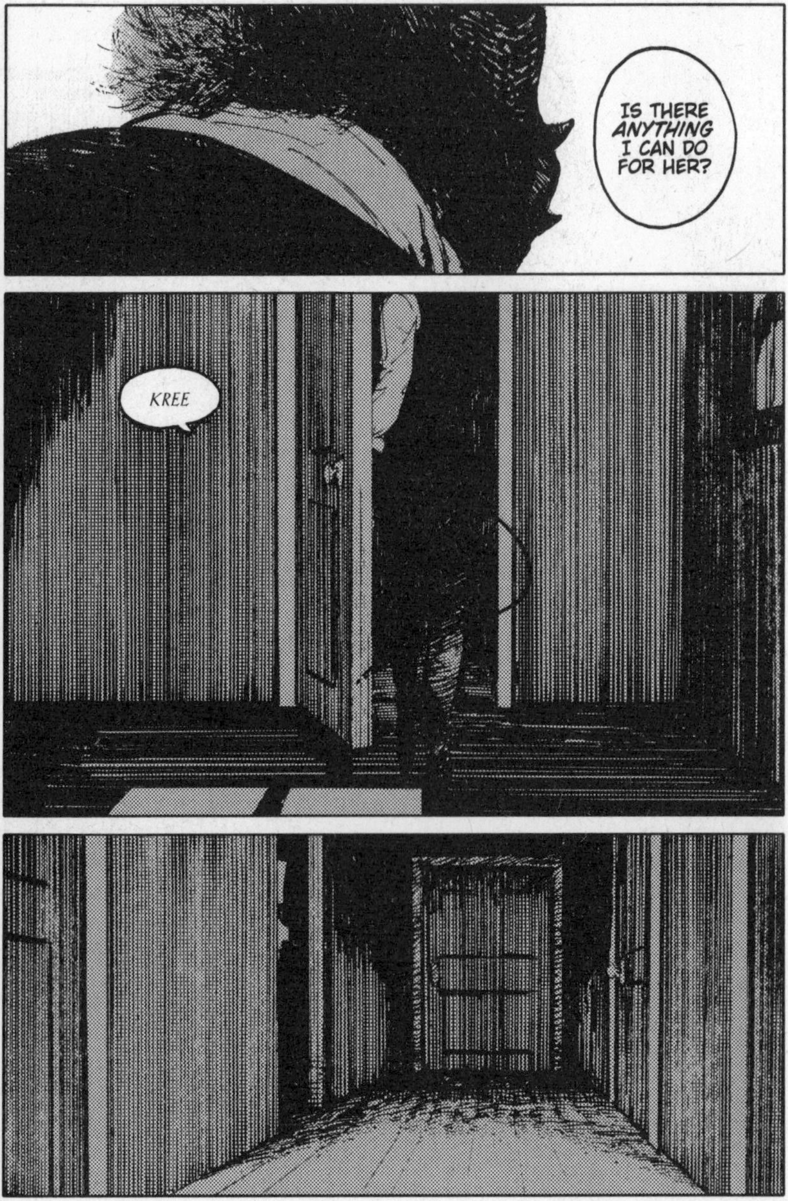
IS THERE ANYTHING I CAN DO FOR HER?
KREE

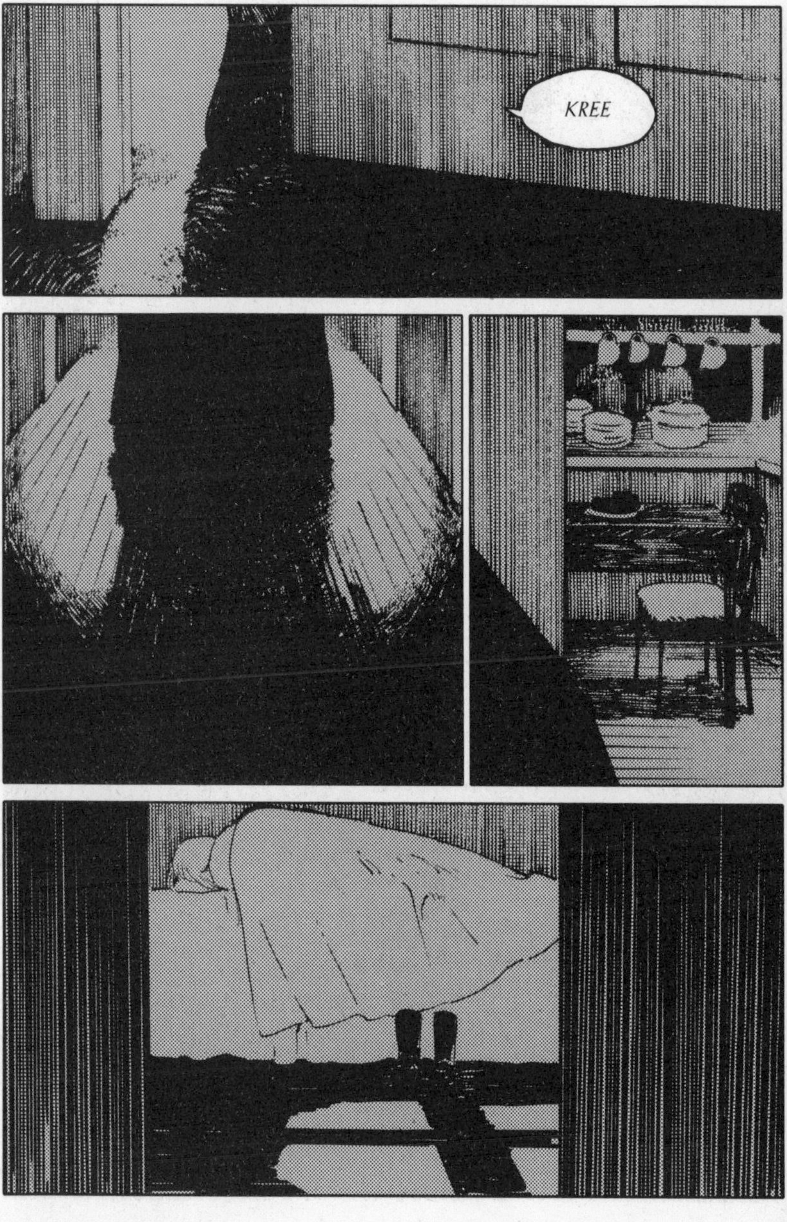
KREE

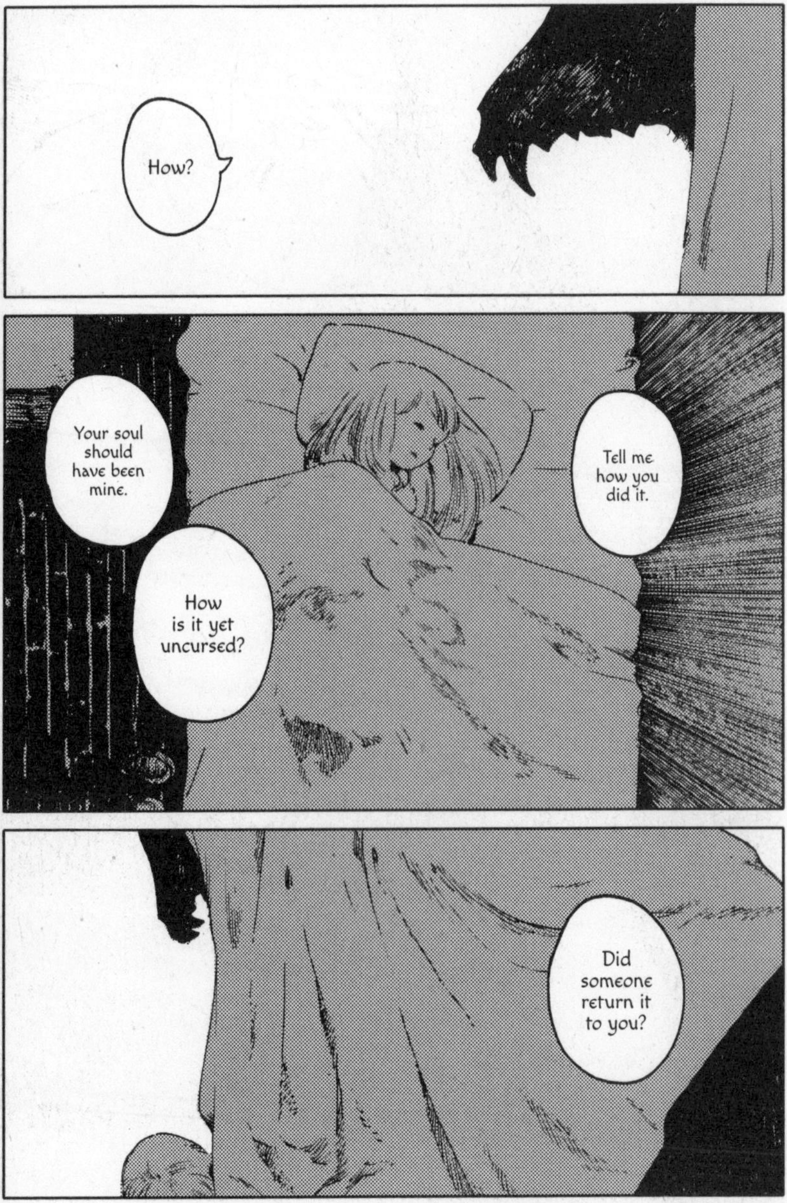
How?
Tell me how you did it.
Your soul should have been mine.
How is it yet uncursed?
Did someone return it to you?

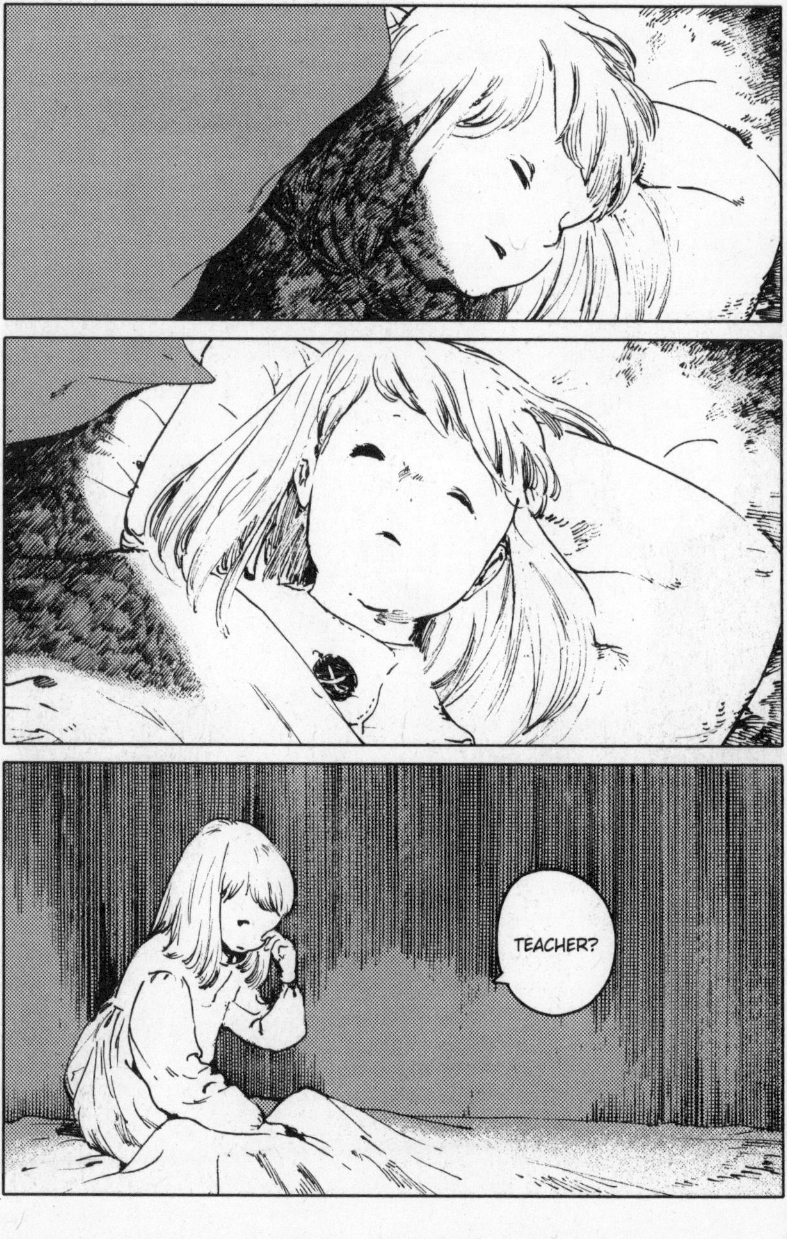
TEACHER?

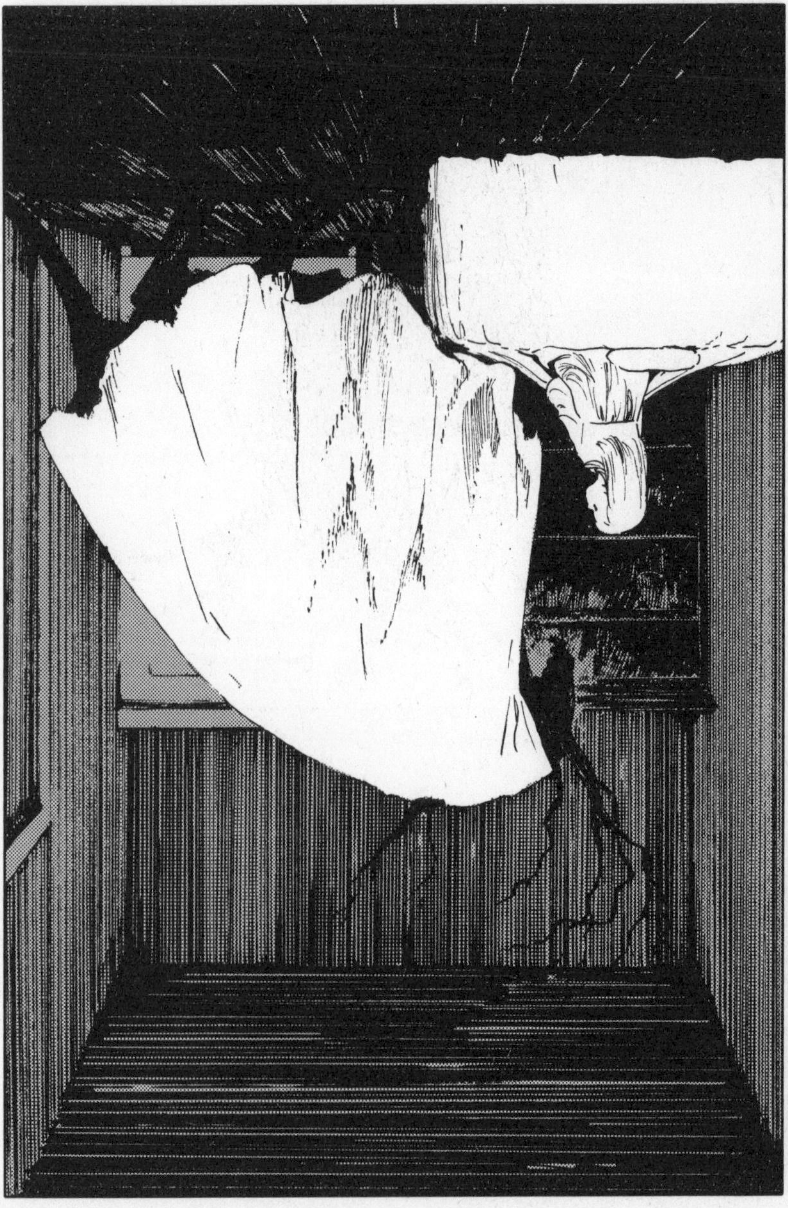

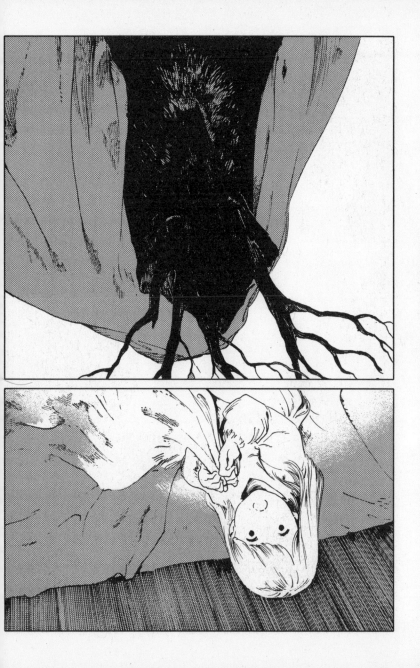

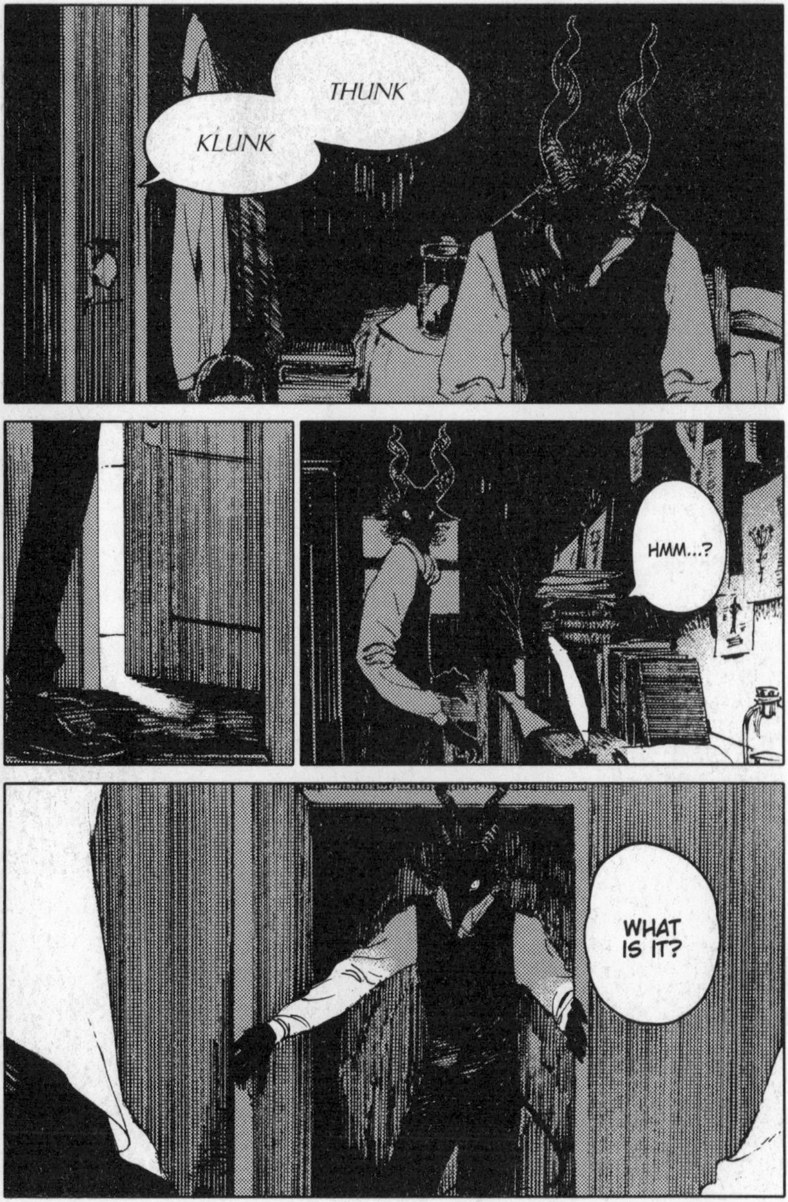
THUNK
KLUNK
HMM...?
WHAT IS IT?

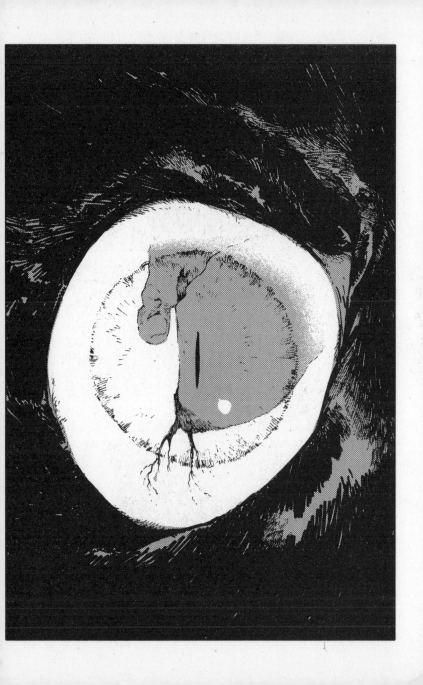

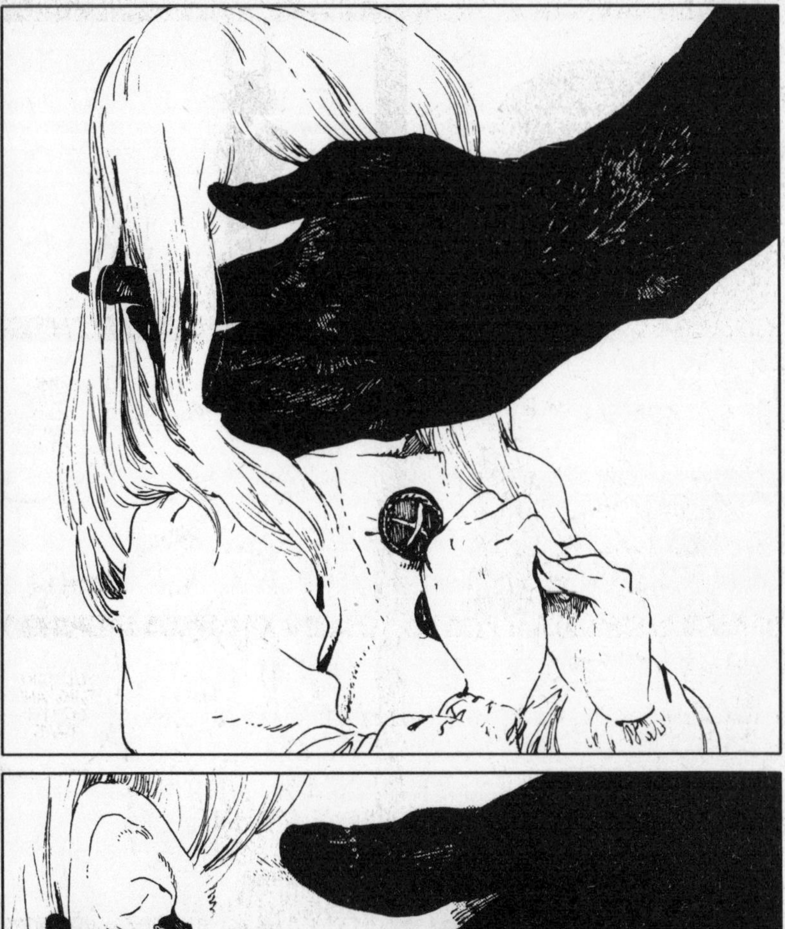

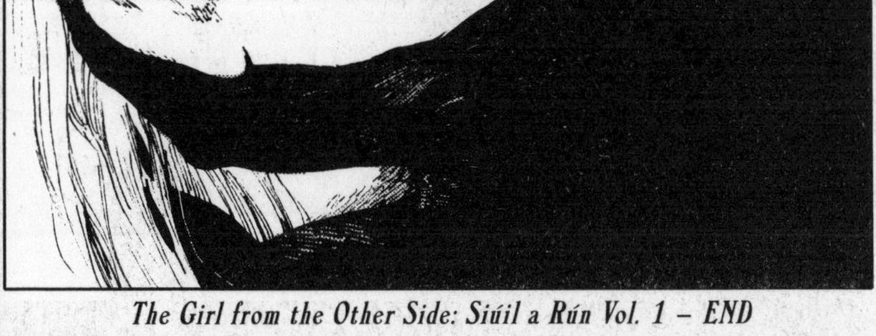

The Girl from the Other Side: Siúil a Rún Vol. 1 – END

A Bonus from the Other Side

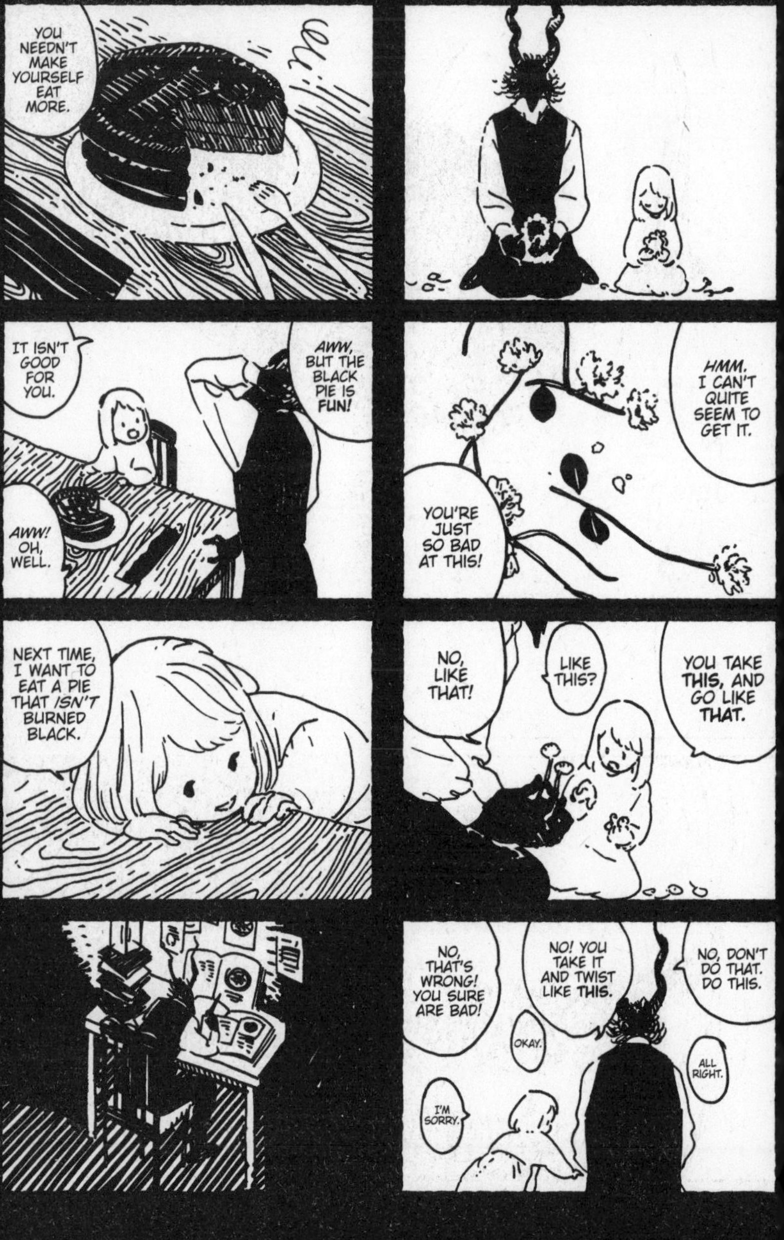

YOU NEEDN'T MAKE YOURSELF EAT MORE.
HMM. I CAN'T QUITE SEEM TO GET IT.
YOU'RE JUST SO BAD AT THIS!
AWW, BUT THE BLACK PIE IS FUN!
IT ISN'T GOOD FOR YOU.
AWW! OH, WELL.
YOU TAKE THIS, AND GO LIKE THAT.
LIKE THIS?
NO, LIKE THAT!
NEXT TIME, I WANT TO EAT A PIE THAT ISN'T BURNED BLACK.
NO, DON'T DO THAT. DO THIS.
NO! YOU TAKE IT AND TWIST LIKE THIS.
NO, THAT'S WRONG! YOU SURE ARE BAD!
OKAY.
ALL RIGHT.
I'M SORRY.

They must never, ever touch-- or so they thought.

The clawed, frigid black hand that touched Shiva's cheek did not belong to Teacher. To be touched by an Outsider was to be cursed to become an Outsider oneself.

What will happen to this frail young girl now? And what meaning does the creepy murmuring of this new Outsider truly hold?

A tranquil fairy tale about those human and inhuman.

VOLUME 2 COMING SOON!

SEVEN SEAS ENTERTAINMENT PRESENTS

Siúil, a Rún
The Girl from the Other Side

story and art by **NAGABE** vol. 1

TRANSLATION
Adrienne Beck

ADAPTATION
Ysabet Reinhardt MacFarlane

LETTERING AND RETOUCH
Lys Blakeslee

LOGO DESIGN
Karis Page

COVER DESIGN
Nicky Lim

PROOFREADER
Shanti Whitesides
Jocelyne Allen

PRODUCTION MANAGER
Lissa Pattillo

EDITOR-IN-CHIEF
Adam Arnold

PUBLISHER
Jason DeAngelis

THE GIRL FROM THE OTHER SIDE: SIUIL, A RUN VOL. 1

Originally published in Japan in 2016 by MAG Garden Corporation, Tokyo.
English translation rights arranged through TOHAN CORPORATION, Tokyo.

ISBN: 978-1-626924-67-3

Printed in Canada

First Printing: January 2017

10 9 8 7 6 5 4 3 2

FOLLOW US ONLINE: ***www.gomanga.com***

READING DIRECTIONS

This book reads from ***right to left***, Japanese style. If this is your first time reading manga, you start reading from the top right panel on each page and take it from there. If you get lost, just follow the numbered diagram here. It may seem backwards at first, but you'll get the hang of it! Have fun!!

1
2
3
4
5
6
7
8
9

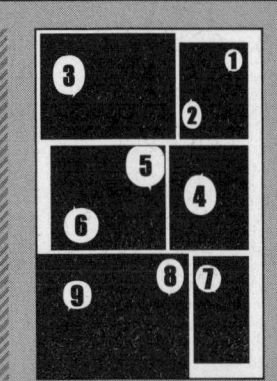